TOYS and TOOLS
IN PINK

TOYS and TOOLS

IN PINK

Cultural Narratives of Gender,
Science, and Technology

———■———

CAROL COLATRELLA

THE OHIO STATE UNIVERSITY PRESS
COLUMBUS

Library of Congress Cataloging-in-Publication Data
Colatrella, Carol.
 Toys and tools in pink : cultural narratives of gender, science, and technology / Carol Cola-
trella.
     p. cm.
 Includes bibliographical references and index.
 ISBN 978-0-8142-1147-2 (cloth : alk. paper)—ISBN 978-0-8142-9248-8 (cd-rom)
 1. Women in literature. 2. Women in motion pictures. 3. Women in science. 4. Sex role—
Social aspects. I. Title.
 PN56.5.W64C65 2011
 809′.933522—dc22
                              2010040892

This book is available in the following editions:
Cloth (ISBN 978-0-8142-1147-2)
CD-ROM (ISBN 978-0-8142-9248-8)

Cover design by Jennifer Shoffey Forsythe
Text design by Jennifer Shoffey Forsythe
Type set in Adobe Minion Pro
Printed by Thomson-Shore, Inc.

♾ The paper used in this publication meets the minimum requirements of the American
National Standard for Information Sciences—Permanence of Paper for Printed Library Materials. ANSI Z39.48-1992.

9 8 7 6 5 4 3 2 1

Contents

Acknowledgments

I appreciate that a number of editors and publishers have granted me permission to incorporate my previously published material for which they hold copyright. Portions of chapters 1, 2, 5, and 6 are based on "Representing Female-Friendly Science and Technology in Fiction and Film," by Carol Colatrella, in *Women and Technology: Proceedings of the 1999 International Symposium on Technology and Society (ISTAS 1999)* (New Brunswick, NJ: IEEE, 1999), © 1999 IEEE. Portions of chapter 1 are from Mitcham (editor), "Science, Technology, and Literature," *Encyclopedia of Science, Technology, and Ethics.* © 2005 Gale, a part of Cengage Learning, Inc. Reproduced by permission. www.cengage.com/permissions. Portions of chapter 2 appeared in Carol Colatrella, *Literature and Moral Reform: Melville and the Discipline of Reading* (Gainesville: University Press of Florida, 2002), 68–73, and are reprinted with permission of the University Press of Florida. Portions of chapter 3 appeared as "The Significant Silence of Race: *La Cousine Bette* and 'Benito Cereno,'" in *Comparative Literature* 46.3 (Summer 1994): 240–66; and as "At optraevle kniplingen," translated by Jakob Stougaard and Thomas Teilmann Damm, in *Passage* 20/21 (December 1995): 141–55. Portions of chapter 4 appeared as "Emerson's Politics of the Novel," in *Emerson at 200,* edited by Giorgio Mariani (Rome: Aracne, 2004), 265–77; and as "Come trasformare l'assistenza medica nell'età dell'AIDS," translated by Cinzia Scarpino in *Ácoma: Rivista Internazionale di Studi Nordamericani* 28 (2004): 114–26. Portions of chapters 3 and 4 appeared as "Representing Liberty: Revolution, Sexuality, and Science in Michelet's Histories and Zola's Fiction," in *Nineteenth-Century French Studies* 20.1–2 (Winter 1991–92): 27–43. Portions of chapters 4 and 6 appeared as "Work for Women," in *Research in Science and Technology Studies (Knowledge and Society,* vol. 12, JAI Press, 2000), 53–76. Part of chapter

6 appeared as "Fear of Reproduction and Desire for Replication in *Dracula*," *The Journal of Medical Humanities* 17.3 (Spring 1996): 179–89, which appears with the kind permission of Springer Science and Business Media. Part of chapter 6 appeared as "From *Desk Set* to *The Net*," *Canadian Review of American Studies* 31.2 (2001): 1–14, and is reprinted by permission of the journal and the Canadian Association of American Studies. Part of chapter 6 appeared as "Feminist Narratives of Science and Technology: Artificial Life and True Love in *Eve of Destruction* and *Making Mr. Right*," in *Women, Gender, and Technology*, edited by Mary Frank Fox, Deborah Johnson, and Sue Rosser (Champaign: University of Illinois Press, 2006), 157–73.

I am grateful to the Library Company of Philadelphia, the Oregon Center for the Humanities, the Emory Center for Public Culture, the Newberry Library, the American Antiquarian Society, the Council for the International Exchange of Scholars' Fulbright Senior Scholar and New Century Scholars (NCS) programs, and the Zentrum für Literatur- und Kulturforschung (Zfl) in Berlin for providing funding and research facilities; I thank their staffs for assistance. I owe special thanks to Sabine Flach of Zfl for arranging a critical period of support in June 2008. Georgia Tech's Ivan Allen College provided a publication grant; I thank Jay Telotte and Kenneth Knoespel of the School of Literature, Communication, and Culture for securing this funding.

I am grateful to those who responded to earlier drafts of this work presented at conferences, including the Coloquio Internacional Montevideana, the Modern Language Association, the Northeastern Modern Language Association, the History of Science Society, the International Society for the Study of Narrative, and the Society for Literature, Science, and the Arts. I also appreciate opportunities to present material to faculty and students at Emory University, Kennesaw State University, Aarhus University, the University of Southern Denmark, Roskilde University, Case Western Reserve University, Armstrong Atlantic State University, Rensselaer Polytechnic Institute, Rose-Hulman Institute of Technology, Virginia Polytechnic and State University, the University of Virginia, the University of California at Merced, Chapman University, and SciTrek.

This work grew from my participation in 1987 School of Criticism and Theory seminars at Dartmouth led by Sacvan Bercovitch and Michael Riffaterre and National Endowment for the Humanities seminars led by James Phelan (The Ohio State University, 1991), Jackson Lears (Rutgers University, 1996), and Lee Clark Mitchell (Princeton University, 1999); I thank seminar leaders and participants. Thanks are also due to 2005–6 NCS Fulbright seminar participants, particularly Nelly Stromquist, Manuel Gil-Antón, Elizabeth Balbachevsky, Reitu Mabokela, Anna Smolentseva, seminar leader Philip G. Altbach, and administrator Patti McGill Peterson.

Many other scholars, including Deepika Bahri, Jamie Barlowe, Helen Burke, Dale Carter, Inger Hunnerup Dalsgaard, Ellen Esrock, Kirsten Gomard, Celeste Goodridge, Shirley Gorenstein, David Hess, Deborah Johnson, Linda Layne, Lis Møller, Alan Nadel, Laura Otis, Kavita Philip, Peter Rabinowitz, Priscilla Wald, and Priscilla Walton, offered critical advice and counsel. I appreciate their insights, patience, and encouragement. I also thank Georgia Tech colleagues Angela Dalle Vacche, Nihad Farooq, Narin Hassan, David McDowell, Anne Pollock, Matthew Realff, Carol Senf, and Lisa Yaszek; and Sandy Crooms, Senior Editor, The Ohio State University Press.

It has been a privilege to collaborate on related research and initiatives with Mary Frank Fox and Mary Lynn Realff, including serving with them as co-directors of the Georgia Tech Center for the Study of Women, Science, and Technology (WST). They have been role models and insightful critics, and I thank them for their understanding and assistance. I have also appreciated discussions with students, including WST-supported researchers Laura Cofer Taylor, Jessica Dillard, and Jimia Head; students enrolled in my courses at Georgia Tech and Aarhus University; and residents of the Georgia Tech WST Learning Community, particularly alumnae Erin Robinson, Komal Patel, and Christina Lurie.

Many others were also willing to think with me about this project and to offer encouragement and tips, including Beth Gibson, Susan Farrell, Lorie Grisham, Leigh Juliano, Leah McLeod, Megan Missett, Corey Greenwald, Rose Appignani Spahr, Jinger Simkins-Stuntz, and Lauren Waits; I thank them for their help. The extended Colatrella and Denton families and parents and students associated with Atlanta Girl Scout Troop 3531 and Inman Middle School Girls Excelling in Math and Science club (GEMS), led by Kelly Schlegel and Mary Lynn Realff, and the Inman Robotics club, led by Jim Stapp and Melissa Nunnink, have also been supportive. I thank my mother, Marie Caufield, for sharing her interest in classic Hollywood films, and my children, Charlie and Lena Denton, who always tell me what they think about games, books, films, and television shows. My greatest appreciation is for my partner Rick Denton, whose copy-editing, critical acumen, and generous debate informed me every step of the way.

Introduction

CULTURAL NARRATIVES AND THE
"LEAKY PIPELINE"

This book analyzes the ways in which fictional and cinematic narratives consider "the leaky pipeline problem": that women drop out of science, technology, engineering, and mathematics (STEM) at a number of stages of education and career. The question of what keeps women from participating in proportional numbers in scientific and technical fields has generated much scholarly and media attention in recent decades. Although witnesses at 2002 and 2009 U.S. Congressional hearings offered testimony documenting barriers and facilitators for women working in science, engineering, and computing and discussed applying Title IX to scientific and technical education, more media attention was paid to Lawrence Summers's remarks in January 2005 characterizing the "intrinsic aptitude" of women as domestic rather than scientific.[1]

Then-president of Harvard University, Summers addressed the National Board of Economic Review (NBER) Conference on Diversifying the Science and Engineering Workforce in January 2005, telling participants, according to Elizabeth Spelke and Ariel Grace, that

> three factors . . . might account for the underrepresentation of women in mathematics, science, and engineering (Summers, 2005). First, sex differences in motivation may produce more men who are drawn to the single-minded pursuit of knowledge. Second, sex differences in cognition may yield more men who are capable of mathematical and scientific thinking at the highest levels. Third, discrimination may cause men to have more favorable career outcomes in these fields. (57)[2]

Summers's speech appeared to dismiss decades of scholarship documenting the effects of socialization, suggesting instead that innate sex-related biological traits and individual choice could be more responsible for differences in performance outcomes than education, parenting, peer relationships, and other social influences.

In response to Summers, critics pointed to social and cultural factors as salient influences on individuals' decisions to avoid or leave STEM fields. The American Sociological Association's statement listed a range of relevant environmental factors, including peer stereotypes and media representations:

> Decades of social-scientific research provide a solid base of empirical knowledge about the power of unequal opportunities, limitations in access to formal and informal training, a lack of social and domestic supports, and lowered expectations about women's capacity to achieve that sap their educational and professional confidence. Studies also show that peer pressures to conform to stereotypical behavior and exposure to popular media affect women's and men's choices and opportunities in the occupational world. These changeable social factors, not innate biological differences, provide the most powerful explanation for the continuing gap between women's abilities and their occupational attainments.[3]

About a month after President Summers's January 2005 talk, Gwen Ifill of PBS's show *The News Hour* opened a news segment detailing the continuing controversy about aptitude and performance in science, asking "So, how big is the Pandora's Box the Harvard debate opened? What do we know about women and scientific achievement, biology and learned behavior?"[4] Ifill's tongue-in-cheek reference to "Pandora's Box" points to a classical myth describing women as troublemakers in science, suggesting that literary and cultural accounts also shape perceptions of women's capabilities.

Pandora, the archetypal woman, according to Hesiod's *Works and Days,* illustrates why females are the "Other" sex, for she "introduced plurality, dissent and disharmony into human existence."[5] In *Theogony* (ca. 700 b.c.e.), Hesiod explains that Prometheus's brother married the beautiful Pandora, who was created as punishment by Zeus. She releases a host of miseries on humanity when she opens a jar that Zeus demanded remain closed. Feminist critic Kate Millett allows that "Pandora . . . represents—a perilous temptation with 'the mind of a bitch and a thievish nature,' full of 'the cruelty of desire and longings that wear out the body,' 'lies and cunning words and a deceitful soul,'" a snare sent by Zeus to be "the ruin of men."[6]

Classicist John Ferguson characterizes the Titan Prometheus as "an ambivalent figure" (121), a master inventor and trickster whose rebellious intelligence helps humans rise above animals.[7] Aeschylus' fifth-century drama *Prometheus*

Bound posits that Zeus grew angry at human achievements made possible by Prometheus; in the play, Might claims that Prometheus committed a "sin" in stealing fire to give to man and that his punishment, being chained to a rock, will teach him "to endure and like the sovereignty of Zeus and quit his man-loving disposition."[8] Whereas Prometheus' heroic rationality resists Zeus and preserves the mortal race, Pandora exemplifies transgressive, destructive aspects of female curiosity about technology.[9] The feminine story is cautionary and neither heroic nor redeeming, for Pandora's actions inhibit human progress instead of encouraging innovation and invention.

Literary and Cultural Accounts

Fictional narratives help shape our understanding of individual achievements and social institutions. As stories entertain us, they also inform and instruct us about social norms and cultural values. Novels and films discussed in this book depict gendered aspects of settings, situations, and individuals while commenting on scientific and technical achievements or failures. Texts reference gender stereotypes to describe scientists' attitudes, actions, and abilities, while plots about scientific research question characters' authority, expertise, and morality, frequently by emphasizing their gendered qualities. Labs and other settings associated with scientific research and technical development appear as socially marginal or even deviant sites in many fictions and films that acknowledge gender norms.[10]

Bernard de Fontenelle's *Conversations on the Plurality of Worlds* (1686), an early modern text of fictionalized dialogue between a male philosopher and a female interlocutor, invites "female participation in the almost exclusively male province of scientific discourse."[11] Other Western European texts were used in teaching scientific and mechanical principles to young women, who, like the female pupil in Tom Stoppard's play *Arcadia* (1993), were educated at home before the mid-nineteenth-century. A number of textbooks on mathematics, chemistry, and physics were published such as Jane Marcet's *Conversations on Chemistry* (1805) and *Conversations on Natural Philosophy* (1819), detailing a female tutor's dialogues with her two female pupils. These works were pitched to women, but their accessible, entertaining scientific explanations appealed to both sexes.

Since the Industrial Revolution, American and Western European narratives referencing science and technology have proliferated. Considering gender in fictional narratives about science and technology published after Mary Shelley's *Frankenstein* (1818), my argument focuses on texts describing female scientists and technologists rather than their male counterparts; in most, but not all, cases these female characters are white. Aspects of the feminine are elaborated as cultural memories, metaphors, and myths about gender, science, and technology that have been naturalized as "truths" for audiences. Characterizations of female scientists and technical experts in news media, drama, film, and science fiction blend issues of expertise, authority, and morality in science and technology with ideologies of masculinity and/or femininity. The narratives considered here associate gender with issues of competence and integrity, link specific features of gender identity with aspects of scientific and/or technical acumen, and outline normative scientific and social roles for characters.

The link between the feminine and disharmony associated with Pandora reappears in Shelley's novel, subtitled *The New Prometheus*. Like Prometheus (and Faust), Victor Frankenstein is brilliant, brave, and overly ambitious. His experiments with artificial reproduction, which could eliminate the need for human pregnancy and procreation, identified in the fictional world as feminine, cause him to ignore his family and friends and disavow the creature he has produced.[12] Victor's egocentric ambition to supersede human reproduction results in death and destruction, as *Frankenstein* warns readers of the dangers that ensue when science and technology are pursued without a concomitant assessment of possible consequences.

Informed by feminist theories, this book considers narratives, beginning with *Frankenstein,* that reference women's participation in and authority over science and technology. Annette Kolodny points out that feminist criticism possesses

> an acute and impassioned *attentiveness* to the ways in which primarily male structures of power are inscribed (or encoded) within our literary inheritance; the consequences of that encoding for women—as characters, as readers, and as writers; and, with that, a shared analytic concern for the implications of that encoding not only for a better understanding of the past, but also for an improved reordering of the present and future as well.[13]

In a similar vein, Robyn Warhol considers that "the point of feminism has always been to ask 'what difference does gender make?' in how we see, feel, know, and are known."[14] Social conventions and stereotypes represented in literary and cinematic texts acculturate men and women into following, resisting, or reconfiguring cultural scripts in practicing science and in designing and using technology.

Fictional characterizations of female scientists reveal complexities and contradictions influenced by women's expected social roles and public perceptions of science and technology. Women appear transgressive in being associated with science and technology, often by not following gender norms. A number of narratives represent science as opposed to domesticity, nurturing, and romantic love, hallmarks of femininity. For example, Walt Disney's classic children's cartoon *Snow White* (1937) offers a frightening image of the jealous stepmother-queen using science and supernatural powers to kill her stepdaughter. After the queen finds out from a magic mirror that the forester did not murder the infant princess as she instructed him, she retreats to her lab to create a poisonous apple. The elegant queen transforms into a hag-like witch, experimenting with beakers and test tubes and mixing deadly ingredients to produce a poison. The film represents chemistry as a malicious pursuit associated with female revenge; however, Snow White is saved by the Prince, as the plot points to the superiority of love and domesticity over jealousy and scientific villainy.

Narratives exploring women's engagement with science and technology demonstrate Protean durability in Western literary and cinematic traditions. Readers/viewers are exhorted by various science fictions to delve into science and control technology for individual and social improvement. In Marge Piercy's *He, She, and It* (1983), Margaret Atwood's *Oryx and Crake* (2003), and other fictions, male and female scientists act on ethical principles that align with stereotypes of femininity: preferring cooperation over competition, valuing social progress as opposed to individual profit, and eclectically employing diverse modes of accessing knowledge rather than limiting one's methodological approach. Negative and positive gender stereotypes in fictions and films connote women's status as scientific and technical outsiders, providing details about environments that help shape views of readers and filmgoers.

A number of scholars have already analyzed how gender matters in science fiction.[15] Because the genre tends to speculation rather than realistic representation, I consider only a few science fiction examples in chapters 6 and 7 and concentrate on the intersections of gender, science, and technology in realistically conceived fictional worlds. My argument tracks race in narratives about female characters who develop or use science or technology, and it delineates gender stereotypes in characterizations, plots, and settings that may also be replicated, reconfigured, or resisted in fictions focusing on underrepresented minorities.[16] Empirical research in social science and science provides a context for discussions of gender, science, and technology in fictions and films.

Science and Gender

Scientific and social scientific research shows more overlap than difference in male and female cognitive abilities. Linda Birke outlines constraints affecting research on cognitive sex difference: how psychological tests are constructed or administered, what they measure, and how "inferences and assumptions" often hold sway in interpretation of data (319).[17] Contributors to *Why Aren't More Women in Science?* acknowledge cognitive differences between males and females, including differences in performance on IQ tests, verbal abilities, spatial and problem-solving abilities, and brain architecture, but a clear majority agree that such slight differences do not explain why there are few women in science.[18] Some experts note the success of females in Singapore and Great Britain who outperform males on mathematics tests as evidence that more than biology is at stake. In sum, while studies show few cognitive differences between men and women, these are not as salient as social and cultural factors in influencing who becomes a scientist.[19]

Sylvia Ann Hewlett of the Center for Work Life Policy conducted a 2006–7 poll of almost 2,500 male and female workers in STEM (1,493 women and 1,000 men). Her report "paints a portrait of a macho culture where women are very much outsiders, and where those who do enter are likely to eventually leave."[20] Poll data indicate that although women working in STEM "do well at the start with 75 percent of women age 25–29" receiving excellent performance evaluations, 52 percent of women exit their STEM jobs "around ages 35 to 40," "some leaving for 'softer' jobs in the sciences' human resources rather than lab bench work . . . and others for different work entirely." This exit rate is twice that of men in STEM and "higher than the attrition rate of women in law or investment banking." STEM fields "have in common" a masculine culture that is "at best unsupportive and at worst downright hostile to women": 63 percent of Hewlett's respondents report harassment on the job, 53 percent dismissive attitudes of male colleagues, and 51 percent a lack of mentors.

Media coverage of the challenges facing women in science has real-world impact, particularly for individuals working in STEM organizations, but also for the public and for prospective scientists and technologists. Mary Frank Fox notes, "The participation, status, and advancement of women in academic science and engineering have been pressing social concerns in the United States."[21] Unpacking narrative representations of women scientists, mathematicians, and engineers offers a potent means of confronting climate issues and transforming environments.[22] Feminist intepretation of texts about science and technology demystifies theories and practices that too often have been obstacles for women. Analyzing texts about women, science, and technology prepares women for working in fields traditionally dominated by men and could help reduce bias and negative attitudes toward women.[23]

Science and technology often appear in novels and films as domains of knowledge accessible in different ways to men and women. Texts link scientific and technical understanding and abilities of characters to aspects of masculinity or femininity, while concomitantly developing dynamic plots concerning the morality of characters' actions and behavior. Scholars of literature, film, and mass media have inventoried such depictions in a number of texts, sometimes in conjunction with surveying and interviewing readers and viewers.

Collaborative research reports by British scholars published by the United Kingdom Resource Center for Women in Science, Engineering, and Technology (UKRC) look at responses of females and males in a variety of age groups to portrayals of scientists and technologists appearing in recent television shows, films, newspapers, and other media.[24] Considering role models in the media, the first report in the UKRC series analyzes interview data with 26 women working in science, engineering, and technology and responses of focus groups consisting of another 60 women training, returning, or teaching with STEM.[25] The UKRC project collaborators and other scholars recognize that increasing the number of female role models and diversifying their representation to reflect different ethnicities and ages could improve access for women in professions now dominated by white males. United States scholar Jocelyn Steinke agrees: "There is also evidence that images and messages conveyed by the mass media contribute to the 'masculine image of science.'"[26] Interpreting stereotypical images and their postfeminist reconfigurations could encourage those studying and working in scientific and technical fields to consider dimensions of equity and level the playing field for women and underrepresented minorities.

Predicting what appeals to audiences' tastes is not easy. The women interviewed in the UKRC project discussed the lack of role models for women of different ages and ethnicities among presenters in news shows and scientists in fictional shows. Respondents offered mixed interpretations and recommendations for future programming. They "were . . . keen to challenge the image of women in SET as socially isolated or geeky. However, promoting role models which might be too unattainable or unrealistic for the average scientist was also seen as problematic[;] . . . some media role models could be unrealistic and not particularly encouraging."[27] Viewers appeared to prefer watching shows offering aspirational realism rather than glamorous fantasy or pessimistic assessments of conditions, but more research is needed concerning audience reactions to particular representations.

Cultural Narratives

Print and film narratives are part of what Graham Dawson, among others, calls "a cultural imaginary," "those vast networks of interlinking discursive themes, images, motifs and narrative forms that are publicly available within a culture at any one time, and articulate its psychic and social dimensions." Dawson acknowledges that "cultural imaginaries furnish public forms which both organize knowledge of the social world and give shape to fantasies within the apparently 'internal' domain of psychic life."[28] My argument considers selected American and European texts to map the terrain of the cultural imaginary in which science and technology appear as gendered pursuits. Representations of gender, science, and technology in fictions and films influence our ideas of who should study, practice, and deploy science and technology. Looking closely at how gender matters in literary and cinematic characterizations, plots, and settings reveals that narrative structures establish political and ethical claims concerning the status of women's participation in scientific and technical fields.

Why Pink?

The title *Toys and Tools in Pink* emphasizes how females and feminine versions of science and technology appear always marginal, sometimes deviant, and often quirky. Because "toys and tools" denotes both children's playthings and "tech toys and tools," the phrase serves as shorthand for a variety of material cultural phenomena. "Toys and tools in pink" describes technoscience coded as feminine. Literary references to pink famously include the pink hawthorn and the lady in pink in Marcel Proust's *Remembrance of Things Past* (1913–27). Historical associations with the color pink include the pink triangle of the Holocaust reserved for gays and lesbians and the pejorative label "pinko" for Communists. In recent years, pink ribbons identify the campaign ("Think Pink," "Pink Zone") for breast cancer awareness.

According to Lynn Peril, since the late 1950s, pink denotes "for girls."[29] Pink is not essentially pro- or antifeminist of any wave (what color could be?), but it has been eschewed by those resisting traditional stereotypes and has been replicated or reconfigured by others. Items in pink are feminized, which seems patronizing to some who regard such marketing "as rampant and unacceptable gender stereotyping," and hip to others, including some female science, computing, and engineering majors in my classes who wear Pink Chuck Taylors or carry laptops in pink cases, or to those who grew up with a pink Nintendo DS or a strawberry iMac.[30] High-profile women also embrace pink's distinctive appeal. Business author Gail Evans asked that her book emphasizing how women should play as team members in business be packaged in pink to attract women.[31] Designer Donatella Versace gave up her pink matched luggage and replaced it with purple because she felt that pink became tired, like black, while others, like MaryJane Butters, an activist and "life style brand" who drives a pink biodiesel truck, prefer "the juxtaposition of rugged and really pretty, grit and glam, diesel and absolutely darling."[32]

Many education scholars perceive girls' interest and success in scientific and technical fields as related to their experiences with material culture and influences of parents, peers, and teachers, and media.[33] In the United States the color pink identifies toys for girls and tools designed to appeal to women. Not all representations and material objects used by women are pink, but they become so metaphorically and in practice. Consider the choice a parent in 1999 had between the Hot Wheels PC in primary colors of red, yellow, and blue or the Barbie PC in white and shades of pink. The first package included a steering wheel for racing games, while the Barbie version was sold with a digital camera and software that allowed the user to put photographed subjects in the same frame with a digital Barbie.[34] Both PCs were cool toys, but the different configurations convey messages about appropriate activities and aesthetics for girls and boys.

The toy industry depends on stereotypes (i.e., marketing demographics) distinguishing gender differences in consumers, as visiting a toy store or the toy section of a department store or shopping via printed catalog or the Internet reveals.[35] Boys' toys are louder, flashier, and more stimulating. They are often adventure or heroic toys as opposed to the domestic and friendship toys offered in the girls' aisle, which is dominated by pink, purple, and sparkly effects. Trying to persuade girls and women to purchase and use their products, manufacturers and retailers of toys and tools attempt to instill "feminine" aesthetics or philosophies, but they may risk alienating other customers who find such associations distasteful or pandering.[36] Mattel decided to omit "Math class is tough" as a phrase uttered by a talking Barbie, but Dentist Barbie and Computer Engineer Barbie are still pretty in pink and blue.[37] Although parents can resist purchasing objects they perceive as referencing negative stereotypes, designers' and manufacturers' perceptions of children's tastes, which are themselves affected by interactions with peers, parents, and media, drive the development and sales of gendered merchandise and, increasingly, the production of tie-in television shows, films, and books pitched to children.

Gender stereotypes remain salient, even when contradicted in practice, because they provide individuals, as well as institutions, with formulas for living. LEGO® and other construction-build kits are often cited as instilling familiarity with physical concepts important for scientists and engineers. During a 2000 visit to Lego headquarters in Billund, Denmark, I spoke with representatives about the company's research and marketing. Lego developed three lines marketed to girls: two lines (the Scala and Belville series) consisted of white, pink, and other pastel pieces to build fantasy homes and castles, while Clikit pink and purple interlocking pieces create frames, purses, and other personal items. A Lego marketing representative acknowledged that their child development research indicates that "kids get older younger," and that by ages seven to nine, some boys and many girls stop playing with toys. That boys appear to play physically and girls more cooperatively is another insight influencing Lego's design, manufacturing, and marketing.

The Lego marketing division atrium was home in 2000 to a banner admonishing "Remember half the children in the world are girls."[38] While most employees involved with engineering research and development at Lego are male, many in marketing are female. All are under pressure to increase their sales to girls, especially those between eight and twelve years of age, a group that buys fewer toys than their male peers. Lego observes that adolescent girls are more interested in social relationships with each other than in fantasy play with toys. Playing with toys is often connected with tinkering (taking apart and constructing) behaviors connected to a developing interest in technology. Many women and men who succeed in science, math, and engineering report that Legos and similar tinkering toys were foundational for them.[39] Some speculate that girls might want a different kind of Legos, in more attractive colors, easier to put together, and more useful.[40]

Lego's financial problems in 2008 increased the company's motivation to sell products appealing to larger markets. The *International Herald Tribune* on March 7, 2008, reported that Lego's chief executive planned "to challenge Mattel and Hasbro, the U.S. companies that dominate the toy market. Girls are a market where 'we'll never stop trying,' said Knudstorp. . . . 'I think there is something that genetically skews us towards boys, but we can do better.'" Assessments of Lego's balance sheet in 2009 indicate that the company's strategy to incorporate Hollywood storylines into its merchandise and to open "concept stores" have increased its profits while other toy manufacturers have been less successful during the most recent recession.[41]

Product color affects consumer appeal. Some male and a few female students in a cultural studies of gender, science, and technology class at the Georgia Institute of Technology reported anxieties concerning the Lillian Vernon pink tool set, the iMac computer in fruit flavors, and the Black and Decker Mouse sander, identifying such items as too "cute," "wimpy," and "feminine" to qualify for purchase.[42] Referring to these objects in classroom discussion and looking at catalog illustrations caused some students to shiver dramatically and enunciate "Ugh!" because they perceive using them as gender-bending behavior and want to perform this assessment for their peers.[43]

Gendered boundaries are demarcated in texts for children as well as in toys, as books such as *The Daring Book for Girls* and *The Dangerous Book for Boys* are marketed to one sex or the other.[44] In my fall 2007 "Introduction to Gender Studies" course, I asked approximately 30 students to determine the intended audiences for these and other books such as Danica McKellar's *Math Doesn't Suck,* which was designed to teach middle school math, and *Fly Girls,* which presents short biographies of early women aviators, along with a number of books about science fair projects and famous scientists as well as popular periodicals directed toward children (*Nickelodeon Magazine, National Geographic Kids, Popular Mechanics*) according to the sex and age of the intended audience.[45] There was no disagreement among students as they regarded topics and packaging colors as key indicators of intended masculine, feminine, or gender-neutral audiences. Any book with pink, fuschia, or purple on the cover or with many illustrations of girls was seen as produced for girls, while books with mostly boys depicted were considered written for them. A book with neutral colors and a balance of illustrations of girls and boys was judged as designed for both sexes. Literary and cinematic narratives also reflect and refract cultural codes regarding gender-appropriate identities and behaviors, as this book demonstrates.

Historical Accounts of Gender, Science, and Technology

Social and textual analyses create "crossover" between disciplines concerned, respectively, with practices and discourses, as historical and social scientific accounts of gender, science, and technology illustrate.[46] Carolyn Merchant's *The Death of Nature* was path-breaking in categorizing science as a male pursuit that "managed" nature, itself identified with women.[47] David Noble describes early modern science as "a world without women" in his book of that title.[48] Margaret Rossiter's *Women Scientists in America* considers how the professionalization of science and the development of scientific societies excluded and marginalized women as researchers and professors in a range of fields.[49] Evelyn Fox Keller's *A Feeling for the Organism* tracks Barbara McClintock's success as related to her marginal status. Cynthia Russett's *Sexual Science* studied the sexual discrimination incorporated in Victorian scientific texts.[50] Barbara Ehrenreich and Deirdre English's book *For Her Own Good* reviews "two centuries of the experts' advice to women" to explain the exclusion of women from the practice of medicine, "the sexual politics of sickness," and "the pathology of motherhood," among other subjects.[51] Nina Baym's *American Women of Letters and the Nineteenth-Century Sciences* acknowledges the contributions of female scientists and writers, explaining their styles and contexts.[52]

Studies of gender and technology have also explored gendered aspects of technological development, production, and reception. In *Feminism Confronts Technology* and *Technofeminism,* Judy Wajcman theorizes the ways men and masculinity are associated with technology.[53] Michèle Martin explains how early developers of the telephone discounted women's preferences for informal conversation as a trivial use of the new technology.[54] Virginia Scharff considers how marketing for the electric car for women in the early twentieth century feminized the product in advertising and in the popular consciousness.[55] Finding that technological innovations raise hygienic and emotional standards associated with housekeeping, Ruth Cowan's *More Work for Mother* revolutionized how historians of technology think about domestic work. Developing and marketing a superior microwave, as Cynthia Cockburn and Susan Ormrod argue, became a site of conflict for one British company in the 1980s because the process replicated and reinforced the male/female division of engineer/home economist in the company; this conflict had its own color code of "brown" electronic goods designed for male consumers and "white" domestic appliances designed for females.[56] *Boys and Their Toys?*, a collection taking its title from Ruth Oldenziel's essay about boys building model cars to enter into the Fisher Body craftsmen guild competition, includes various essays about male work and play that analyze connections between technology and masculinity.[57]

These texts illustrate historical constraints placed upon women interested in science and technology. Identifying past exclusions helps to contextualize my analyses of narratives and offers an ethical opportunity to evaluate the progress and challenges associated with women's history. Studying literature and history allows readers to consider strategies toward eliminating existing barriers. Women still confront questions concerning whether STEM fields offer appropriate work for women, whether women should hold executive/managerial appointments, and the difficulty of pursuing STEM work and raising children, as social scientists document.[58]

Social Studies of the Leaky Pipeline

We live in a period witnessing both decreasing public understanding of science and technology and growing skepticism about the motives and outcomes of these fields in many industrialized nations. The Organisation for Economic Cooperation and Development (OECD) notes that "social acceptance of new avenues for scientific research increasingly requires a permanent dialogue with an informed civil society,"[59] for it is civil society that foots most of the bills for research in engineering and science. A cross-cultural survey of individuals from 40 countries revealed that "people who are more scientifically literate have more positive attitudes to science in general, but are not necessarily more positive about specific technological applications or specialized areas of scientific research."[60] Movements to expand science education and to incorporate consideration of science and technology in schools are promoted as ways of enhancing citizens' scientific and technical literacy and attracting more minorities and girls to these fields.[61] As previously noted, the majority of social scientists find that environmental (social and cultural) factors affect the leaky pipeline and outweigh any slight outcomes due to genetic differences between girls and boys.

Despite initiatives designed to increase diversity in the STEM workforce, questions about the proportional representation of women in science have simmered for decades.[62] Robert K. Merton's 1963 analysis of gender differences in science formulated the Matthew effect as the outcome of cumulative advantages accruing to a male scientist in the meritocratic hierarchy of science, while Margaret Rossiter described as a 1993 corollary to Merton's formulation the Matilda effect, which "consists of the cumulative disadvantages accruing to a female scientist" by "undercutting, undercounting, and minimizing" the achievements of women.[63] Social and political changes in the 1970s opened up access to university degrees and careers for women and ethnic minorities, and the proportions of girls and women studying and working in STEM have increased since; however, many talented women and minorities pursue work in non-STEM fields (business, education, and law, largely) or stop working outside the home rather than continue in science or engineering.[64]

Recognizing the significant roles played by science, mathematics, engineering, and technology in society and its changing demographics, some educational institutions have worked to create programs to assist female and minority students by developing more welcoming university environments.[65] Research studies in the United States document the problems of access, retention, and promotion that have given rise to the terms "chilly classroom" and "hostile workplace" for women studying, teaching, and practicing science, mathematics, and engineering.

Programmatic transformations are necessary to advance women in these fields.[66] In the United States, statistics and testimonials support the need to make more effective efforts at recruiting, retaining, and promoting women in scientific and technical fields, a problem that is linked to maintaining a diverse workforce. The National Science Foundation (NSF) has tracked progress and provided grants to encourage the continued participation of women in science, computing, and engineering. Since 2001, NSF has also awarded ADVANCE funds to universities to "transform" institutional climates and to model leadership programs to make these higher-education environments more equitable for women, a change that improves institutional environments for all.[67]

Grades in core university math and science courses are the most reliable predictor of which American students will remain in scientific and technical fields; not surprisingly, students who have taken more high school courses in these subjects tend to have higher achievement test scores and better grades in university courses, as well as better rates of retention in universities. Female STEM majors at some institutions have higher grades and test scores as well as higher retention levels than their male counterparts, but disproportionately low numbers of women in STEM are due to environmental hurdles. Sandra Hanson's *Swimming against the Tide: African American Girls and Science Education* sums up a situation that many students in STEM majors recognize as prevalent in their institutions: "the culture of science continues to be a white male culture that is often hostile to women and minorities."[68] Among the strategies to improve the number of undergraduate and graduate students in STEM are bringing in notable women to serve as role models and mentors; enlisting parents, employers, and faculty as supporters of girls and women in STEM; coordinating living and learning programs for female students in on-campus housing and offering events and activities directed toward their interests. Intervention programs offer initiatives in advising, mentoring, career counseling, and strategizing for success to help warm the chilly climate for women on campus.

Many industrialized nations experience gender stratification in some areas of STEM education and employment. In the United States, women and men earn undergraduate degrees in some fields of science and engineering in nearly equal numbers, with women surpassing men for the first time in 2005, according to NSF's *Women, Minorities, and Persons with Disabilities 2007*.[69] Women make up more than 50 percent of graduate students in social sciences, psychology, and biology, but they fall short of proportional representation in computing, engineering, and physical sciences.[70] NSF 2006 figures indicate that "46 percent of Ph.D. degrees in the biological sciences are awarded to women (compared with 31 percent two decades ago); 31 percent of the Ph.D. degrees in chemistry go to women (compared with 18 percent 20 years ago)."[71] NSF reports "Women received 46% of all research doctorates awarded in 2008," while "23% of the U.S. citizens and permanent residents who earned research doctorates . . . are members of racial/ethnic minority groups."[72]

As faculty in doctoral institutions, women are less likely than men to hold full-time appointments (34 percent in 2005–6), tenure-track appointments (40.9 percent), and tenured appointments (25.8 percent).[73] In STEM fields, the numbers of women faculty are lower; the American Society of Engineering Education cites an average of women faculty in engineering as 11.3 percent in 2006.[74] Christina Hoff Sommers noted in 2008:

> Women comprise just 19 percent of tenure-track professors in math, 11 percent in physics, 10 percent in computer science, and 10 percent in electrical engineering. And the pipeline does not promise statistical parity any time soon: women are now earning 24 percent of the Ph.D.'s in the physical sciences—way up from the 4 percent of the 1960s, but still far behind the rate they are winning doctorates in other fields.[75]

Yet Sommers, a conservative scholar at the American Enterprise Institute, does not believe that such disparities owe to the organizational environment of science, and she resists proposed efforts to review faculties. She regards the application of Title IX as potentially eroding a successful, merit-based system, arguing that this process would harm science because "[d]epartments of physics, math, chemistry, engineering, and computer science have remained traditional, rigorous, competitive, relatively meritocratic, and under the control of no-nonsense professors dedicated to objective standards."

Referencing research on genetic differences in intelligence and women's roles in caregiving, Sommers speculates that persistently low numbers of women in science are more likely related to inherent differences and preferences that account for the different performance outcomes for men and women. She cites a poll in which 1,417 professors were asked "what accounts for the relative scarcity of female professors in math, science, and engineering?" Sociologists Neil Gross of Harvard and Solon Simmons of George Mason University report, according to Sommers, that "1 percent of respondents attributed the scarcity to women's lack of ability, 24 percent to sexist discrimination, and 74 percent to differences in what characteristically interests men and women." She concludes from the poll's results that applying Title IX is a mistake because "[t]hese proposed solutions assume a problem that might not exist." However, poll responses indicate 24 percent noticed discrimination and 74 percent identify different career interests for men and women, a perception that might be seen as related to socialization (i.e., that men and women are acculturated to choose different career paths).

Formulas connecting gender, science, and technology frequently appear in media. Dorothy Nelkin finds, "The overwhelming message in these popular press accounts is that the successful woman scientist must have the ability to do everything—to be feminine, motherly, and to achieve as well."[76] Marcel LaFollette considers how students react depictions of scientists:

> Studies of U.S. school children, from the 1950s to the 1980s, show that both boys and girls see the "typical" scientist as male. Some of these attitudes simply reflect statistical reality—far fewer women than men work as scientists—but they also indicate continuing, deep-seated bias against science as an appropriate activity for women. It is not just that science is regarded as a masculine occupation. Historical analysis of American culture shows that, throughout this century, the mass media have also purveyed a strongly negative image of women scientists, depicting them as atypical scientists and atypical women.[77]

Since LaFollette's 1988 article, some national newspapers and general-interest magazines have covered a more equitable balance of female and male scientists and inventors. Profiles and interviews of scientists, engineers, and information technology gurus appear with some frequency in major U.S. national newspapers and on television. Achievements such as the 2009 Nobel prizes in medicine and in economics to women are widely reported as notable by national newspapers and television news shows.

National Academy of Sciences and NSF findings indicate that fewer women rise to higher levels in science and engineering.[78] LaFollette's "deep-seated cultural bias" has become a component of a modern paradox. Scientific and technical discoveries, processes, and products are pervasive and are more likely to be used in the home and workplace. At the same time, many citizens are disinclined to pursue STEM study and work, and scientific and technical institutions remain challenged in recruiting and retaining a diverse workforce.

Film as Culture

A number of scholars speak to the cultural power of film as a mirror illustrating social reality while also creating it. Film is known as a medium that can get "inside the head" of viewers. Sociologists Peter Weingart, Claudia Muhl, and Petra Pansegru argue that "the images, clichés, and metaphors used by filmmakers and scriptwriters to portray science and scientists are a reflection of the popular images of science, insofar as their films are a reflection of popular culture. At the same time their films reinforce these images and provide them with imaginative detail and decorum."[79] Robert Rosenstone acknowledges the power of film images "that run in our head over and over again," indicating that "such images function deeply within us as memories, and also as metaphors."[80]

Film scholars emphasize how the medium reports, promotes, and contains social change. Angela Dalle Vacche explicates the early Italian diva film's concern "with history—namely time—since its primary topic was the change from old to new models of behavior in the domestic sphere and between the sexes."[81] Feminist film critics Laura Mulvey, Tania Modleski, and Mary Ann Doane argue, respectively, that many Hollywood films objectify the female by "the male gaze"; reveal "male paranoid fears, developed during the war years, about the independence of women on the home front"; and make woman "the subject of a transaction in which her commodification is ultimately the object."[82]

Contemporary films and television productions set in hospitals and labs include at least a token representation of women, including African Americans, Asians, and other minorities, working in scientific and technical fields. Documentary and fiction films and TV shows offer numerous representations of women who work as professional scientists, usually as medical caregivers and researchers or as forensic pathologists playing minor roles in ensemble dramas as on *ER* (1994–), *Grey's Anatomy* (2005–), the *Law & Order* franchise—*Law & Order* (1990–2010), *Law & Order: Special Victims Unit* (1999–), *Law & Order: Criminal Intent* (2001–)—and the *CSI* group—*CSI* (2000–), *CSI: Miami* (2002–), *CSI: NY* (2004–). Productions such as *Bones* (2005–) and *Hawthorne* (2009) focus, respectively, on a forensic anthropologist in a research institute and a head nurse in a hospital. Female characters appear as exceptional in comparison with male peers and with women in other professions. Women adept in the use of science and technology appear anomalous in their upbringing or outlook and sometimes socially trangressive in their sexual, social, and political attitudes.[83]

Glamorous, heroic television depictions of women and men are understood to attract individuals to study and enter certain fields. For example, the scientific knowledge and engineering ingenuity displayed in the U.S. television show *MacGyver* (1985–92) led to a spike in applications to engineering schools. National newspapers report increased interest in college programs in criminal forensics because of television programs such as *CSI, Crossing Jordan* (2001–7), *Bones, The X-Files* (1993–2002), and other shows featuring pathologists as criminologists.[84] Jay Siegel argues "Women see this [criminal forensics] as a scientific field they can get into and make a difference without worrying about the gender-equity question."[85]

As the following chapters illustrate, fictions, television shows, and films that represent women in STEM incorporate characterizations emphasizing stereotypical gendered assumptions about scientific authority, expertise, moral integrity, and professional ethics. Characterizations of scientists and technologists and the plots in which they appear shape practices and cultural conventions of how women and men in science and technology learn and work. Stories of transgression, achievement, success, or failure become salient models that discourage or inspire readers and viewers.

According to sociologists and media scholars, cultural stereotypes in literature and other media affect audience acceptance of which professions are appropriate for women and perceptions of women's accomplishments. A *Sex Roles* article about female athletes explains:

> Thus, the media frame, at least in part, our thoughts, attitudes, and behaviors (Kane et al., 2000). In addition, the mass media, in concert with one's peers and family members, acts as a socialization agent, in that it shapes the emotional and moral development of youth (Moore, Raymond, Mittelstaedt, and Tanner, 2002). . . . Rintala and Birrell (1984) argued that the media provide girls with possible role models. . . . [I]f girls and women are not represented in an equitable fashion by the media, then girls are not afforded the necessary exemplars to emulate.[86]

Jocelyn Steinke points out that "[e]xamining images of female scientists in the mass media is an important first step in understanding the role these images may play in shaping adolescent girls' perceptions of scientists and engineers and their perceptions of careers in SET [science, engineering, and technology]."[87]

Steinke and collaborators argue that "images of scientists in popular culture as depicted by characters and images in books, movies, television programs, magazines, comics, video games, clip art, Web sites, and a variety of other media sources . . . may be considerable sources of influence that shape children's view of the appearance, characteristics, traits, and lifestyles of scientists."[88] Steinke and Marilee Long analyze female characters in fictional and nonfictional children's educational science programs referencing scholarship documenting "the underrepresentation of women in scientific careers and the barriers to educational and professional advancement in science for girls and women."[89]

Texts representing gendered engagement with science and technology do so in diverse ways. Some narratives discussed in this book show how women's interest in science and technology identifies their criminal deviance (*La Cousine Bette, La Curée*) or intersects with feminine motivations in love and marriage (*Dracula, Making Mr. Right*), while other narratives identify heroic aspects of women subjected to or deploying science ("Hilda Silverling," *Lorenzo's Oil, Contact*) and technology (*Christopher Strong*). Some works, including *Contact* and *IQ*, identify specific structural barriers for women and men working in scientific and technical environments, while even popular television cartoon shows such as *The Adventures of Jimmy Neutron, Boy Genius* and *The Simpsons* connect aspects of masculinity and femininity with scientific and technical expertise. *The Governess* (Dir. Sandra Goldbacher, 1998), a historical film with actors Minnie Driver and Tom Wilkinson, depicts an extramarital affair between a governess hiding her Jewish ancestry and her employer, who is a photographer; after the governess demonstrates her photographic talent, the photographer ignores her contribution to his research and breaks up their relationship, motivating the governess to set up her own successful studio. A number of recent films set in the present similarly illustrate how scientifically and technically minded women resist conforming to social norms set for their gender (*Laurel Canyon, Kettle of Fish,* and *Yes*).

Gender Coding in Literature and Film

Gender codes in literature and cinema reflect a cultural imaginary that readers and viewers rarely question. The process of recognizing the connections drawn among gender, science, and technology allows us to reconsider what appears at first glance to be common sense. Jonathan Culler explains that

> what we speak of as conventions of a genre . . . are essentially possibilities of meaning, ways of naturalizing the text and giving it a place in the world which our culture defines. To assimilate or interpret something is to bring it within the modes of order which culture makes available, and this is usually done by talking about it in a mode of discourse which a culture takes as natural.[90]

Cultural codes are apparent in the narrative rules known to authorial audiences.

Peter Rabinowitz terms these rules of notice (what we pay attention to in narratives) "signification" (what it means), "configuration" (how pieces of stories fit together), and "coherence" (figuring out the ways the text makes sense). Rules "tell us where to concentrate our attention" and are further reinforced by cultural observation.[91] This book explores how fictional and cinematic narratives incorporate gender codes and schemas related to science and technology in narrative elements (characterizations, plots, and settings).

As James Phelan argues, characterization and plot are closely connected in narratives, even those focusing on science and technology.[92] Male and female characters in the texts under consideration emulate or transgress cultural codes concerning gender-appropriate identities and behaviors, while narrative plots link characters' expertise in science and technology to gender norms and schemas.[93] Recognizing the dynamics of plot as "a structuring operation," textual analyses demonstrate that fictional and cinematic plots about science and technology rely on gendered associations to evaluate moral outcomes.[94]

Feminist critics identify gender codes in narratives ranging from folktales to Hollywood cinema. Marina Warner's work on fairy tales surveys representations of women, situating Cinderella stories within social historical contexts for different generations of women who were economically and legally dependent on men and forced to get along in the same household.[95] In *Backlash,* Susan Faludi includes chapters on 1980s Hollywood television shows and films that demonstrate how production executives in television networks and film companies resisted positive representations of feminism and colluded in offering media products saturated with conservative depictions of women.[96]

Susan J. Douglas's *Where the Girls Are* provides a cultural history of the 1960s and 1970s, a period when female characters in films and television shows struggled with their limited social roles.[97] Douglas updates her analysis of media portrayals of women in her contribution to *The Shriver Report* (2009), in which she argues, "Women's professional success and financial status are significantly overrepresented in the mainstream media, suggesting that women indeed 'have it all.' So what much of the media have been giving us, then, are little more than fantasies of power."[98]

Including female characters in narratives set in scientific, medical, or technological environments highlights gender as a prominent function. Mieke Bal points out that "referential characters . . . act according to the pattern we are familiar with from other sources. Or not."[99] Popular representations reinforce or resist views of who should study, practice, and apply scientific and technical tools and procedures. Myths, literature, and films frequently portray male scientists and engineers as modern Frankensteins, egocentric, socially deficient, morally flawed, temperamentally eccentric, or power-hungry in seeking to increase their scientific and technical knowledge and fame. James Cameron, writer/director of the *Terminator* films and a former physics major, produced a science documentary; he claims that Hollywood films "almost never get their facts right. They always show scientists as idiosyncratic nerds or . . . villains."[100] His film *Avatar* (2009) offers a corrective, sketching a future in which the U.S. military and corporate executives join forces to exploit natural resources of the planet Pandora only to be defeated by an eco-friendly group of scientists with a highly ethical female leader (Sigourney Weaver) and a subversive Latina pilot (Michelle Rodriguez).

Typologies of scientists offered by scholars cover a range of genres, often presenting characters as mediating between science and the public. Roslynn D. Haynes's *From Faust to Strangelove* surveys "representations of the scientist in Western literature," starting with "evil alchemists" and "Bacon's new scientists."[101] Haynes discusses fictional godless and inhuman scientists of the eighteenth and nineteenth centuries such as Frankenstein, and classifies Victorian, post-Romantic scientists as efficient and powerful, adventurous, heroic, dangerous, impersonal, amoral, out of control, and rehabilitated. In 2003, Haynes acknowledged seven stereotypes of fictional portrayals of the male scientist as the "evil alchemist," the "noble scientist," the "foolish scientist," the "inhuman researcher," the "scientist as adventurer," the "mad, bad, dangerous scientist," and the "helpless scientist."[102] Kristen Shepherd-Barr begins her 2006 survey of drama, *Science on Stage,* with Faustus, considering plays about physics, mathematics, and thermodynamics and evaluating their appeal for contemporary audiences. Shepherd-Barr's penultimate chapter discusses eighteenth- and nineteenth-century plays about medical doctors by European and American authors, while her last chapter reviews "the challenge of engaging science on stage," comparing this task to that of the translator.[103]

Media scholars identify stereotypes related to cultural ideologies of femininity. Myra Macdonald groups representations of women in films and television shows according to qualities identified as "four myths of femininity": "enigmatic and threatening," "nurturing and caring," "sexuality," and "refashioning the body."[104] These qualities are incorporated in characterizations and plots in many literary and cinematic works that emphasize gendered aspects of engaging with science and technology. For example, Eva Flicker argues that romantic potentials of the female scientist are incorporated into a film "to develop suspense."[105]

Many texts identify supernatural, romantic, criminal, and/or natural qualities as essentially feminine aspects of how characters, whether playing major or minor roles in narrative plots, engage with science and technology. As chapter 5 illustrates, sex-typed traits of female scientists are often prominent in films, as these women appear more emotionally sensitive, socially marginalized, and interested in social good than their male peers.[106]

Narrative representations depict, provoke, or resist cultural change, thereby identifying tensions regarding sex roles, scientific and technical expertise, and ethics. Like consumers' reactions to colors, individual readers' responses to plot, character, setting, and theme are difficult to predict, given the variety of personal and cultural experiences individuals bring to stories and the abilities of individuals to read narratives for different purposes.[107] Acknowledging that a variety of influences affect interpretation of any text or object, Lori Kenschaft argues:

> One cannot rely on a cultural product to be, in itself, subversive or liberatory. Too much occurs during the process of interpretation for a cultural product alone, outside a tradition of critical conversation, to carry such weight. That critical tradition—be it located in a classroom, a newspaper column, a circle of friends, or a parent's whisper into a child's ear—crucially affects what people see and hear in any cultural product.[108]

Today's Hollywood producers survey particular audience reactions to a film and cut it to suit audience preferences, but many interpretive processes remain more elusive.[109]

Identifying cultural narratives of science, technology, and gender reports how ideology assists in determining interpretation. Reader response critics provide a set of principles, methodologies, and theories concerning narrative conventions and strategies, capabilities of readers, and the deeply contextual understanding of text. Agreeing with Hayden White, Peter Rabinowitz notes that narrative "conventions . . . are one of the grounds on which the politics of art is mapped out; often invisible, they serve as enabling conditions for literature's ideological structures. Thus, the study of literary conventions can help illuminate the connections between politics on the one hand and interpretation and evaluation, as the academy currently practices them, on the other."[110]

Feminist theorists interpret cultural proscriptions raised within texts as formative. Patricia Clough claims that "African-American feminists, Third World Feminists, feminist post-colonial critics, and queer theorists are reinventing the literary by making clear how the literary is not merely a matter of fiction. . . . showing how . . . modern narrative form . . . provides the logic or the ideologies by which social relationships are made intelligible."[111] Narratives incorporating stereotypes could replicate the hostile environments girls and women face in science, mathematics, and engineering, or they could provoke interventions or correctives. Cultural critique opens up representations and their social contexts to reveal ideological claims and suggest counterarguments.

Children's Viewing

Researchers at the UK Resource Centre for Women in Science, Engineering and Technology investigated what children watch and how they understand and react to nonfictional and fictional representations of female scientists, technolologists, engineers, and mathematicians on U.K. children's television. They found that there was "a substantial amount of STEM on five . . . British TV stations in the two sample weeks" (35); however, the sample of British and U.S. shows produced for children and shown on British TV infrequently include "'authentic' and 'diverse' portrayals, in terms of gender (also age, ethnicity and not only those who conform to the slim, attractive, bespectacled emerging image)" (36). *The Simpsons* (1989–), *Futurama* (1999–), and *Arthur* (1996–) were among the U.S. television shows included in this study.

Baby boomers, and their children who watch such shows on the TV Land network or online at Hulu, can easily identify caricatures of scientists in 1960s U.S. situation comedies. For example, *Gilligan's Island* (1964–67) and *Lost in Space* (1965–68) stereotype the nerdy male scientist—the Professor and Dr. Smith, respectively—and showcase women as sex objects (Ginger, Judy Robinson) or nurturers (Mary Ann, Maureen Robinson) who rarely assume authority over science or technology.

Contemporary animated films also incorporate gender stereotypes of science and technology, sometimes to question their force. For example, following in the tradition of science fiction films linking experimentation to apocalypse, *Lilo and Stitch* (2002) represents the genetic engineer as an "idiot scientist" with aspirations to be an "evil genius" and his alien product Stitch as a rather odd household pet. The film thereby conflates a popular stereotype about science (that it is an esoteric body of knowledge with dangerously inhumane outcomes) with the hopeful sentimentalism of romance (that love can reconcile all). The story of how the seemingly monstrous product of genetic engineering reveals itself to be more human than the earthlings melds the "orphan" story of the created alien life form with a plot about an orphaned Hawaiian girl left in the care of her older sister. At the end of *Lilo and Stitch,* the alien scientist, the life form, and the Hawaiians become a wacky and loving family, protected from both the authoritarian alien government and the intrusive social services of Hawaii. Despite this happy ending, the film leaves unreconciled the opposition between the masculine world of science (represented by both the male scientist and his alien product) and the feminine world of "family" that is all too fragile until stamped with approval by government bureaucrats.

The popular children's books and television program *The Magic School Bus* (1994–98) center on a teacher who enthusiastically instructs elementary schoolchildren about science. Ms. Frizzle is a rather wacky young woman (her voice on the show is supplied by Lily Tomlin) with a strange way of transporting her charges into mind-blowing situations in which they are miniaturized (cruising through a classmate's bloodstream or digestive tract, wandering in an old log along with many other organisms usually not visible to the naked eye, traveling inside a storm). This teacher comes across as a bizarre woman with amazing technical expertise and a bent for teaching science, gifted with remarkable powers to reach her audience.

Ms. Frizzle is the rare popular example of a woman who understands science and the scientific method, even if she has rather flaky, and sometimes determinedly feminine, ways of exhibiting her knowledge. Her outfit exemplifies the lesson of the day; in one episode she wears earrings fashioned as rocket ships and a dress with the solar system on it. Her favorite phrases ("Take chances." "Get messy." "Make mistakes.") are uttered as reminders that science is challenging, frustrating, risky, and full of failures that produce knowledge. Her powers are both analytical and magical: she seems to understand intuitively the structure and function of the organism, system, or science studied, without revealing her research. The audience learns, like her budding scientist students, about principles of biology, chemistry, physics, and earth science. But as one cover illustration of a Magic School Bus book about the principles of flight shows, these scientific and technical lessons come packaged in pink, in this case a pink airplane.[112]

Because Ms. Frizzle's unusual behavior and her wacky way of demonstrating scientific concepts are narrative features appealing to the primary target audience of elementary-school-age children, it might be difficult for viewers to see her as a realistic role model of how a female scientist should act. Rather, her example is iconically inspirational. Adults and children know that real scientists do not have magic buses or humanlike lizards helping them. Ms. Frizzle's enthusiasm, broad knowledge, and interactive style of teaching motivate her students to pursue scientific investigations. Tim, Keesha, Dorothy Ann,

Arnold, Phoebe, Carlos, Wanda, and Ralphie learn to put their observations of phenomena together with their research and to formulate a testable theory, one which might take into account the ways an old log disintegrates or how an airplane moves. Forming hypotheses that explain how the natural world and machines work, Ms. Frizzle's class works as a team in combining common sense and skills to analyze scientific ideas and technological products. Students display human frailties and talents. Phoebe and Arnold tentatively engage in adventures but always come up with interesting perspectives on problems that the more gung ho Ralphie and Wanda consider more cautiously. Each day's scientific adventure has all children participating and contributing to the group's effort and successful outcome. That the students work together is crucial because they are able to complement each other's strengths and weaknesses just as real-life collaborators in university classrooms and labs do. Not surprisingly for a production receiving some funding from NSF, the show educates children and adults by framing complicated scientific concepts in logical and entertaining ways.

The Nickelodeon cartoon show *The Wild Thornberrys* (1998–2001), a commercially supported production that includes a film (2002), also educates its audience about science but in a looser way as it concentrates more on entertaining than teaching. The British-American Thornberry family travels through exotically underdeveloped natural landscapes full of strange plants and wild animals so that parents Nigel and Maryann Thornberry can film their nature documentaries. Nigel is a brilliant but absent-minded natural scientist who calmly explains to his wife when they are in deadly danger. He is fascinated by the creatures he observes and comically describes his own physical and mental characteristics using pedantic scientific language. Maryann is the cameraperson, who lugs heavy equipment and superintends her husband to set up the best photo opportunities; her direct language often deflates her husband's pompous statements. Nigel and Maryann are a good team because they put together their knowledge about a species and combine their talents, consisting of Maryann's technical camerawork and Nigel's voice-over scientific analysis.

The three Thornberry children (Debbie, Eliza, and Donnie) and one chimpanzee named Darwin tag along with the grown-ups. The twist in this series is that daughter Eliza develops a magical power to talk with animals, including her chimp friend Darwin, so that even in the most remote locations she can set off on her own adventures while her parents are busy with their work.[113] Unlike her sister Debbie who is primarily concerned with hair, boys, and being left alone, Eliza has strong observational skills, an interest in learning, and a supernatural ability to converse with all creatures—attributes that make her an excellent science student.

Eliza is adventuresome enough to take risks to gain new knowledge, and she revises her hypotheses according to the new information she develops. Her adoptive brother Donnie helps her out when she does not recognize clues or dangers in the jungle. Found in the bush by the Thornberrys, Donnie has no discernible language and only erratically demonstrates a familiarity with social conventions, but his understanding of nature exceeds his communication skills. This family is composed of idiosyncratic individuals who need each other to survive. As in Ms. Frizzle's class, everyone has something to contribute.

Unlike *The Magic Schoolbus, The Wild Thornberrys* does not present explicit lessons about natural phenomena that analyze scientific principles or methodologies. Instead, *The Wild Thornberrys* concentrates on describing certain aspects of animal behavior discovered by the family. Both shows demonstrate that anyone's scientific abilities can be improved by experience, even for those of us without magical powers. These cartoons stimulate interest in science while teaching viewers about the construction of scientific hypotheses and conditions that affect how scientists work. In both shows, serendipity affects the scientific process as chance injects creativity into the careful synthesis of facts and evidence on which science relies. Random circumstances initiate the inquiry of the day for Ms. Frizzle's pupils and force Eliza Thornberry to refine her understanding of her family, her environments, and her abilities. These scientists-in-training learn to cope with chance, seeing it in relation to scientific frameworks that provide a sense of control over what might otherwise seem overwhelmingly dangerous. Science is represented as in the personal and social interest of everyone—experts and nonprofessionals.

■　■　■

This book applies critical theories elaborated by feminist critics, narratologists, and social studies of science scholars to identify particular constellations of narrative references to gender, science, and technology. Each chapter presents a set of fictions and films, organized topically according to various roles enacted by females using science and technology. Chapters 2 through 6 identify science and technology with specific roles assigned to women engaging with science and technology (ethical observer, criminal deviant, mother/caretaker, babe scientist, and technical innovator). The concluding chapter discusses examples of classic adolescent fiction and several recent television shows pitched at children, adolescents, and adults that revive and/or reconfigure stereotypical characterizations of how girls and women engage with science and technology. Characterization, emplotment, and thematics in the narratives replicate, reinforce, or occasionally resist gender stereotypes, as these narratives sketch sex roles at home and at work and portray how scientists interact with others according to familiar stereotypes.[114]

The argument presented in chapter 2, "The Ethics of Feminist Science," considers nineteenth-century fictions that rely on classical myths in troping science as a masculine project with dangerous and even deadly outcomes for women, contrasting these with Lydia Maria Child's short story "Hilda Silfverling," which identifies science and technology as beneficial to the eponymous woman. Referring to the Pygmalion myth rather than the story of Prometheus, Nathaniel Hawthorne outlines the dangers of scientific ambitions and technological tinkering in stories such as "Rappaccini's Daughter" and "The Birthmark."[115] Chapter 2 concludes with a discussion of woman's aptitude for science and technology represented in Herman Melville's stories about marriage and home and his poem "After the Pleasure Party," and Sena Jeter Naslund's modern adaptation of Melville's *Moby-Dick*, *Ahab's Wife or, The Stargazer*.

Chapter 3, " Female Criminals and Detectives," compares the representation of technologically adept female criminals in Honoré de Balzac's *La Cousine Bette* (1846) and in Emile Zola's *La Curée* (1872). In contrast, Mina, a central character in Bram Stoker's *Dracula* (1897), patriotically employs communication technologies to protect families and nations, identifying scientific progress with imperialism. Female scientists and detectives in recent television documentaries and dramas face updated versions of Mina's challenges.

Chapter 4, "Mothers and Medicine," discusses narratives by Zola, William Dean Howells, Charlotte Perkins Gilman, and the film *Lorenzo's Oil*. These texts reference femininity, marriage, maternity, and medicine. Chapter 5, "Babe Scientist: Science and Sex," details common elements of film romances about female scientists after Mervyn LeRoy's *Madame Curie*, looking closely at the protagonists and plots of *Contact*, *IQ*, *Twister*, *The Saint*, *Laurel Canyon*, *Kettle of Fish*, and *Yes*.

Chapter 6, "Femininity, Feminism, and Technology," considers Charlotte Perkins Gilman's fictions about women's technical innovation and three Katharine Hepburn films that image women's engagement with technology. Films connect femininity and technology in diverse ways, ranging from representing technology as violent (*Eve of Destruction*) to showing how technology makes romance possible (*Making Mr. Right*). The book's conclusion in chapter 7 considers several U.S. cartoon series (*Powerpuff Girls*; *Dexter's Laboratory*; *The Adventures of Jimmy Neutron, Boy Genius*; *My Life as a Teenage Robot*); two novel series for adolescents (Mary Norton's *The Borrowers* and *The Borrowers Afield* and Madeleine L'Engle's *A Wrinkle in Time* and *A Wind in the Door*); and other works that point to improving prospects for girls interested in science.

Time will tell whether these narratives might be responsible for motivating children to study science in elementary, middle, and high schools and at universities, or for raising public awareness of science, but we should not minimize the powerful effects of combining entertaining role models and messages (lively young women make good teachers for young children) with educational information meant to increase knowledge, understanding, and confidence.[116] Fictions, television shows, and films appeal to general audiences in the United States and have some capacity to affect the need for a diverse workforce in science and technology that developed countries feel most acutely. But these narratives might also speak to audiences elsewhere who are interested in how ideas about science undergird cultural assumptions of gender identity and behavior.

For children and adults who may be tentative about exploring science and technology, critical engagement with cartoons, fictions, and films enhances how we understand science and technology. As my interpretations argue, narratives linking gender, science, and technology explore values of self-reliance, innovation, and inclusive multiculturalism, while often replicating and sometimes resisting gender stereotypes. Although many narratives support perceptions of gender equity by overrepresenting women in STEM professions, they also sketch representations of feminine "intrusion" into the mostly male worlds of science and technology. The following chapter details the ways in which feminine interventions in science and technology often appear in fictions as ethically principled and reasonable, although these views are sometimes cast as signs of weakness or vulnerability. Texts ranging from *Frankenstein* to *Ahab's Wife* consider feminine motives, opportunities, and outcomes in science and technology.

The Ethics of
Feminist Science

Nineteenth-century fictions following in the steps of Mary Shelley's *Fran-kenstein* illustrate consequences that ensue when women are subjected to science and technological innovation or engage with science and technology. Although Shelley and Nathaniel Hawthorne depict scientific passion and ambition in conflict with sentimental domesticity in their narratives, Lydia Maria Child and Herman Melville describe women who benefit from science and technology. The bleak outcomes for females affected by science, outcomes that are apparent in *Frankenstein* and in Hawthorne's "The Birthmark" and "Rappaccini's Daughter," contrast with the more beneficial outcomes for women in scientific plots described in Child's "Hilda Silfverling" and in Melville's "Jimmy Rose," "I and My Chimney," and "The Apple-Tree Table." More recently, Sena Jeter Naslund's retelling of *Moby-Dick* in *Ahab's Wife or, The Star-Gazer* sketches how historical and fictional female characters succeed as result of their engagement with science and technology in ways that resonate with contemporary ethical arguments about women's participation in science.

Philosopher of science Sandra Harding in "Just Add Women and Stir?" claims an ethical basis for opening up scientific and technical fields to women, arguing that sustainable development issues must be considered from the perspective of women's lives. The rationale is clear: scientific and technological "changes that are designed only from the perspective of men's lives cannot produce an overall improvement in women's conditions nor, consequently, can they generate sustainable human development for men or the communities that both constitute."[1] Harding asserts, "A form of the democratic ethic clearly states the moral grounds for such a solution: <u>those</u>

who bear the consequences of a decision should have proportionate share in making it" (307).

Other feminists examine values in scientific practices and theories that in part determine gender equity. Philosophers Alison Wylie and Lynn Hankinson Nelson explain: "Feminists engage the sciences not only as critics of bias and partiality but also as practicioners who recognize that systematic empirical inquiry has an indispensable role to play in understanding and changing oppressive conditions."[2] Wylie and Nelson recognize "complex relationships between science and values," maintaining

> The problem we face, if we are committed to understanding and improving scientific practice, is no longer that of cleansing science of intrusive values but, rather, that of determining what kinds of contextual factors, under what circumstances, are likely to advance the cause of science in specific ways, where the goals and standards of science are themselves evolving and open to negotiation. (79, 78)

Assessing values in the contexts surrounding scientific actors, investigations, and outcomes acknowledges various perspectives and interests. Feminist philosophical arguments about the ethics of science endorse women's participation in STEM and are consonant with fictions that applaud women's authority in science and technology and criticize gender discrimination and racial marginalization.

Scientific Ambitions

Shelley's *Frankenstein* (1818) characterizes the failed ambitions of a scientist who seeks new scientific knowledge without thinking about the consequences or responsibilities associated with discovery. George Levine writes about *Frankenstein* that it "is about the inevitability of solipsism, the alienation of the self from the world, and the necessity and desperation of the quest to rejoin it."[3] As previously noted, the novel's subtitle, in referencing Frankenstein as the new Prometheus, indicts egoism, particularly of hubristic men risking family and friends for the sake of ambitious invention. Feminist interpretation recognizes Shelley's incorporation of gender polarities in the novel: the masculine pursuit of science and technology ignores and threatens sentimental attachments identified with women and children.[4]

The novel's three concentric narratives call into question the scientific experiment as a heroic enterprise, presenting perspectives of the educated observer, the scientist, and the object of study. An epistolary novel, *Franken-*

stein provides Walton's letters to his sister as the outermost frame of Victor Frankenstein's account of his ambitious scientific career and his neglect of family. Victor's narrative incorporates the monster's tale, describing his lonely search for companionship after Victor abandons him; Shelley contrasts Victor's insensitivity to others with the monster's initial emotions. The creature's "natural" and "intuitive" sympathy for others prompts him to seek companionship, but the DeLaceys' horror at the creature's appearance and Victor's refusal to create a mate for his "offspring" provoke the monster's revenge.

Instead of concluding with the scientific triumph of Frankenstein or the redemption of his creature, Shelley's novel ends with Walton's decision to make a safe return to home, domesticity, and order, values identified within the novel as feminine.[5] *Frankenstein* approves the pursuit of scientific knowledge while protecting self and others, as Walton is a scientific investigator who compromises scientific inquiry when its risks become too great. Walton sacrifices his ambitious dreams to extend explorations in the polar regions; he responds instead to his crew's pleas and turns his ship homeward. He will not risk his crew's lives, even for the sake of pathbreaking exploration, and thus avoids the sad fate of the ambitious, obsessed Victor Frankenstein, who dies seeking revenge on his creature.

Because Victor resisted marriage and familial connections in favor of pursuing science, many readers perceive his creature's appreciation of community as more natural, sympathetic, and worthy of respect than Victor's single-minded attempts to find fame as a great scientist. The creature's sensitivity, like Walton's care of his crew, is aligned in the novel with the feminine. If we imagine reading *Frankenstein* and excluding the first-person narrative of "the monster," Walton's decision to turn his ship back could signify weakness. However, having noted the massive destruction resulting from Victor's invention and subsequent abandonment of his creation, most readers understandably pause when he endeavors to persuade Walton's crew that important scientific discoveries require dangerous risks. Walton's sense of responsibility toward his crew and his decision to turn back appear more admirable than scientific ambition.[6]

Presenting Victor's experiences as learning opportunities, Shelley's novel instructs readers as to how scientists and inventors should act. Victor's first-person narrative influences Walton, who serves as the text's exemplary reader in judging his new friend's and the monster's actions. *Frankenstein* warns us that if practicioners do not exercise caution, science and human invention could force unintended consquences on society. The Frankenstein myth suggests that science has the potential to go awry and that there might not be a suitable home in our world for technological products. The novel aligns masculine ambition with interest in science and technology, and feminine care of friends and family with more cautious exploration.

Nathaniel Hawthorne's "The Birthmark" (1843) is also a cautionary tale about masculine scientific obsession and ambition. The protagonist Aylmer ("a man of science—an eminent proficient in every branch of natural philosophy")[7] stops practicing science when he marries. The narrator evokes what Carolyn Merchant describes as a Baconian understanding of science's control over nature:[8]

> In those days, when the comparatively recent discovery of electricity and other kindred mysteries of nature, seemed to open paths into the region of miracle, it was not unusual for the love of science to rival the love of woman, in its depth and absorbing energy. The higher intellect, the imagination, the spirit, and even the heart, might all find their congenial aliment in pursuits which, as some of their ardent votaries believed would ascend from one step of powerful intelligence to another, until the philosopher should lay his hand on the secret of creative force, and perhaps make new worlds for himself. (259)

Aylmer loves his wife, but he suggests to her that a peculiar mark on her cheek mars her beauty: "dearest Georgiana, you came so nearly perfect from the hand of Nature, that his slightest possible defect—which we hesitate whether to term a defect or a beauty—shocks me, as being the visible mark of earthly perfection" (260). The narrator explains that this mark "deeply interwoven . . . with the texture and substance of her face" is called a fairy handprint by suitors and "the Bloody Hand" by women; it fades or emerges when Georgiana respectively blushes or pales (260, 261).

Convinced that science can improve on nature, Aylmer wishes to eliminate his wife's birthmark. For him, it is the sole defect of her nearly perfect beauty, one that is "intolerable," for it "colors" the totality of their relationship (261). Georgiana responds that many previous suitors found the mark resembling a tiny hand to be a charm rather than a defect, and she wonders what might happen if her husband removes the mark. Despite questioning whether removing it would result in her deformity or death, she nevertheless submits to the operation because she recognizes that Aylmer views the mark as "a frightful object" (262). Georgiana's feelings scarcely matter, as "her husband was inexorably resolved to cut or wrench it away" (263).

Her birthmark encourages Aylmer to view his wife as a scientific muse, for, as he tells his wife, "Georgiana, you have led me deeper than ever into the heart of science" (264). Aylmer's pursuit of science as a masterful manipulation of nature links him both to Enlightenment scientists, who according to Merchant, understood science as a means of unveiling the powers of nature, and to alchemists, whose works led Victor Frankenstein astray.[9] Allison Easton finds Aylmer's fatal flaw to be his prioritizing of science over love: for him, "'science' is always more important than love. He fails to recognize Georgiana as a subject in her own right. Instead, impossibly, she must be both 'Nature' and the 'Ideal,' a sexual, potentially childbearing being who must also be physically flawless, self-denying, all-loving."[10]

Hawthorne's references to Aylmer's scientific powers and knowledge of alchemy suggest that he formed his assistant Aminadab (the name backwards is "bad anima"), called "thou human machine" and "thou man of clay" by Aylmer (273). Aminadab is "A man of low stature, but bulky frame, with shaggy hair hanging about his visage." Aylmer's imposition of science on nature appears misguided to the dark, subordinated Aminadab, whose only line of dialogue expresses disagreement with his master: "If she were my wife, I'd never part with her birth-mark" (266). More sensitive than his master, the assistant understands the futility and destructiveness of the scientist's quest, which raises readers' suspicion that Aylmer is unreasonable in forcing his wife to submit to an operation removing her birthmark.

Cindy Weinstein points out that "Georgiana fails to see Aminadab," for "he is neither human nor machine but . . . invisible." As "an ideal of immobility, stability, and submissiveness," Aminadab is a model for what Aylmer wishes Georgiana to become.[11] After Georgiana submits to her husband's performing surgery, Aylmer "was confident in his science, and felt that he could draw a magic circle around her, within which no evil might intrude" (266). But Aylmer's experiment is a miserable failure; in seeking to "perfect" his wife, he kills her.

Hawthorne's allegorical plots in "The Birthmark" and "Rappaccini's Daughter" employ binaries—masculine vs. feminine, science vs. nature, and ambition vs. love—familiar from *Frankenstein*. "Rappaccinni's Daughter" (1844) adds another binary (north vs. south) to this set in describing a student who observes firsthand an Italian Renaissance experimentalist's projects. Dr. Rappaccini's work in Padua produces living poisonous plants as an environment suitable for his similarly poisonous daughter Beatrice, for his science controls nature with malicious effect. Giovanni Guasconti, a Neapolitan, meets Beatrice, and unknowingly participates in the lifelong experiment Dr. Rappaccini conducts on his daughter. Beatrice warns Giovanni that her father "is a man fearfully acquainted with the secrets of nature . . . and at the hour when I first drew breath, this plant sprang from the soil, the offspring of his science, of his intellect, while I was but his earthly child. Approach it not!" (416). She allows that "my father's fatal love of science . . . estranged me from all society of my kind" (416). Giovanni's entrance into the story enables Dr. Rappaccini to provide Beatrice with a companion by making sure that the young man also becomes transformed into a poisonous being.

"Rappaccini's Daughter" presents a love story as an emplotment of scientific critique, as romance and science converge in destruction when the woman dies due to overreaching masculine ambitions. Because the couple "stand in utter solitude," Giovanni asks Beatrice to ingest, as he plans to, an antidote developed by Rappaccini's rival Baglioni (418). Dr. Rappaccini emerges from the shadows after Beatrice swallows the antidote and hears her complaint: "wherefore didst thou inflict this miserable doom on thy child?" (420). Rappaccini underscores her supernatural powers, which Beatrice discounts: "I would fain have been loved, not feared" (420). Baglioni's powerful antidote turns out to be poisonous and causes Beatrice's death, an event welcomed only by Baglioni who emerges to call "loudly, in a tone of triumph mixed with horror . . . 'Rappaccini! Rappaccini! And is *this* the upshot of your experiment?" (420). Baglioni, Rappaccini, and Guasconti share responsibility for Beatrice's death because they subject her to their desires, both scientific and romantic. Baglioni and Rappaccini provide material causes effecting her destruction, while Guasconti aids and abets them to fulfill his love. Destructive scientific experiments in technologies of poisons and antidotes in "Rappaccini's Daughter" are akin to the deathly operation depicted in "The Birthmark," as both procedures are identified with man's scientific repression of woman's agency.

Cultural Readings

Aylmer's and Rappaccini's experiments could not be replicated in contemporary scientific laboratories. Yet, as allegories of human engagement with science and technology, the plots and characters of Hawthorne's fictions have long cultural lives in being referenced as evidence in contemporary political debates about scientific investigations. To read a fictional text as a statement relevant to the real world is to offer it as a fragment of ideology, albeit an unstable ideology, as Terry Eagleton asserts:

> All literary works, in other words, are "rewritten," if only unconsciously, by the societies which read them; indeed there is no reading of a work which is not also a "re-writing." No work, and no current evaluation of it, can be simply be extended to new groups of people without being changed, perhaps almost unrecognizably, in the process; and this is one reason why what counts as literature is a notably unstable affair.[12]

Ideologies crystallize when close readers of literary texts of the nineteenth century debate scientific and technological controversies of the twenty-first. Recent political and media attention paid to Hawthorne's stories illuminates a case of fictional interpretation supplying "evidence" of the need for caution in scientific investigation.

There is no more charged environment in which to examine the real-world consequences of analyzing fictional representations of gender, science, and technology than in the political debates surrounding fetal tissue and cloning research. At the first meeting of President George W. Bush's Council on Bioethics in January 2002, its then-chairman Dr. Leon R. Kass asked panel members to discuss Hawthorne's "The Birthmark." Legislative debates in the U.S. Congress in fall 2001 about fetal tissue research focused on fears of human cloning, and the president initially opposed human cloning on any grounds. Therefore, it not surprising that the 18 members of the Council on Bioethics weighed ethical considerations about such science during their first meeting. As Sheryl Gay Stolberg reported in the *New York Times,* "Dr. Kass said that while the panel's work was delayed by the terrorist attacks of September 11, those events had also created a new moral seriousness in the nation."[13] After the meeting, the president suggested that the council members "can help the conscience of the country." The outcome of the council deliberations tilted toward upholding caution and morality over risk and discovery, but they did not recommend a permanent ban on such research.[14]

Other reports indicated dissension within the council. Stolberg's mention of "The Birthmark" in her January 18, 2002, article about the Council's first meeting provided a clue that the council would slow, if not halt, research on fetal tissue: "As an icebreaker, Dr. Kass scheduled a discussion of . . . 'The Birthmark,' a tale of a scientist who marries a beautiful woman with a tiny blemish on her left cheek and then kills her in trying to remove it." On July 26, 2002, *The Chronicle of Higher Education*'s Jeffrey Brainard wrote that a ten-member majority of the members on the Council on Bioethics favored "a four-year moratorium on attempts to create cloned cells for medical research, putting the panel at odds with President Bush . . . who has strongly supported a permanent ban on research cloning."[15]

Kass's choice of "The Birthmark" as an initial reading for the Council on Bioethics struck a cautionary note and acknowledged the power of literary representations to codify and inspire reactions to scientific and technological pursuits. The bioethicist George Annas wrote in May 2002 about "The Birthmark" in the *New England Journal of Medicine:* "The moral of this 1843 short story is that the quest for human perfection is doomed to fail and that scientific hubris can lead to death and destruction."[16] Annas identified Aylmer's "real crime" as "being unable to separate his love of science from his love of his wife" (1602).

Few observers of the fetal cell debates considered that Hawthorne's story illustrates a gendered and racialized myth about science and technology: Aylmer's patriarchal, scientific authority is invoked when he operates on his wife, asserting his masculine will to control nature, assisted by Aminadab and medical procedures. The absence of feminist viewpoints in media coverage of debates about fetal cells and cloning could be explained as a refusal to present a position seen as close to promoting eugenics or as a disinclination to "taint" pro-choice positions on abortion with arguments about cloning. Philosophers Wylie and Nelson assert that "the goals and standards of science are themselves evolving and open to negotiation," pointing the way toward continual reconsideration of values and interests in science, whether these involve procedures related to fetal cells (78) or other matters.

Cloning cells evokes Frankenstein's scientific experiments to create life, to allow a male to reproduce without women. While Shelley's novel and Hawthorne's stories align scientific mastery, particularly the control of nature's appearance and reproduction, with misguided male investigators who ignore the interests of women and others identified as socially marginal, it would be a mistake to generalize from *Frankenstein* and Hawthorne's stories that fiction always doubts scientific authority as suspect or dangerous, for, as discussed in the next section, some nineteenth-century fictions regard science as empowering and socially beneficial.

Feminist Science

Lydia Maria Child, who was well-known during the early nineteenth century for her political journalism advocating for the rights of Indians, African Americans, and women, found appealing the idea that scientific techniques enable social progress. She promoted reform by publishing sentimental fiction about social issues that blends radical political criticism, practical domestic advice to individuals, and the histories of minority achievements. Child's *Fact and Fiction: A Collection of Stories,* first published in 1846 and later reprinted within the collection *The Children of Mount Ida,* includes short stories resembling Greco-Roman myths, American historical tales, Indian legends, and science fictions challenging readers to correct abuses affecting African Americans, Native Americans, women, and immigrant Irish.

Providing a more positive spin on science and technology than Shelley's and Hawthorne's fictions, Child's story "Hilda Silfverling" explores how a young woman benefits from being subjected to scientific experimentation. "Hilda Silfverling: A Fantasy," originally published in the *Columbian Lady's and Gentleman's Magazine* in October 1845, connects science and social progress by imagining how science and technology help one woman escape cultural constraints. The story represents how technological innovations free Hilda from the social bonds of patriarchal oppression and shows how science can assist in relieving oppression, for Child imagines that progressivism in human history and culture would allow for the gradual improvement of cultural conditions for women.

Premised on the principle that history progresses reasonably, Child's short fictions in *Fact and Fiction* bear similarities to G. W. F. Hegel's theory of history. R. G. Collingwood describes Hegel's assumptions about the retrospective logic of causality:

> [S]ince all history is the history of thought and exhibits the self-development of reason, the historical process is at bottom a logical process. Historical transitions are, so to speak, logical transitions set out on a time-scale. History is nothing but a kind of logic where the relation of logical priority and posteriority is not so much replaced as enriched or consolidated by becoming a relation of temporal priority and posteriority. Hence the developments that take place in history are never accidental, they are necessary; and our knowledge of an historical process is not merely empirical, it is *a priori,* we can *see* the necessity of it.[17]

Illustrating historical shifts regarding social progress, Child's story "Hilda Silfverling" limns cultural progress in ways that fit comfortably within a Hegelian vision of history, one that imagines expanding rights for women.

Child was not dogmatically religious, but her journalism and fiction reveal her faith in a kind of Christian pantheism which accepts that organic processes of nature influence progress for humanity. Along with her optimistic faith in natural processes, Child's reformist idealism supports her representation of favorable aspects of technology. Unlike Hawthorne's and Shelley's fictions, which illustrate the excessive costs of scientific experiment and technological innovation, Child's story recounts how scientific and technological discoveries improve society in enhancing social conditions for women.

Child chose Scandinavian settings to tell Hilda's story, identifying how characters of different nationalities can be drawn together in affection and support each other. The narrator of "Hilda Silfverling" describes how the title character, "the daughter of a poor Swedish clergyman"[18] whose original name was "Hilda Gyllenlof," suffers first the deaths of her parents and then rejection by distant relations who see her as a burden. Fending for herself, Hilda finds work as a seamstress and maid in Stockholm, where she falls in love with a Danish sailor, Magnus Anderson. Soon after meeting Hilda, Magnus sets sail from Sweden and is lost in a storm at sea. Pregnant by him, Hilda gives birth to a baby whom she is ill-equipped to care for. She manages to find a good woman, Virika Gjetter, who adopts the ten-day-old baby and moves with the infant to Virika's own native village in Norway.

After someone discovers an infant's corpse, "strangled with a sash very like one Hilda" wore (207), Hilda is assumed to have killed her baby. She is imprisoned and sentenced to die. Like the judgment placed on Justine, who is wrongly executed for killing Victor's brother William in *Frankenstein*, Hilda is convicted by scant circumstantial evidence. She has no defense, for Virika cannot be located to provide any testimony on Hilda's behalf. But the court spares Hilda from execution because a scientific solution is proposed to effect the legal punishment: a chemist suggests that instead of beheading her, the community might learn more and lose nothing if she were to be frozen and reanimated 100 years later. The chemist has already practiced his freezing technique on a bear and a wolf, so he asks the government to grant his request to test the suggestion of "a metaphysician" to see "how extremely interesting it would be to put a human being asleep thus, and watch the reunion of soul and body, after the lapse of one hundred years" (208). The narrator tells us, "His request, being seconded by several men of science, was granted by the government; for no one suggested a doubt of its divine right to freeze human hearts, instead of chopping off human heads, or choking human lungs" (208).

Although afraid of the freezing process, Hilda is grateful to escape death. She is brought to "a tomb-like apartment" where she falls asleep while being frozen. With a deference to the scientific subject that Aylmer and Rappaccini do not exhibit, the chemist accommodates her desire to sleep on a shelf away from the crocodile and "handed her up very politely" (211). The narrator relates, "On the shelf where she lay was pasted an inscription: 'Put to sleep for infanticide, Feb.10, 1740, by order of the king. To be wakened Feb.10, 1840'" (211). The chemist's scientific experiment proves a boon to Hilda, who remains frozen until the chemist's great-grandson, also a chemist, reanimates her.

Having served her sentence, the still-young Hilda is free to do as she pleases and takes a new name to escape approbation. She travels to Upper Tellemarken, Norway, the homeland of her friend Virika, where Hilda finds a wooden trumpet called a *luhr* that she remembers was owned by Virika; it is "the only visible link between her present life and that dreamy past" (217). Hilda is told that this instrument was given to the current homeowner by one Alerik Thorild. When Hilda meets Alerik, she notices his resemblance to her lover Magnus (222), including their similar voices (230).

Indeed, Hilda realizes that Alerik is her own great-grandson, a fact that she relates to him when she turns down his first marriage proposal. Described as a persistently engaging and unusually spirited young man, Alerik insists on marrying Hilda. He believes what she says, that she is his great-grandmother returned to life, although not by science: "I have no doubt the fairies carried thee off some summer's night and made thee verily believe thou hadst slept for a hundred years" (235).

Unwilling to let any scientific experiment defeat his plan to marry her, Alerik argues by means of a loosely scientific, mystical philosophy that nature would not oppose their union. He describes how the human body changes its matter over time and that reincarnation inevitably recycles old matter, demonstrating that he and Hilda are no more closely related than any two other people. Citing Lessing's idea "that our souls keep coming back again and again into new bodies," Alerik asks Hilda, "If these things are so, how the deuce is a man ever to tell whether he marries his grandmother or not?" (233). Hilda is exasperated by her lover's perversity at turning around all arguments and complains that his fantasies are nothing compared to the truth of the Christian religion. But Alerik counters with another question, asking "what [does] the Christian religion [have] to do with penning up young maidens with bears and crocodiles?" (237).

After a time, Alerik overcomes Hilda's resistance, and the couple marries. During the course of their married life Alerik jokingly refers to Hilda as his great-grandmother, but their friends remain puzzled by his remark. Their marriage is not understood, perhaps because it is based on sexual pleasure and ignores social boundaries. As Carolyn Karcher writes, "Flouting all patriarchal taboos, the bawdily incestuous ending foreshadows a future that will give free play to sexual pleasure," a future made possible because scientific innovation, being frozen until social mores change, permits the crime of one century to be rewarded in the next.[19]

Hilda finds a different world in 1840, one friendlier to single women from foreign countries. Suspended animation has protected her from the narrow-minded suspicions of her past society by allowing her to move anonymously to a different one. While Child does not describe what scientific information was gained from the experiment of freezing a human being, she assumes that refrigeration effects social engineering. She imagines how a technology that is still experimental during her own time improves the lot of a woman from an earlier century and shows how scientific knowledge and techniques enable Hilda's romance and happiness.

Child's fantasy identifies technological developments as progressive. According to historians of refrigeration technology, inventors worked out many of the modern principles of man-made refrigeration in the late eighteenth and early nineteenth centuries. Accomplishments of two American inventors were widely reported in the European and U.S. press in the 1830s and 40s. In 1834, Jacob Perkins of New England provided one solution to "the mechanical production of cold" in obtaining a British patent on a closed-cycle volatile-liquid compressor and condenser.[20] In 1844 Dr. John Gorrie, director of the U.S. Marine Hospital at Apalachicola, Florida, "described in the Apalachicola Commercial Advertiser . . . a machine ice maker to insure his hospital fever patients that ice would always be available" (32).

Child does not delve into the exact means of refrigeration employed by the chemist in her story; rather, she creates an optimistic vision of how this technology, one her audience would have some awareness of, might reshape relations between men and women. The first modern refrigerators were developed in the early 1840s as a means of preserving meat and dairy products, a technological improvement that revolutionized agricultural distribution and consumption. Like other household innovations, the refrigerator influenced the way women worked at home and their contributions to family life. The fictional freezing process referenced in the story makes "Hilda Silfverling" a utopian fairy tale recognizing social equality as a benefit of refrigeration.

Child's fantasy is an allegory demonstrating how improvements in a domestic technology empower women socially and sexually. Refrigeration is thus imaged as a sexually charged trope, for freezing Hilda is the process substituting for imprisonment to confine her as a sexually loose, dangerous woman. But Hilda overcomes the frigidity forced on her, a condition that patriarchal culture associates with the condition of being woman, to find happiness. Hélène Cixous argues, in "Laugh of the Medusa," that writing allows a woman to retrieve her sexuality,

> giving her access to her native strength; it will give her back her goods, her pleasures, her organs, her immense bodily territories which have been kept under seal; it will tear her away from the superegoized structure in which she has always occupied the place reserved for the guilty (guilty of everything, guilty at every turn: for having desires, for not having any; for being frigid, for being "too hot"; for not being both at once; for being too motherly and not enough; for having children and for not having any; for nursing and for not nursing . . .)."[21]

Child rewards Hilda with a second chance at life, permitting her greater freedom and happiness. The story demonstrates how science and technology enable individual liberation and social progress in freeing women from cultural constraints. Child's vision of potentials unleashed by scientists in this story differs from the dangers imagined by Shelley and Hawthorne, as "Hilda Silfverling" reconfigures science and technology as pursuits beneficial to women, although not authorized and controlled by women.

Feminine Domestic Authority

Exemplifying Deborah Tannen's characterization of competitive, hierarchical male discourse, the television show *Home Improvement* (1991–99) represents Tim "The Tool Man" Taylor, host of a home fix-it show, as one step above

Neanderthal in his inability to understand the complex, sensitive philosophy of life shared by his wife Jill, his assistant Al, and his neighbor Wilson.[22] Tannen's prescription to men and women that "[u]nderstanding genderlect makes it possible to change" the way couples communicate (297) is enacted in each television episode, which shows how Tim raises his consciousness. He does so by learning (usually from his wife or his feminist neighbor Wilson) a different vocabulary inflected with more sensitive and practical values, a sociolect that helps him to decode his errors and understand aspects of female culture so that he can become more successful as husband, father, and friend.

Rehearsing nineteenth-century models of domestic power, *Home Improvement* acknowledges that a woman should control the security and stability of her home by exercising her intuitive ability to guide those in her domestic circle. Because our contemporary culture privileges, at least rhetorically, consensus over competition as a model for social progress, each show conveys Tim's realization that his wife was always already aware of what he later comes to learn: that her understanding of home and family exceeds his own and that he should defer to her judgment in these matters. Like *Home Improvement,* three of Herman Melville's stories—"I and My Chimney" (1856), "The Apple-Tree Table" (1856), and "Jimmy Rose" (1855)—represent gender conflict regarding home renovation as a pretext for miscommunication between husband and wife. In these stories Melville describes home improvement as a battleground in the war between men and women, suggesting that shared understanding generated from communication promotes domestic harmony.

The New England and New York domestic scenes represented in these three Melville stories are free of the dark and imprisoning aspects of domestic family life that haunt other Melvillean narratives.[23] While some critics resort to gender stereotyping in describing William Ford and his wife (he is rationally masculine, and she is too assertive to be adequately feminine, according to conventions of the time),[24] I argue that this couple negotiates common household problems in a fairly cooperative manner as they communicate their different philosophical approaches regarding home improvement. The stories consider how marriages function through periods of disagreement because the partners are committed to each other and do not resist expressing their conflicts. The Fords communicate according to a model that reconfigures power relations between wife and husband to create a modern domestic ideology. In short, the narrator's pessimism regarding the virtues of domesticity permit him to represent flexibility and compassion as virtues in his portrait of marriage.[25]

Husband and wife in Melville's "Jimmy Rose" disagree about whether the old city house they have inherited should be newly decorated. The narrator-husband's sentimental associations with the previous owner of the house prevent him from putting up new wallpaper. To convince his wife to preserve the home, he tells how Jimmy Rose's generosity before bankruptcy does not protect him after his financial ruin. Those who had been eager guests at his table resent the charity their former host later seeks from them. Yet Jimmy's aspect flourishes even though his pocket is empty: the "roses in his cheeks; those ruddy roses in his nipping winter. How they bloomed . . ." (343).[26] The wallpaper, with its "wilted resplendence of those proud peacocks on the wall," make the husband think of "the withering change in Jimmy's once resplendent pride of state" (345). The husband is more sentimental about his friend than many women, who are less sensitive to the needs of the poverty-stricken bachelor.[27] The narrator wishes that Jimmy Rose's life and house were memorialized and appreciated, rather than cast aside by his friends.

"I and My Chimney" presents presumably the same first-person narrator in a much more gruff and self-assertive mood, but with similar inclinations to preserve past technical achievements. The narrator identifies himself with the large, old-fashioned chimney standing at the center of his domicile and insists that the chimney must not be renovated or demolished, even though previous renovations to the house have changed the roof and chimney. The narrator's wife objects to the odd appearance of the "wax nose" of the chimney, but her husband claims to prefer the "picturesque" quality of "decay" (356). Only when the mortgagor of the property demands that the wax nose be removed does the narrator agree to the demand, but this lost battle motivates him to persevere in protecting the chimney from his wife, who calls in a builder to support her case. Like the basement of the city house in "Jimmy Rose," which resembled "the ancient tombs of Templars" (337), the cellar in the country house has noble qualities because the base of the chimney predominates. However, the husband's sentimental meditations on the stateliness and magnitude of this chimney conflict with his wife's plans to modernize the house by eliminating its "endless domestic inconveniences" (359).

The wife's health and energy outstrip the narrator's, but her plan does not recognize "the realities of architecture" that her husband voices: "if you demolish the foundation, what is to support the superstructure?" (360). Unlike the husband, the wife has a youthful spirit and excellent hearing, and she does not suffer from sciatica. She focuses on improvement and progress and, unfortunately for the narrator, seems inclined to fix problems as soon as possible, a principle that does not hold for the indolent narrator who expresses a preference for "oldness in things" (361). The husband's criticism of the wife does not demean her as he comically points out their differences, emphasizing his affection for his energetic, clever wife even as they battle.

The war over the chimney proceeds as the wife tries to redesign her domicile by omitting her husband's favorite part of it. Encouraging a mason to send her husband a letter indicating that the chimney might enclose secret passages, she hopes that the narrator will give in to his own curiosity, if not her desire to improve the house, but her husband refuses to be taken in by her schemes. Finally, he takes action and pays the mason to write a note verifying that the chimney is safe and has no secret passages. This document does not end the war, as the wife cannot abide the husband's attachment to the chimney. While "Jimmy Rose" and "I and My Chimney" ostensibly privilege his sentimental conservativism over her preference for renovation, in both stories the wife reasonably and convincingly articulates her views. The husband's sensitivity becomes a sympathetic characteristic that questions stereotypical sex roles concerning building renovation and serves as a foil to the wife's doggedness.

Melville's "The Apple-Tree Table" can be similarly read as an argument considering whether scientific rationalism supersedes supernatural and superstitous claims. The story commences with a lengthy description of how the husband, the first-person narrator of the tale, found the table in the attic of his newly purchased house, rumored to be haunted. His wife supports her husband against their daughters, who believe the table to be supernaturally affected (381). For a short time, the family accepts the table as a household fixture. But one Saturday night in December, while drinking and reading, the husband realizes that he hears a strange ticking coming from "one cloven foot of the little apple-tree table" (384). The narrator wakes his wife up to tell her about the ticking, but she persuades him to come to bed rather continuing his investigations. The next morning the wife and daughters listen to the ticking with predictable results: the girls believe it is the physical manifestation of spirits, while the wife maintains a commonsense pragmatism and doubts the supernatural explanation.[28]

The wife manages to be "mistress" of her house despite the unreasonable fears of the supernatural evidenced by her daughters, husband, and maid. Her strength of mind is not appreciated by her more fearful husband because he questions her war against the spirits. Yet the narrator changes his behavior around the table because he wants to imitate his wife, who remains logical when confronting a mystery. His newfound patience rewards him one night while he is alone; he watches a bug shining "like a glow-worm" and catches it under a tumbler "as it was just on the point of escaping its prison" (389). After the narrator explains how the bug came out of the table, his wife retains her composure in the face of her daughters' hysteria. The narrator expects his news to fluster his spouse, but she exhibits "scornful incredulity . . . worthy of Democritus himself" (392) and tells the maid to rub down the table with roach powder. After the more passive husband assumes the mystery has been solved, the wife questions whether there might be another bug in the table. The narrator puts another tumbler on the table and decides to wait for the bug, encouraging his family to stay up with him. The wife's resolve allows her to remain calm while waiting, although her husband and daughters cower at every noise, including the cider going off and the baker delivering the bread. Eventually, all are rewarded in seeing a bug "flashing in the room's general dimness, like a fiery opal" (396).

The story illustrates how female and male characters reveal attitudes about science and technology that defy gender stereotypes. The girls refuse to let go of their supernatural explanation of spirits in the face of material reality, but their mother prevails in sending her husband to consult with Professor Johnson, the male naturalist, instead of Madame Pazzi, the conjuress. Professor Johnson hypothesizes that insect eggs had been encased in the table for about one hundred fifty years. The narrator teases his daughters that their faith in spirits has not been vindicated, while his wife and the professor silence his gloating by suggesting that the husband's speculations have encouraged his daughters' fantasies.

Despite the scientific account supported by the wife, the husband continues to represent women as more inclined to accept irrational explanations than men are, a conclusion that readers cannot easily accept in view of his confessed irrational anxieties. Instead we understand him to be an unreliable narrator. Demonstrating his conviction that women are less likely to trust logic, the narrator recounts how his daughters take pride in exhibiting the insect to "whatever lady doubts the story" (397), but he neglects to praise his wife's calmness and common sense regarding the table, held despite her husband's and daughters' emotional outbursts.[29]

Melville's three stories reverse gender stereotypes in identifying sentimentality and affection with the male narrator and independence and rationality with the wife who is forced to indulge her husband's wishes. The wife in these fictions is correct and able to understand scientific and technical concepts in a superior way to her spouse, revising conventional associations. As Tannen remarks, "experience has shown that given the tool of understanding, individuals are able to devise ways of addressing and often solving their problems" (314). In *Home Improvement*, the domestic conflict demonstrates the cultural lesson that "men and women were not meant to live together, and therefore, married life is a series of consequences couples face for having defied fate."[30] Yet, as the actress who plays the wife on the show notes, "The fact that you see two people from different points of view coming together and working out their problems with humor and tolerance is of course comforting."

Melville's stories recognize the consequences of gender difference (i.e., understanding that women sometimes know more about and are superior authorities over science or technology) as empowering men and women to achieve fulfillment in domesticity. Negotiations between husband and wife suggest that self-claimed authority over technology should be treated suspiciously and that a dialogue constructed between variant points of view offers a collaborative interpretation superior to either individual's position. As Tannen notes, "looking at communication from the point of view of differing conversational styles is reminiscent of the principle of complementarity in physics, which was fundamental to the work of Niels Bohr. You have to look at things from two points of view, he explained, to really understand it" (317). Like marriage, science is enhanced by dialogue and courteous debate between differing perspectives.

Science and Romance in *Ahab's Wife*

Sena Jeter Naslund's novel *Ahab's Wife, or The Star-Gazer* (1999) takes up the conjoined challenges of representing the woman who is married to Ahab, one of Melville's most famous characters, and the noteworthy female scientist Maria Mitchell. Naslund's historical romance reworks Melville's canonical *Moby-Dick* (1851) to include heroic fictional role models for girls; she incorporates the life stories of other women along with "discovering" the woman who married Ahab, Una Spenser. Naslund revised Melville's narrative in creating a romance, a genre identified as feminine, in celebrating feminist networks and women's participation in occupations traditionally identified with men, such as whaling, philosophy, astronomy, and writing. Una even suspects that her second husband, Ahab, would not object to the idea of a woman captain, for "[h]e was not conventional, and I did not anticipate this idea, or any idea, would shock him."[31] Providing a female perspective on Ahab and the *Pequod*'s crew, Una, as her literary name foretells, becomes a writer.

Naslund's opening came to her as an epiphany of words and image: the sentence "Captain Ahab was neither my first husband nor my last" and the image of a woman standing on a Nantucket widow's walk watching sea and stars. *Ahab's Wife* tracks Una's quest for fulfillment, an odyssey incorporating Ahab's quest for revenge in chasing the white whale as one tale among many. Naslund's novel satisfies the most ardent Melvillean in weaving together characters, events, and refigured passages from *Moby-Dick* while also referencing numerous historical persons and political issues such as women's suffrage, abolition, penal reform, and public education. In addition to Margaret Fuller and Maria Mitchell, who befriend Una and become role models for her, other famous writers appear, including Nathaniel Hawthorne, Ralph Waldo Emerson, Frederick Douglass, and "Ishmael," the only sailor to survive Ahab's last voyage, who becomes Una's companion at the end of the novel. That Ahab and most of his crew converse in dialogue taken from *Moby-Dick* or in phrases consonant with it encourages readers to appreciate Una's story as the feminine, feminist complement to Melville's narrative epic.

Allusions to other works blend with unexpected turns in Naslund's narrative. Early in *Ahab's Wife,* Una spends a night in bed with Susan, who has escaped from slave catchers by sneaking into Una's Kentucky cabin. The relationship between the women is somewhat like Ishmael and Queequeg's in *Moby-Dick* in that conventions are upturned as Susan takes Una's surname for her own and and they call each other sisters. Elements of Susan's story also parallel those in narratives about runaway slaves, such as Eliza in Harriet Beecher Stowe's *Uncle Tom's Cabin,* and those in freedom narratives, such as Harriet Wilson's *Our Nig* that describe slaves' ingenious escapes.

Una is an appealing, heroic protagonist who is game for any adventure and sensitive to others' needs, and Ahab is humanized in being represented in a loving relationship with a young, vibrant wife. Una confronts cannibalism, the lunacy of two husbands, the desertion of her first, and the deaths of both parents and a newborn before hearing about Ahab's death.[32] Her life appears against a broad background representing many different people with a variety of political and religious views. Her politics generally agree with those of Fuller, who argues in the novel, "One must be able to imagine what it is like to be a woman, or a slave, if one is moved to remove artificial barriers. To remove unjust legalities" (378), an assertion linking womanhood and slavery that helps explain why the life story of the runaway slave Susan frames Una's narrative.

In the book's opening, the pregnant Una visits her mother in Kentucky while Ahab is on a long voyage. Una's labor pains send her mother driving off in a snowstorm to fetch a doctor. While waiting for her mother to return, Una opens the door to slave catchers who insist on fruitlessly searching the cabin for a slave before they head off in further pursuit. Unbeknownst to Una, the slave had sneaked into the cabin and inserted herself between two mattresses to hide from the slave catchers. After Una wails in childbirth, Susan crawls out from the bed and serves as midwife to Una, whose child is born, is named Liberty, and dies in quick succession. Una learns the next day that her mother has also died, for the old buggy she was driving turned over and she froze to death before she was found. Susan sets off for the North after Una provides her with outergarments and ice-shoes. Demonstrating technical ingenuity, they fit a pair of shoes with nails serving as crampons so that Susan can escape across the icy river before the floes melt. Susan and Una are kindred spirits who seek liberty and happiness and use found items to fashion homemade technology.

Una periodically wonders in the book what happened to Susan after she left Kentucky. The novel's last pages reproduce Susan's letter explaining that after a time she headed South to free her mother. Finding that her mother's foot was cut off after she tried to escape, Susan realized she could not leave with or without her lame mother, so she returns to the overseer, who brands

Susan to prevent her from again escaping. Susan's letter nevertheless ends on a hopeful note: she has faith that one day she and her mother and child, also named Liberty, will be free. No other character in the narrative suffers from "the unjust legalities" discussed by Fuller as much as Susan does, for her ingenuity, bravery, and kindness cannot protect her from being treated as property.

By referencing Fuller and the celebrated astronomer Maria Mitchell in her novel, Naslund naturalizes woman's participation in philosophy and science. Naslund explains in an interview how including details from Mitchell's life inspired the novel's genesis:

> Melville had written the quintessential sea story. I needed something more vast—the heavens. The first time I visited Nantucket (which was Ahab's home), I went from the wharf into a tour guide mini-bus, and the guide immediately began to speak of the historical woman Maria Mitchell, who was the first person in the world to discover a comet using a telescope. She did this from her roof-walk observatory in Nantucket. For a moment I thought she might be Ahab's Wife, but as I learned more about her, I saw this was impossible. Melville also amazingly enough was struck by Maria Mitchell and wrote a long poem, "After the Pleasure Party," based on the woman astronomer. In my book, Maria becomes a good friend of my totally fictional character Una Spenser, who does marry Captain Ahab.[33]

Melville met Mitchell and her father during a visit to Nantucket. Biographer Laurie Robertson-Lorant comments that Melville's poem "After the Pleasure Party"

> voices the anguish of a woman torn between her passion for science and her sexual desires. Her soul split in two with longing, the astronomer Urania has retreated to the terrace of a Mediterranean villa in a state of confused arousal after feeling sexually attracted to a man she observed walking arm in arm with a peasant girl at a picnic. She fears Amor "may wreak his boyish spite" on "her turbulent heart and rebel brain," and racked by "sensuous strife," she suspects her devotion to the cold stars is barren "self-illusion self-sustained."[34]

That Maria Mitchell, who lived on Vestal Street, lived a constrained life because of her dedication to her scientific work is a thought that also occurs to Una: she contemplates that Maria gives up conjugal bliss to view the stars, something Una would never do (464).

Naslund depicts Mitchell living and working within a loving Quaker family; she is close to her parents and to the younger siblings she tutors. Visiting the Mitchells, Una enters into an astronomy lesson with models of the solar system Maria has set up for her younger siblings. Maria's mother is "unexceptional" (462) in terms of intellectual pursuits, perhaps because she is the primary caregiver for her children, but Maria works for limited periods in a small closet that she calls her office. These appear meager circumstances to Una, but Maria's eyes "glisten" (463) with excitement, as she allows, "I am doing exactly what I love to do" (464).

Naslund describes how Maria Mitchell waited on the eve of her celebrated observation of a comet, the moment that began her career as a professional scientist. Her waiting occurs during the beginning of Una's marriage to Ahab. During this time Una blossoms as a writer, for she recounts her experiences and her friends' in philosophically meditative letters to Margaret Fuller. Spending time with the Mitchell family allows Una to recognize that her education, and Fuller's, were directed by fathers less playful and spontaneous than Mitchell's, a crucial distinction that seems to Una to account for Maria's passion for science:

> I reflected that I, too, had been very happy in the midst of their curiosity about observable phenomena. But what of the inner life and what of the dark issues of our time—of slavery, of the position of women, of temperance, of the crisis in religious belief? William Mitchell had spoken as an ardent abolitionist at the dinner table, but he mainly invested his time in science. Maria seemed content merely to focus on what she herself wanted to do. Perhaps that was as good an answer as any to the question of the status of women. (466)

Maria works in tandem with her father, who teaches her astronomical observation so that she can help him set ships' chronometers for captains passing through Nantucket, and she never doubts her abilities. She announces to Una that by observing Halley's comet, Maria will meet the challenge set by the king of Denmark: she will be the first in the world to observe a never-before-seen comet through a telescope (482). When Una wonders whether Mr. Mitchell might do this first, Maria disagrees: "I think it will be I, for Father is not so ardent as I" (482). Una wonders whether Maria is up to the task, fearing her friend might confront her own failure or that of others to recognize her.

Despite Una's fears, Maria does observe the comet "telescopically," as mentioned in chapter 151. This achievement was celebrated as a victory for American science and for women scientists struggling to prove themselves as equal to male counterparts. Historian of science Sally Gregory Kohlstedt explains Mitchell was

> a symbol to her contemporaries, men and women alike, of the contributions women were able to make in science. Her discovery of a comet in 1847 and her

calculations of its exact position at the time of discovery brought her a gold medal from the king of Denmark and led to her membership in the American Academy of Arts and Science, "in spite of being a woman." One result of these honors was Lucretia Mott's citation of Mitchell's achievement at the Seneca Falls Women's Rights Convention in 1848 as evidence of women's capability in all occupations.[35]

Mitchell later taught a new generation of female astronomers at Vassar and became an active supporter of women in science by participating in the Association for the Advancement of Women.[36] Mitchell advocated enlisting a wide audience of women club members to support female education and women's colleges, and she headed AAW's committee on science, which monitored the status of women practicing in the sciences and medicine.[37] Kohlstedt concludes that Mitchell identified "success" as "dependent on women working cooperatively to advance the situation of women" (143).

Characterizations of Una's relatives (her father the stern Protestant, her mother the inveterate reader, her feminist aunt, her abolitionist cousin Frannie) and friends (Susan, the dwarf bounty hunter David Poland, her first husband's former girlfriend Charlotte, Captain Maynard's wife, first mate Starbuck's wife Mary, and the elderly Phoebe Folger) provide a spectrum of the lives of women and other socially marginal figures. Female characters establish women's diverse roles, choices, values, and potentials. Naslund acknowledges the power of motherhood to change the course of individual and social destiny, as a number of characters, including Una, see motherhood as an ethically developmental experience.[38] Experiencing feminine rituals of love, marriage, pregnancy, and motherhood, Una behaves unconventionally, notably when she dresses as a boy to stow away on a whaling ship and again when she decides to trust David Poland. Una first lets him share her one-room Kentucky cabin and then allows him to accompany her while she journeys east by foot and donkey.

Incorporating elements of Maria Mitchell's and Margaret Fuller's biographies into a retelling of *Moby-Dick* lets readers view Una within a panorama of women's experiences.[39] Many women in the novel, including Una, Susan, Fuller, and Mitchell, pursue individual passions, intellectual and romantic, to varying degrees while supporting others. They connect social progress for women with scientific and technical achievement. Fuller and Mitchell are models for Una, who recognizes that even famous women resist social conventions to become celebrated for pursuits traditionally identified as masculine (458), just as Una herself ran away to sea and became familiar with whaling.[40] Fuller particularly suffers criticism from conservative characters who prescribe domestic duties and constrained lives for females. For example, kind Judge Lord dismisses Fuller to Una: "I should rather have you, my dear . . . describe to me exactly what you are seeing and thinking at this moment than listen to Margaret Fuller's dusty learning" (376).

Una hears more criticism of Fuller from Nathaniel Hawthorne, who is initially disinclined to speak with Una until he learns she bears a name he wishes to give to his future child. Naslund's account of the meeting between Hawthorne and Una melds critical and political issues, illustrating tensions evoked in Hawthorne's fictions and critical accounts of them. Jamie Barlowe argues that

> Hawthorne scholarship has, through its exclusions and often intimidating and silencing impositions, exposed the excessive fears that these exclusions and impositions have attempted to hide. When such texts/contexts are continuously recontextualized and reread, they become sites where identity, agency, and power dynamics are contested, and where differences are allowed to emerge, rather than already claimed territory where identities of the Other can be rigidly constructed and maintained by the dominant group.[41]

In Naslund's novel, Hawthorne and Una meet in the forest as Una is on her way to look for Fuller at Emerson's home. That Hawthorne stormed out of Emerson's house after Fuller dared to disagree with him exemplifies the power dynamics Barlowe identifies.

Hawthorne and Una engage in conversation about his prose that empowers her as a critical peer, while offering a sympathetic dimension to Hawthorne as a result of their interaction. Although their meeting might seem like a slight detail blending history in fiction, the episode has great poignancy and offers a hint of repressed eroticism familiar to readers of *The Scarlet Letter* (1850) who remember how Hester and Dimmesdale meet in a forest outside Salem. Una later learns that Hawthorne bought her nightgown after her friend David Poland finds her forgotten valise (497).

Reviewers offered generally positive responses to *Ahab's Wife,* which became a bestseller, but each pointed to different virtues. A number noted the passionate eloquence of the prose and favorably remarked on its epic sweep. Pico Iyer in *Time* indicated that the novel "[p]ossesses the reader like an unholy fever," and James Urquehart in *The Times* (London) described it as "[c]rammed with travel, childbirth and rearing, unorthodox liaisons and a rigorous engagement with the scientific, cultural, religious and moral issues of the day."[42] More provocatively, Walter Kirn labels *Ahab's Wife* as footnote fiction, suggesting that while Melville's masculine adventure story remains timeless and powerful, the feminine romance is derivative, a kind of "artistic affirmative-action program."[43] Kirn's review concludes that the novel is "a diverting work in its own right, decidedly minor but charmingly determined to say something major, to stick up for itself." He diminishes the interpretive capacities of *Ahab's Wife,* noting that Naslund's Ahab could be "any grumpy old sea captain" instead of "Melville's great creation" and that Una is an indomitable heroine who is ultimately a bore.

In contrast, feminist reviewers point to Una as the central unifying force of a woman-centered novel that stands side-by-side with *Moby-Dick,* rather than offering commentary on it. Una becomes a star-gazer, but her domestic trials and tribulations remain the focus rather than professional trials or attempts to balance personal and professional lives. Naslund's and Melville's narratives are complementary epics, as Melville's tells of men's lives in the nineteenth-century and Naslund's tells of women's.

The division between marriage and work noted in *Ahab's Wife,* that most women look for love and most men for professions, resembles generic divisions assigned to different fictional forms, generic conventions that Naslund flouts in true Melvillean spirit. As Steven Cohan and Linda Shires explain the romance:

> The modern romance genre can be more properly termed a 'feminine narrative.' For it structures the meaning of gender difference through a narrative representation of female subjectivity in much the same way that masculine narratives such as the thriller and western structure the meaning of gender difference through narrative representations of male subjectivity. Though their structures differ, both feminine and masculine narrative genres rationalize the normative values of heterosexual relations—in the household (for the female) and in the workplace (for the male). In the case of feminine narrative, the story places gender in a field of signification so that, at the level of events and actors, representations of sexual difference acquire meaning by reinforcing the values of love and marriage, of emotional vulnerability and domesticity, and by making them appear natural, inevitable, and desirable as culturally legible signs of "femininity." In the case of masculine narrative, the story structure promotes the values of competition, physical power, and authority as irrefutable signs of "masculinity."[44]

Ahab's Wife is both a romance and an adventure about Una, blurring the generic boundaries and gendered modes of appeal that Cohan and Shire categorize. Like *Moby-Dick,* a multicultural epic of whaling that puts Ahab's obsession and Ishmael's education in its foreground, *Ahab's Wife* has a broad scope in describing Una's life. The novel documents her relationships with individuals whose different genders, races, ethnicities, classes, regions, religions, political viewpoints, and physical challenges prompt Una's reflections.

Applying conventions of heroic narrative used to depict male scientists to characterize Mitchell, and including Fuller's tragic romantic adventure,

Naslund's narrative resists being restrained by generic boundaries, an appropriate stylistic choice considering that *Moby-Dick,* emulating the white whale, slips in and out of genre categories.[45] Child's and Melville's fictions identify women's powers to access science and technology in ways consonant with Naslund's account, contradicting the view of science and technology as a male domain uncongenial to women as represented by Shelley and Hawthorne. *Ahab's Wife* acknowledges women's interests in science and technology as cooperative and progressive, not transgressive.

In the works discussed in this chapter, women's scientific and technical aptitudes are exceptional rather than typical, but the most recent among them offers optimism for the potential of future generations to emulate Maria Mitchell's achievements and the fictional Una Spenser's adventures. As Henry David Thoreau wrote at the end of *Walden* (1854) in his parable of a bug, an anecdote like that of Melville's "The Apple Tree Table," "Who knows what beautiful and winged life . . . may unexpectedly come forth from amidst society's most trivial and handselled furniture to enjoy its perfect summer life at last!" (312).

Female Criminals
and Detectives

The stereotyping of emotion as feminine is "a bedrock belief" in Western culture according to psychologist Stephanie Shields.[1] Similarly, the distinction between feminine emotion and masculine reason has become an essential element characterizing criminals and crime solvers in fictional narratives. Nineteenth-century legal scholar Francis Lieber endorsed this distinction in his commentary on rehabilitation in penitentiaries: "The two sexes have been destined by the Creator for different spheres of activity and have received different powers to fulfill their destiny. The woman destined for domestic life, and that sphere in which attachment and affection are most active agents, has been endowed with more lively feeling and acute sensibility: she feels, man reasons."[2]

A number of nineteenth-century novels represent criminality according to gendered schemas, recognizing deviant behavior in men of the lower classes and madness as "the female malady."[3] Writers described men as evolutionary throwbacks prone to violence, and female criminals as aberrant and prone to hysteria. At first mirroring popular associations of under-class criminality and heredity, details from fictional accounts were later incorporated into the science of criminal anthropology dating from the publication of Cesar Lombroso's *L'uomo delinquente* in 1876. In our own day, images of criminality incorporating stereotypes of atavism and sexuality in films and television testify to the continuing power of gender, race, and class stereotypes in crime narratives.

Scientific theories of deviance in the United States and Europe developed to help governments identify criminals and administer criminal justice. Stephen Jay Gould's *The Mismeasure of Man*, a history of pseudo-scientific theories of human intelligence based on physiognomy, and Simon Cole's *Suspect Identities,* a history of criminal identification, consider how personal biases and cultural values influenced the development of criminal science and the ways in which scientific techniques such as fingerprinting and anthropometry informed national practices in criminal justice.[4] During the eighteenth and nineteenth centuries, a period marked by political revolutions in Great Britain, France, and the United States, politicians and moral reformers worked to create effective systems to identify and rehabilitate lawbreakers.

According to Michel Foucault, French prison reformers developed the penitentiary system of enforced discipline as a rigid hierarchy crafted to control deviant behavior; criminals were seen as abnormal individuals whose persistent aberrant behavior could be rehabilitated through an enforced system of control.[5] Reformers portrayed criminal behavior as akin to physical and mental illness and described delinquency as a lower-class abnormality that could be controlled if it were isolated and treated in the same manner as a physical contagion.[6] The criminal's inability to mask physiological symptoms indicative of immorality exposed him or her as an impaired individual like the lunatic or the cholera victim.

The nineteenth-century narratives discussed in this chapter incorporate principles of phrenology and physiognomy, pseudo-sciences predicated on the assumption that criminal tendencies and behavior could be predicted and revealed by genealogy and physical appearance. Novels by Honoré de Balzac and Emile Zola include stereotypes of race, class, and gender in their presentations of criminal contagion. Bram Stoker's *Dracula* conceptualizes transgression as vampirism and suggests that scientific and technical efforts of Anglo-American men and women, particularly Mina in *Dracula,* make it possible to stamp out its foreign influence. Contemporary television shows about crime link female investigators with emotional sentimentality and supernatural powers as feminine methods of detection assist science and technology.

Unraveling the Lacemaker: Balzac's *La Cousine Bette* and Zola's *La Curée*

Like phrenologists and criminal anthropologists, Balzac and Zola asserted the primacy of visual "scientific" evidence in their representations of the born-criminal female. Their fictions portrayed the female criminal as a masculinized woman whose passion for crime negated any sexual or maternal instinct. In *La Cousine Bette* (1846) and *La Curée* (*The Kill,* 1871–72), two novels about speculation and greed, born-criminal females appear sexually ambivalent because their "natural" feminine qualities are distorted by their perverse predispositions to crime. Characterizations of Bette Fischer and Sidonie Rougon incorporate assumptions of female sexuality prevalent in early psychological and physiological studies of criminal behavior; they are described as bearing physically masculine traits, as sexually neutral, and as passionately devious, exhibiting personality characteristics that sociologists and criminal anthropologists linked to the unnatural criminality of women.

Nineteenth-century novelists who represented characters as realistic types relied on associations of moral and physical characteristics conventionalized by phrenologists and physiognomists. For instance, Victor Hugo portrayed Madame Thénardier of *Les Misérables* (written in the 1840s and published in 1862) as a type of masculinized woman whose love for her children exists in parallel with her criminal leanings. Watching her two daughters at play, Madame Thénardier was "a woman whose appearance was somewhat rather forbidding, but touching at this moment . . . swinging the two children by a long rope, tenderly following them with her eyes for fear of accident with that animal yet celestial expression peculiar to motherhood" (146–47).[7] Madame Thénardier's physique reveals her criminal tendencies; she

> was a red-headed, large but angular woman, the soldier's wife type in all its horror with, strangely enough, a languid air gained from novel reading. (She was a masculine simperer.) If this woman, now seated bending over, had been upright, perhaps her towering form and her broad shoulders, those of a movable colossus, fit for a market-woman, would have dismayed the traveller, disturbed her confidence, and prevented what we have to tell. (150)

This description mixes maternal affection and masculine aggression, combining feminine and masculine traits that later criminal anthropologists also identified in some female offenders.

According to social scientists, giving birth to and caring for children muted the criminal impulses of some women. Thus, the female criminal frequently appears in many nineteenth-century fictions as a spinster or a childless woman whose social marginality motivated and encouraged her to carry out dangerous schemes. Describing the fictional female offender's "unnatural" propensities for crime, novelists contributed evidence illustrating scientific and pseudo-scientific theories that classify human behavior according to physiological characteristics.[8] Balzac acknowledged his interest in works of Johann Casper Lavater and Franz Gall, and Zola affirmed his belief in the scientific theories presented by Cesar Lombroso and Prosper Lucas. Lavater and Gall were primarily concerned with identifying physiological indications of mental health, while Lucas's biological theory linked heredity to crime by introducing the concept of atavism, the reappearance of a characteristic in subsequent generations.[9]

Nineteenth-century phrenological and criminological theories of deviance and femininity offer a context for Balzac's and Zola's fictional treatments of criminal behavior.

Phrenologists' linking of physiology and temperament provided novelists and criminologists with a pseudo-scientific system for classifying deviant behavior.[10] Describing the field as an "uncultivated science," Lavater, the father of phrenology, first published his essays in German in 1772; he claimed that physiological features cannot be changed and that "these are . . . decisive marks of the temper and character of man."[11] He argued that phrenologists could discern various moral characters of animal species,[12] and he maintained that "[c]onsideration and comparison of the external and internal make of the body, in male and female, teaches us that one is destined for labour and strength, and the other for beauty and propagation" (241). Gall and George Combe agreed with Lavater that men and women are phrenologically distinctive. Gall and Combe pinpointed areas of the brain responsible for character traits and indicated more specifically than Lavater which traits were likely to be stronger in women (parental love, adhesiveness, and veneration).[13] They also argued that women who exhibited masculine features (a heavy jaw, a piercing gaze, thick neck, etc.) were more likely to behave in a masculine manner than women who appeared more delicate and fragile.

Social scientists produced case studies and statistical analyses that cast a positivist light on the subject by claiming that race, age, and sex determined criminal tendencies of the individual. Adolphe Quetelet's 1833 survey of national crime statistics concluded that educational background and economic conditions could not alone account for criminal behavior, but that "the different races of men" and climate were important factors linked to crime, for these genealogical and geographical considerations determined criminal opportunity.[14] His description of the individual type most likely to commit a crime (a young man in his twenties from a coastal region) and his comments on differences between the sexes influenced novelists who incorporated such realistic details in crime stories. In 1833 Quetelet argued that upper-class women, who were presented with fewer criminal opportunities, were less likely to commit crimes; however, he acknowledged that female criminals could be as vicious as male counterparts.[15] He held that the type of crime differed with the sexes because women were far more likely to indulge in devious schemes than their male counterparts: "Woman, without doubt out of a sense of weakness[,] commits crimes against property rather than against persons; and when she seeks to destroy her fellow creature, she employs of preference poison" (65).

Influenced by phrenological theories and sociological studies, nineteenth-century French novelists depicted male criminals as atavistic animals. Balzac described the superhuman criminal Vautrin as a primitive savage, and Hugo represented the angry Jean Valjean as an instinctive criminal. Stendhal also depicted in his writings young lower-class men whose transgressions against society resulted from their violent impulses. Yet the brutish, violent character-istics assigned to the fictional male criminal did not prevent him from being sympathetically viewed by the general populace, for the fictional offender's revolt against the law was regarded as a sign of justifiable political rebellion by the marginalized working class.

Novelists who represented criminality as the popular revolt of the laboring classes understood, Louis Chevalier argues, "the working classes' conviction that they constituted, on the edge of the city and its civilization, a different, alien and hostile society."[16] Journalists and novelists described criminals as men whose physical strength exemplified the political power of the masses. The superior intellect and abilities of Balzac's Vautrin and Hugo's Jean Valjean mark them as heroic figures. Fictional characterizations of heroic criminals relied on historical precedents. Vidocq, a once-powerful criminal, published a cel-ebrated memoir (whether he wrote the four volumes or not), relating how he became head of the Sûreté, a transformation of Crime into Justice, a story that Balzac could not resist incorporating into his characterization of Vautrin in *La Comédie humaine*.[17] Although Balzac's character Jacques Collin, alias Vautrin, was capable of vicious murder, he was also depicted as generous and loyal to his fellow thieves. Chevalier describes Vautrin as the first criminal character to symbolize the frustrations of the working classes.

Whereas male criminals were compared with animals, children, and women, the typical female criminal was described as an unnaturally mascu-line woman whose transgressions against the law and ethics resulted from her sexual perversity. In *Splendeurs et misères des courtisanes* (1839–47), Balzac argued that "[p]rostitution and theft are two forms of vital protest, male and female, of *the state of nature* against society."[18] Like sociologists of his time, Bal-zac assumed that these "forms of protest" pointed to distinct characters of the sexes: women were passive by nature; therefore, their habitual crime, prostitu-tion, consisted of the utmost passivity. All men are acquisitive by nature and desire to own property; an evil man will act on this impulse without impunity. Balzac claimed that criminals become stupid (like animals, women, and chil-dren) because all of their energies are devoted to their profession:

> Not only, the crime once committed, do their troubles begin, for they are as bewildered by the need to hide their booty as they were formerly oppressed by poverty; but also they are weakened like a woman recovering from childbirth. Frightening in their energy at the time of action, they are like children from the moment of triumph. Their nature, in a word, is that of wild animals, easy to kill when they've fed. (460–61)

The novelist drew connections among criminal, woman, child, and animal, basing his view of deviance on a theory of sexuality positing female weakness and deceitful female motivations.

Alluding to phrenological theories and assumptions of early criminology, both Balzac and Zola noted the aggressive temperament and masculine physical features of the born-criminal female, including her darker complexion and coloring. Of all criminals, only prostitutes, who were represented in sociological literature as the most feminine of women, managed to escape being seen as androgynous and asexual. Like phrenologists and criminologists who noted physiological attributes, notably the shape and the size of the head and peculiar facial anomalies, as signs of criminal tendencies, these novelists distinguished the born-criminal female by physical characteristics, including color of skin and facial aspect, which revealed her primitively masculine predisposition to commit criminal acts.

La Cousine Bette describes Lisbeth Fischer, the bitter cousin of the pure and beautiful Adeline Hulot, as a "peasant girl from the Vosges, with everything that implies: thin, dark, with glossy black hair, heavy eyebrows meeting across the nose in a tuft, long and powerful arms, and broad solid feet, with some warts on her long, simian face: there is a quick sketch of the spinster."[19] The reference to the Vosges, a department associated with revolution and rebellion, is pointed: after the Franco-Prussian War and until the end of the First World War, part of the Vosges became German territory. Even for a reader unfamiliar with the plot of the novel or with French history and geography, the physical description indicates Bette's inclination to crime by pointing to her darkness and superabundance of strength, which are suspicious traits. Her dark, abundant hair, her bitter vengefulness nurtured over a long period, and her great strength are her most prominent features, and they metonymically represent her as of a lower class and race in betraying her instinctive criminality. According to the racialized discourse of the novel, criminals are savages; Bette is a dangerous natural force (83) whose name connotes beast ("une bête") and stupidity. Animal metaphors in the novel indicate her criminal tendencies; at various times, the narrator describes her resemblance to a mule, a monkey, a tiger, and an ape, animals associated by phrenologists with vicious character traits.[20]

Bette's illiteracy does not constrain her devious intelligence, and her obsessive jealousy of her virtuous cousin Adeline motivates the spinster to scheme for the downfall of the Hulot family. A lacemaker by trade, Bette engages in complicated financial and legal intrigues that would not have succeeded if planned by someone who was less patient or less passionate about achieving her destructive goal. Her ability to work secretly for a long time on an elaborately devised plan can be seen as a realistic detail drawn from Quetelet, who viewed a woman's typical crime as committed within a small circle, for reasons of "shame or modesty," and by devious means.[21]

According to Balzac, Bette's virginity provided her with the power to intrigue against the Hulots:

> Virginity, like all abnormal states, has its characteristic qualities, its fascinating greatness. . . . When celibate persons make demands on their bodies or on their minds, need to resort to physical action or thought, they find steel stiffening their muscles or knowledge infused into their minds, a diabolical strength or the black magic of the Will. (118)

Virgin and celibate, Bette resists marrying a man who might control her. For much of the novel, Bette's ambivalent and masculinized sexuality makes her a curious, but not dangerous, woman to her family.

Until the young Polish sculptor Wenceslas Steinbock enters her life, Bette seems uninterested in marriage except as a business proposition. Bette's affection for him reverses the norm of sexual relations: the narrator describes her as the man of the relationship, while Wenceslas's passivity and gentleness mark him as "female" (107). Bette is outrageously jealous when the sculptor falls in love with Adeline's daughter Hortense, although the spinster can't explain her own desire. Bette wants to be his all-consuming and domineering mentor or even mother, not his lover or his wife, and she is willing to fight to the death to prevent her young cousin Hortense from enjoying a happy marriage with Wenceslas. To achieve her goal of destroying the Hulots, Bette provides Wenceslas with a mistress, Valerie Marneffe, a woman also involved with Baron Hulot.

The novel describes other women who lie, cheat, and steal to stay afloat. Even the supremely good Baroness Hulot (Adeline) is willing to sell herself to obtain a dowry for her daughter. Valerie Marneffe manages to convince her husband, the bureaucrat Marneffe, and her lovers Baron Hulot and Crevel that each man has fathered her child, so that she can ask all of them for money. Hulot's mistress before Valerie, the singer Josepha is also a beautiful, greedy woman whose liaisons pay off. Masquerading as Madame Saint-Estève, although sometimes using the alias Madame Nourrison, Jacqueline Collin, the aunt of Jacques Collin, alias Vautrin, appears in *La Comédie humaine* as the woman who keeps a brothel in *La Cousine Bette,* receives stolen goods in *Le député d'Arcis,* and acts as servant to a prostitute in *Splendeurs et misères des courtisanes.* Both Bette and Madame Saint-Estève are masculine women using the younger, prettier women as lures in financial schemes.

Madame Saint-Estève negotiates with Valerie Marneffe's scorned Brazilian lover, Baron Montéjanos, to work against Bette's schemes, leveraging the baron's jealousy to have him punish Valerie. Madame Saint-Estève designs a complicated revenge plan: Baron Montéjanos administers a strange Brazilian disease-causing poison obtained from his "Negro" servants to another woman, who infects the baron. Then Montéjanos infects Valerie, who transmits the disease to Crevel. Balzac identifies Baron Montéjanos as a racial Other, assuming "that animal, Negro, jealousy, passion, criminality, and the New World are metonymically linked qualities."[22]

A similar reference to the female criminal's position as an intermediary arranging sexual liaisons occurs in *La Curée* (*The Kill*), in which Zola describes how Sidonie Rougon acts as an agent for her successful brothers, Eugène Rougon and Aristide Saccard, and secretly plots her revenge against those who cross her. Like Bette, Sidonie is small and dark; she ostensibly earns a living as a trader in lace. Her appetite for money and her need for intrigue serve her well because she makes a career out of negotiating for wealthy families with secrets to hide. Her unattractive appearance (she is "petite, maigre, blafarde," / "short, lean, and sallow")[23] belies her success; in spite of her dowdy clothes that make her less feminine to the narrator, who notes that she "was scarcely female" ("etait si peu femme") (369), Sidonie's biological need for intrigue helps her brother Aristide marry a rich woman who could underwrite his career.

Although Sidonie married at an early age, her preoccupation with litigation after her husband's death makes "the woman die in her" ("la femme se mourait en elle") (371). Other details support this assertion: she infrequently uses her husband's surname; most people refer to her as Madame Sidonie. Her masculine interest in business neutralizes any feminine sexuality in her and makes her a hermaphrodite (373). In an analogy that flatters none of the parties, Zola described her as a species between a businessman and a procuress (373).

Since Sidonie's life focuses on her acting as an intermediary in lawsuits, it is not surprising that she also conducts a brisk trade in shady liaisons between men and women. After Aristide's second wife, Renée Saccard, refuses to act on Sidonie's proposition that she seduce a wealthy nobleman to earn money, Sidonie's rage at being crossed is not quelled until she exposes Renée's affair with her stepson, her husband Aristide's child from his first marriage. Like Balzac, Zola frequently identifies characters by means of animal metaphors. But while Bette appears as a species of spinster with primitively vengeful animal qualities, Sidonie seems a financial monstrosity. With a complexion like paper (371), she was as "sèche comme une facture, froide comme un protêt, indifferente et brutale au fond comme un recors" (372) ("dry as an invoice, as cold as a protest, and at bottom as brutal and indifferent as a broker's man") (42).[24]

Balzac and Zola refer to hereditary characteristics, explicitly contrasting the aggressive criminal acts of Bette and Sidonie with the decadent seductions of the women who serve as their sexual surrogates, Valerie Marneffe and Renée Saccard. Bette and Sidonie are transgressive figures who refuse to enact the traditional social roles assigned to woman—the roles of loving wife and mother understood as natural by the narrators and authors. Avoiding marriage and mothering, Bette and Sidonie remain suspicious figures whose selfish desires make them perverse as well as primitive. The primitive state is, in turn, recognized as the natural condition of savages and persons of color by the novelists and pseudo-scientists, whose theories of human behavior referenced and reinforced narrative discourse.

The fictional female offender's deviance from appearance and behaviors traditionally ascribed to women made her an especially interesting specimen for criminal anthropologists who classified subjects according to race, gender, and class. Published in Italian in 1893 and in French in 1896, Cesare Lombroso's book *La donna delinquente* presented his anthropometric study of women criminals.[25] Physical measurements of cranial capacity and brain size as well as numerous photographs of incarcerated women provided documentary examples of criminal physiology for Lombroso, who catalogued physiological qualities of known and fictional criminals to extrapolate a female criminal type. Familiar with the works of Balzac and Zola, Lombroso relied on their descriptions of fictional characters to support his theories of criminal physiology. The criminologist cites fictional evidence when appropriate. For example, Zola's character Nana, the high-society prostitute, has a mole that Lombroso identifies as an example of a facial anomaly often seen in female deviants.[26] He claims that unlike ordinary women, born-criminal females share a number of physiological traits with men; criminal women have heavier jaws and smaller skulls (18) and are more likely to have facial and cephalic anomalies, such as moles or bumps, than law-abiding females (76). Criminal women appear shorter than women in the population at large, they have deeper voices than average (85), and they are inclined to have abundant hair (71).

Lombroso distinguishes brief episodes of criminal activity from habitual crime. His account of criminal tendencies explains that during political revolts such as the Paris Commune of 1870, women participate with "the greatest of violence."[27] This section of the text ("Epidemic cruelty") concludes by describing how

> all the moral restraints that evolution has built up slowly over time dissolve in a flash, like a fine veil in the flame, with even civilized men becoming killers and cannibals. Women, in these extraordinary, transient, atavistic reversions, become the cruelest of the cruel. They tear out the tongue of the corpse, disfigure its manhood, prolong their victims' agony and demonstrate their thirst for inflicting pain.[28]

The capacity of the female criminal to harm her victims has its analogue in the degree of extreme violence in which even seemingly normal women will participate.

Although Lombroso believed that all women fostered maternal instincts, he argued that the female criminal's masculine aggression and deception could outweigh her natural femininity. His description of the female criminal's predisposition for revenge pivots on his generalization, shared with Balzac, that women are more likely to brood on revenge than men, an assumption neither confirmed nor denied by science. Lombroso revealed his own fear of women by claiming that those who are predisposed to criminal acts merely act upon their natural feminine instinct by waiting for the right time to strike. Occasionally, he uses physical aspects to explain moral degeneracy: differing from male criminals whose great physical strength aids them in spontaneous malice, females cannot afford to be impulsive (155); therefore, women are deliberate criminals whose plans are likely to be mad or absurd (175).

Following Balzac and Zola, whose characters served as examples of the criminologist's theory, Lombroso took pains in his work to distinguish carefully between the pretty, passive prostitute and the rough-tempered, less attractive female criminal, whom he described as a masculinized woman: "even the handsomest female offenders have invariably strong jaws and cheek-bones, and a masculine aspect" (70). While he finds prostitutes inclined to be fair-haired or red-haired (70), more brutal female criminals tend to have dark hair and facial anomalies that detract from their appearance. For novelists and criminal scientists, the prostitute's more comely physical appearance hints at her passivity and her ability to reform her wicked ways. Fallen women could be rehabilitated if they were taught the advantages of living virtuously; since a prostitute's criminal activity did not signify sexual perversity, she might be rehabilitated from a life of crime by appealing to her natural desire to marry and to raise a family. Charles Dickens, an anonymous benefactor of a home for wayward girls, expressed this sentiment in an 1846 letter addressed to the institution's supervisor: "Such girls as these needed to be 'tempted to virtue. They cannot be dragged, driven or frightened'—and the best incentive was the hope of marriage."[29] Chapter 5 of Zola's *Doctor Pascal* describes Sidonie's work late in life at a religious institution designed to rehabilitate seduced, pregnant girls by preparing them for marriage.

Many Frenchmen agreed with Dickens and viewed both criminality and perverse female sexuality as illnesses that could be controlled by proper medical treatment and education. As Jules Michelet indicated in *L'Amour* (*Love*) (1858) and *La Femme* (*Woman*) (1859), woman's energies should be directed toward motherhoood. His theory points to woman's remarkable powers of fecundity and nurturing, which allow her to maintain a close connection to nature. She shares in the expression of universal love by procreating, an activity that kept her mysterious and seductive impulses in check. If a man fails to civilize a woman by making her into a good mother, and therefore a good wife, her dangerous sexuality, metonymically represented by her repulsive menstruation, might be responsible for continued disorder and chaos in the world.[30] Lombroso agreed with Michelet that "when piety and maternal sentiments are wanting," a woman would be inspired by morbid criminal impulses (151).[31]

Criticism directed at female criminals focuses on their ambiguous sexuality.[32] A masculine appearance and an interest in activities identified as masculine—such as Bette's and Sidonie's ambitions to strike it rich and their willingness to do so by illegal or unethical acts—indicate criminal tendencies. Masculine appearance and behavior serve as metonymic signs of sexual deviance, a transgression against society that could not be rehabilitated. Like male criminals whose vices indicate their primitive nature, female criminals other than prostitutes are described as innately seeking to destroy persons and property. Differing from male criminals, these deviant women are seen as biologically inferior because they are sexually deformed.

Blaming characteristics of deviant sexuality on the inherent madness of criminal women, conservative narratives discourage women from crossing traditional social boundaries. The criminal's masculinized sexuality make her fearsome to those who assumed that nature intended women to be passive forces under the direction of their husbands. According to Balzac, Bette Fischer is dangerous because she is not motivated by feminine desire and therefore does not fit into the structure of a patriarchal society. Refusing marriage, Bette lost her opportunity to become a member of a community accepting women as subordinates. Sidonie Rougon also refused to live as her society demanded of women. Zola described her as a sorceress threatening family honor (577), for Sidonie avoids a second marriage and gives up her child to satisfy her greed and yearning for intrigue, which are unnatural desires for a normal woman.[33]

Although Balzac and Zola associate female criminals with lace, a seemingly innocuous symbol of feminine domesticity, lace also symbolizes the complicated webs of deceit woven by Bette and Sidonie, thereby transforming a technological product, a sign of domesticity, into an indicator of the overwhelming power of female corruption. Agreeing that the female offender is a perversion of nature, Lombroso argues that "the born female criminal is . . . doubly exceptional, as a woman and as a criminal" (151). Novelists and criminal anthropologists represented fictional and historical women subverting the patriarchal order as monsters who threaten male hegemony. Women working to destroy the family and patriarchal values, Bette and Sidonie are neutralized within narratives so that readers continue to preserve the family and maintain domestic harmony. Bette must be silenced by death and Sidonie overcome by religious devotion in works enforcing patriarchal notions of feminine sexuality.

Reproduction and Replication in *Dracula*

Although technology is often represented in the post-Romantic British and Continental novel as an oppressive force in conflict with human desire, later-nineteenth-century fictions represent both positive and negative aspects of technological innovation. The irritating noise and odor of the paper mill in Stendhal's *Le Rouge et le noir* (1830) and the suffocating smoke produced by the factories of Dickens's *Hard Times* (1854) give way to subsequent depictions noting the tremendous power of technology to improve human existence. Fin-de-siècle works, such as Zola's *Fécondité* (1899), discussed in the next chapter, link technology to humanitarian ideals by identifying material progress with industrial innovation and domestic use of science and technology. Bram Stoker's *Dracula* (1897) demonstrates how technology and human biology, when properly deployed, can counter even supernatural powers, as the novel explores how dangerous aspects of vampires, especially their erotic power of sexuality, struggle against the restraining forces of communication technologies and the power of human reproduction.

In the novel, Dracula depends on superhuman seductive abilities to extend his influence and survive, while his opponents rely on religious and scientific technologies to eradicate the evil influence of the master vampire. British and American characters in Stoker's novel defend the world from Dracula's contamination by a number of technical means, including transfusing blood and transmitting information about his incredible abilities, his hiding places, and his plans to access a new blood supply. Using a combination of supernatural and scientific means, the mostly Anglo-American collaborative team chases the Eastern European monster out of London back to his homeland, where they confront and destroy him.

The conflict between Dracula and those who battle him reflects differences related to race, philosophy, morality, social values, and scientific principles. Critical interest in the representation of women and ethnic minorities inspires interpretations examining gender, race, and class oppositions in the novel. Polarities that critics discern include the tension between male and female desire (Roth 1982, Dijkstra 1986, Case 1993); the conflict between British imperialism and the foreign Other (Stevenson 1988, Arata 1990, McKee 2002); and the contrast between scientific technology based on rationality and atavistic principles of evolution based on folklore (Auerbach 1982, Dijkstra 1986, Greenway 1986).[34] It has become a critical commonplace to regard Stoker's depiction of vampirism as an illustration of aggressive, foreign, and primitive male sexuality of a racial Other, a force opposed by a collaborative team of male protoganists—the Dutch Dr. Abraham Van Helsing, Brits Dr. Jack Seward and Arthur Holmwood, and the American Quincy Morris—who invoke principles of natural science, notably evolutionary ideas concerning criminal behavior, to support their campaign against Dracula.

But few critics analyze how Dracula's last victim, Mina Harker, becomes the central character of the narrative. Mina's womanly power to procreate and her technical skills, when suitably protected by the supernatural and scientific methods used by the male collaborators, outstrip Dracula's endeavors. The crusade against the monster fought by male Western Europeans and Americans holds the British family dear, regarding marriage and motherhood as sacred institutions threatened by the Eastern European demon who prefers promiscuity to monogamy. Dracula's infamous bloodsucking ritual in some ways resembles an adulterous and bizarre sexual encounter and in others enacts a weird variation on breastfeeding. Stoker encodes forms of human reproduction as being superior to Dracula's method of replication. Religious preventives against vampirism and scientific means of coping with its effects, including medical and communication technologies, are invoked to guard the reproductive powers of woman. Whereas Lucy's sexual proclivities mark her as unable to be saved, Mina's abilities, particularly her aptitude in managing a variety of innovative communication technologies, make her a significant force, as a collaborator and as Jonathan's spouse.[35] Her desire to be a good wife is an explicit assertion of her need to become the mother of future Harkers rather than a bride of Dracula.

Dracula's liaisons contrast with the stable social unions desired by the British and American characters. Dracula's stalking of female victims, in the novel and in some of the films made about this legendary figure, reveal a libidinous sexuality that helps him spread his influence and assure his survival. The infectious process of vampirism employed by Dracula resists the prevailing mores of sexual behavior acknowledged by other characters in the novel; the narrative's worldview implicitly endorses sexual behavior only as a means of procreation. Indeed, at the end of the novel, all the surviving central characters have been married off, with the notable exception of Dr. Van Helsing, whose loyalty to his institutionalized wife commends him to the young men who look on him as a father figure teaching principles of "chaste love."[36] Instead of marrying and producing children, as society dictates, Dracula promiscuously pursues female victims whose blood allows him to remain immortal. By infecting these women through sucking their blood, he thereby produces another vampire with the same extreme need for blood.[37] Dracula's enemies must restrain his biological urges, and Dracula must battle their numerous superstitious and scientific schemes to track and contain his movements.

The first half of Stoker's novel notes Dracula's unusual behavior and its effects on humans, including Jonathan Harker and Lucy Westenra, while the second half depicts how Lucy's and Jonathan's friends and family unite to fight

Dracula. Dr. Seward, Dr. Van Helsing, Arthur Holmwood, and Quincy Morris realize that they must employ all means necessary to fight the foreign threat and work as team. Encouraged by Van Helsing, each man who learns about vampirism guards against attacks by wearing garlic, holding up a crucifix, and securing passages with communion wafers as well as by carrying guns and knives. Even Jonathan Harker transcends his original condescending tone, exhibited in his reluctant acceptance of icons from the Roumanian peasant who tells him to wear a cross "[f]or your mother's sake," and becomes quite religious in bearing wafers, crosses, and garlic as ritual protections when he and the other men enter Carfax, where Dracula has stored his boxes of native earth.[38]

Medicine also appears effective in upholding patriarchy and empire, but the medical research depicted in the novel offers only one means of fighting the enemy of British values, Dracula. Therefore, holy wafers, garlic, crucifixes, and weapons must be supplemented by the use of a cutting-edge medical technology, blood transfusion, and the many communication technologies Mina accesses. The process of direct blood transfusion was developed in the decade before Stoker wrote *Dracula,* and perhaps the author had a greater familiarity with medical innovation than the average man because his three brothers were physicians.

William Stewart Halsted documented his use of the transfusion technique in a paper titled "Refusion in the Treatment of Carbonic Oxide Poisoning," as "one of the earliest proponents" of blood transfusion. Sherwin Nuland describes the direct blood transfusion Halstead employed in 1881 in Albany, New York, during a visit to his sister. He arrived

at her home just as she was giving birth. Shortly thereafter, he found her pale and pulseless due to a massive postpartum hemorrhage. In a note written years later he described his response to the situation: "After checking the hemorrhage, I transfused my sister with blood drawn into a syringe from one of my veins and injected immediately into one of hers. This was taking a great risk but she was so nearly moribund that I ventured it and with prompt result."[39]

Nuland's description of this early transfusion connects love, reproduction, and transfusion in ways that resonate with Stoker's novel.

The novel's scenes of blood transfusion mingle science and passion, as each male donor is called on to prove his declared love for Lucy. Dr. Van Helsing, Dr. Seward, Mr. Morris, and Lord Godalming give blood on a number of occasions to the dying Lucy, but Dracula's repeated nocturnal visits remove what medicine and love provide. Three of the men—Seward, Morris, and Holmwood, who becomes Lord Godalming upon his father's death—have previously asked for Lucy's hand in marriage, a situation causing her to remark on the unfortunate social principle of monogamy that requires her to accept only one, Godalming. After she becomes ill, her former beaus enlist in a campaign for her health orchestrated by Van Helsing, who has been called in as a consultant by his former student, Seward.

After each of Dracula's nighttime visits, Lucy relapses and requires another transfusion. On one occasion since her fiancé is not present, Seward donates his blood and reveals his still-active sexual feelings for her: "It was with a feeling of personal pride that I could see a faint tinge of colour steal back into the pallid cheeks and lips. No man knows till he experiences it, what it is to feel his own life-blood drawn away into the veins of the woman he loves" (128). Later, after Lucy's mother dies and Lucy's condition is at its weakest, Morris also donates blood to Lucy, quickly responding to Van Helsing's assertion, "A brave man's blood is the best thing on this earth when a woman is in trouble. You're the man, and no mistake. Well, the devil may work against us for all he's worth, but God sends us men when we want them" (149). Dracula's persistent attempts to assault Lucy undo the positive results of the transfusions, inspiring the collaborators to avenge her death, protect womankind, and save Britain by driving out vampirism.

After Lucy dies, Van Helsing proposes to kill the Un-Dead Lucy by cutting off the corpse's head and driving a stake through her heart, although the grieving Arthur initially forbids such a mutilation (206). Van Helsing counters Arthur's objection in his non-standard English by calling on his own manly love for Lucy:

> But I beseech you, do not go forth in anger with me. In a long life of acts which were often not pleasant to do, and which sometimes did wring my heart, I have never had so heavy a task as now. Believe me that if the time comes for you to change your mind towards me, one look from you will wipe all this so sad hour, for I would do what a man can to save you from sorrow. Just think. For what should I give myself so much of labour and so much of sorrow? I have come here from my own land to do what I can of good; at the first to please my friend John, and then to help a sweet young lady, whom, too, I came to love. For her—I am ashamed to say so much, but I say it in kindness—I gave what you gave: the blood of my veins; I gave it, I who was not, like you, her lover, but only her physician and her friend. I gave her my nights and days—before death, after death; and if my death can do her good even now, when she is the dead Un-Dead, she shall have it freely. (207)

Van Helsing and the other men believe that giving Lucy blood verges on sharing sexual union with her; for them, the exchange of bodily fluids represents intercourse. Van Helsing's poignant plea to Arthur, couched in sexual language, wins the day, enabling the men to set off on a visit to Lucy's tomb. To accomplish their macabre task, Van Helsing passes out crucifixes, wafers, and garlic and directs Arthur to hammer a stake into his beloved's corpse, performing yet another ritual resonant with sexual associations.

Stoker connects positivist efforts of doctors and other modern men to control Dracula with religious protections supported by Roman Catholic rituals and folk legends. The most successful scientific approach employed by the vampire fighters involves the appropriate, systematic, and timely application of information technologies. In the second part of the novel, after Lucy's corpse is restrained and her soul sent to heaven, her "lovers" band together to destroy her murderer, for Dracula threatens her survivors, especially her good friend Mina. Innovative means of communication help Van Helsing and his collaborators defeat Dracula by allowing them to proceed efficiently and, for the most part, without their enemy's knowledge.

As the plot against Dracula gains momentum, the narrative increasingly depends on the use of replicative communication technologies (shorthand, telegraph, phonograph dictation, typewriting, newspapers, and photography) to fight Dracula and to protect human reproduction. Mina and Jonathan practice shorthand by writing in journals that serve as documentary evidence of Dracula's movements and abilities. For much of the narrative, they record their enemy's behavior without scrutiny; because Jonathan's journal is in shorthand, Dracula does not recognize its threat.[40] Dr. Seward's practice of recording his medical notes on phonographic cylinders provides a thorough record of the madman Renfield's reactions and thoughts regarding his Master's coming. Even Lucy in her last hours recognizes the utility of leaving a written account of her feelings because she is uncertain about surviving her illness.

Jonathan's photographs and architectural plans of Carfax are part of his work for Dracula before the count's nefarious nature is revealed, and the group avails themselves of these renderings when they look for the boxes of earth that hold Dracula's body. Most importantly, Mina's efforts to record notable events at Whitby, including her incorporating conversations with old Mr. Swales, news of the shipwreck, and references to her sleepwalking, and her delineation of Jonathan's recuperation in Roumania, offer valuable clues that are later deciphered by Van Helsing, who provides expert insight into how vampires attack and debilitate human beings.

After Lucy's fate reveals the deadly influence of Dracula, Mina becomes ill at the climax of the narrative. The Dracula fighters have sought to protect her because she is a woman, and a married one at that, but their efforts fail as Dracula surreptitiously infects Mina. Without telling Mina, the men successfully invade Dracula's lair in Carfax and find many significant documents. Van Helsing remarks that Mina has a woman's heart and a man's brain, suggesting that she not be informed about the team's plans because her fragile mind might be overcome with the horrors of confronting Dracula: "You are too precious to have such a risk. . . . We are men, and able to bear, but you must be our star and our hope, and we shall act all the more free that you are not in danger, such as we are" (242). Jonathan is relieved by this turn of events, and he acknowledges Mina's contributions more generously than Van Helsing does:

> Somehow, it was a dread to me that she is in this fearful business at all, but now that her work is done and it is due to her energy and brains and foresight that the whole story is put together in such a way that every point tells, she may well feel that her part is finished and that she can henceforth leave the rest to us. (247–48)

Unfortunately, despite the best intentions to preserve Mina by separating her from the rest of the group, this isolation causes her to be vulnerable to Dracula.

The vampire's contact with Mina occurs without her knowledge; she notes in her journal that she sees a mist creep up to Seward's house, which is next-door to the estate investigated by the men. Mina later describes the course of events, indicating how the mist spreads and her fears increase as she hears Mr. Renfield's screams: "I could in some way recognize in his tones some passionate entreaty on his part. . . . I was so frightened that I crept into bed and pulled the clothes over my head. . . . I was not then a bit sleepy . . . but I must have fallen asleep, for, except dreams, I do not remember anything until the morning, when Jonathan woke me" (258). Mina's entry continues to explain her thoughts while she was asleep, describing how "the mist grew thicker and thicker" and "things began to whirl through my brain" (259). She wonders, "Was it indeed some spiritual guidance that was coming to me in my sleep?" (259), acknowledging that these feelings remind her of what Jonathan wrote about his encounter with the three women in Dracula's castle, a clue for the reader that Dracula has found Mina.

After Renfield informs the doctors that he and Mina have both seen Dracula, Seward and Van Helsing understand she was attacked. They immediately rush over to the Harkers' residence, literally finding the couple in bed with the demon:

> On the bed beside the window lay Jonathan Harker, his face flushed, and breathing heavily as though in a stupor. Kneeling on the near edge of the bed facing outwards was the white-clad figure of his wife. By her side stood a tall, thin man, clad in black. His face turned from us, but the instant we saw it we all recognized the Count. . . . With his left hand he held both Mrs. Harker's hands, keeping them away with her arms at full tension; his right hand gripped her by

the back of the neck, forcing her face down on his bosom. Her white nightdress was smeared with blood, and a thick stream trickled down the man's bare breast, which was shown by his torn-open dress. The attitude of the two had a terrible resemblance to a child forcing a kitten's nose into a saucer of milk to compel it to drink. (282)

Like the children infected by Lucy earlier in the narrative, Mina is small and helpless compared with the vampire. That the process of infection resembles a kitten drinking milk, itself a substitution of nursing, reminds us that vampiric infection appears to be an abnormal means of nursing in that one derives nourishment from blood rather than milk. Dracula serves as a progenitor of vampires who feed on him and others. While the nursing child depends upon the mother's breast, Dracula represents a perversion of motherhood because he forces Mina to partake in what does not benefit her.

By the time Dracula infects Mina while she is sleeping with her husband, the vampire realizes the power of the documents produced and shared by his enemies. On the same evening that Mina becomes "unclean" because Dracula has forced her to drink his blood, he strikes a blow against the growing conspiracy. Arthur notices that Dracula has destroyed all original documents held by the Harkers, although duplicate copies have been preserved in the safe (285). Unlike Lucy who wastes away from her illness and can only record her vague feelings, Mina speaks with her husband and the other men; she tells them what she realizes about the vampire. Her capacity to inform the group about where Dracula goes after he is chased from the Harkers' bed improves over time. Because Mina is infected, she reveals a deep connection with Dracula that permits her to report on his movements only when she is hypnotized by Van Helsing.

Mina's contributions to the processes of collecting and collating information cannot be overstated. Her foresight in clipping newspaper accounts pays off when the group tries to piece together how Dracula might leave England. Her cleverness in preventing catastrophe manifests itself in other ways as well, from memorizing train schedules to sending warning messages to her collaborators when Dracula might find them poking around his property (303). Similarly, telegrams sent between solicitors also permit quick resolution of business so that Dracula's opponents can close in on their prey; in the last pages of the novel, telegrams from the collaborators indicate the location of the ship that holds Dracula's last box of earth, letting the men know where to find their enemy (335, 337).

As already noted, superstitious solutions supplement scientific methods. Without Mina's typewriting and the shorthand journals she and Jonathan write, the team would not be able to compile a collated set of documents confirming Dracula's plans to store his native earth in many locations. Dr. Van Helsing also contributes by maintaining a supply of garlic, stakes, and crosses for the men who confront the monster.[41] Without the telegraph, the collaborators would have had to rely on Dr. Van Helsing's hypnosis sessions with Mina, which reveal only the most general information about the vampire's whereabouts. Mina's unconscious mind reveals that Dracula is near water, and the telegrams provide specific locations for the ship that holds him.

The construction of the narrative as a set of documents, including letters, journal entries, memoranda, telegrams, newspaper clippings, and transcriptions of phonographic dictations, convinces the reader that various communication technologies offer a powerful antidote to counter Dracula's threat. The prefatory note to the text indicates that "how these papers have been placed in sequence will be made clear in the reading of them." The note draws our attention to the question of why the papers and the narrative have been organized in such an odd way. While it is true that collecting contemporary documents and presenting them in a roughly chronological sequence helps to tell the history of Dracula's effects on a particular group of individuals, the collated set of documents preserved in the safe is itself a copy of originals (that is, the copy records individual observations and interpretations of Dracula's presence). That the novel purports to be an authoritative, collated duplicate of the original documents provides a new spin on the necessity and value of reproduction.

The "original" work as represented in the novel is, of course, the monster who threatens England by attacking women, for Dracula infects mostly women. But, unlike humans whose sexual intercourse result in reproduction of an offspring partially related to each parent, Dracula can only transform others into versions of himself. Until the vampire enters their lives, Lucy and Mina anticipate courtship, marriage, and motherhood. The introduction of Dracula and his vampiric practices threaten their abilities to birth and rear children. Lucy's eerie appearance as a seductive bride infecting small children haunts the European and American collaborators, who are forced to admit that they must drive a stake through her Un-Dead body to protect her and themselves. The state of being infected by the vampire can be compared with the state of being pregnant, for in both cases subjects are described as developing a more profound sensory experience. Vampires can hear better than the average human, as Lucy and Mina document in their journals, and they sense Dracula approaching, as Renfield tells. Some pregnant women are more sensitive to the sight, smell, and taste of foods that can cause nausea, and they display strong reactions to other atmospheric influences.[42]

To obtain the blood that sustains him, Dracula woos potential mothers and spirits away their children, thereby destroying families. While the men who court Lucy (Dr. Seward, Quincy Morris, Arthur Holmwood, and, to a lesser extent, Dr. Van Helsing) promise women the opportunity of reproduction, Dracula cannot parent another being; instead, he attempts mastery of the world by duplication. Although he achieves some success with the three women entombed in his chapel and with Lucy, Dracula loses the final battle with his adversaries, whose lives depend on the sheltering of women and the nurturing of children.

Fostering replication of vampires rather than reproducing offspring, Dracula detests those who collaborate against him and their means of opposing his projects. One reason he achieves some degree of success in his plan to take over England is that vampirism is not publicized as a known entity. Only hysterical Roumanian peasants, the rather addled Mr. Swales, the seemingly crazy sailors on the *Demeter,* and the lunatic insect-eater Renfield seem aware of Dracula's powers. Destroying witnesses and their accounts of his existence and powers permits Dracula to maintain his low profile and to concentrate his efforts on possessing Mina, and eventually the entire Western continent, as his own. But the collaborators learn to fight duplication with their own form of copying documents and by relying on their abilities to reproduce themselves.

The conflict between Dracula and the men who rally to fight against him demonstrates the powers of human sexuality and technological duplication as linked advantages. The popularity of the Dracula myth as a basis for horror films ironically recreates the tension between reproduction and duplication.[43] As a cultural icon replicated in many forms, Dracula represents a way of life that is secret and opposed to reproduction. Dracula fails to extend his empire of vampirism because faith in technology's superiority plus religious belief and pagan superstition join together to defeat his plans. While both Dracula and his enemies employ replication and duplication to establish power, the locus of power in the novel remains Mina.[44] She is more adept at employing communication technologies, including thoughts revealed only under hypnosis, a kind of vampiric method of communication, than the men who rely on her assistance. Ultimately, together with her husband Jonathan, she transcends the limits of duplication by reproducing a son, Quincy, whose first name is itself an image of the sacrificed Morris.

The last lines of the novel, in a note contributed by Jonathan that was written seven years after Dracula's destruction, bring the reader up-to-date on the characters' actions. The narrative ends with a quotation from Van Helsing that mentions the Harkers' child and sums up what the survivors expect readers to believe: "We want no proofs; we ask none to believe us! This boy will some day know what a brave and gallant woman his mother is. Already he knows her sweetness and loving care; later on he will understand how some men so loved her, that they did dare much for her sake" (378). "This boy" is Quincy Harker, Jonathan's and Mina's son, who outlives Dracula and even the original set of documents describing the vampire's actions, proving that human reproduction is victorious over monstrous replication.

Dracula is defeated by a team that includes a number of men with different knowledge, expertise, and access and one woman adept with various communication technologies, including supernatural communication. Lord Godalming works his connections, Quincy Morris exhibits his courage, Dr. Van Helsing is a medical expert on vampirism, and Dr. Seward contributes his medical knowledge and provides access to Renfield. But Mina's technical and supernatural abilities, combined with her love and respect for her husband and friends, make her contributions critical to the group's success. In some ways a New Woman, Mina also retains virtues traditionally expected of women: knowing about domestic affairs, deferring to men, and being sensitive to their masculine pride. Dracula's plot ultimately fails because his designated victim shows herself to be smarter, and in this case more technically adept, than her pursuer, while still being traditionally feminine, a formula persisting in television and film narratives about female crime fighters.

Female Crime Fighters

In mass media, women scientists and technical experts are most often relegated to secondary and stereotypical roles within plots that limit women's participation in the public sphere. The television roles in which women engage with science and technology include detectives, lawyers, and doctors. Hospital shows since *Ben Casey* (1961–66) and the soap opera *General Hospital* (1963–) foreground female physicians. More women, and "women's" issues such as professional insecurity, romance and work, and balancing motherhood and profession, appear in *ER* (1994–2009), *Grey's Anatomy* (2005–), and *Scrubs* (2001–). As noted in chapter 1, a number of forensic pathologists appear in ensemble police procedurals—*Law & Order* (1990–2010) and its spinoffs *Law & Order: Special Victims Unit* (1999–) and *Law & Order: Criminal Intent* (2001–); *CSI* (2000–) and its franchises *CSI: Miami* (2002–) and *CSI: New York* (2004–); *Crossing Jordan* (2001–7); *Cold Case,* (2003–); *Bones* (2005–); *Without a Trace* (2002–); and *NCIS* (2003–). These shows illustrate the ways in which women who are experts in science and technology interact with predominantly male colleagues in professional worlds where men and women are roughly equal but always different.[45] As a 2008 UK Resource Centre for Women in Science, Engineering and Technology report asserts, "[S]ystemic overviews of films suggest there are some recurring stereotypes," an observation the researchers documented in their study of 46 television dramas, including episodes from some of the above-mentioned series.[46] Many series portray female (and some male characters) as alternating between their professional competence and the upheaval caused by personal emotional and family crises that make them more vulnerable at work.

A niche field for women on television is psychological profiling, with women appearing as the protagonists in *Profiler* (1996–2000), *Medium* (2005–), and *Ghost Whisperer* (2005–). Profilers have paranormal experiences revealing information about crimes. *Medium*'s central character is suburban wife and mother Alison Dubois (Patricia Arquette) who consults with the Phoenix district attorney's office when she has a vision. *Ghost Whisperer* focuses on the newly married Melinda (Jennifer Love Hewitt) whose paranormal abilities allow her to communicate with earth-bound spirits, help them "cross over," and solve various mysteries. Melinda's ability to see ghosts causes tensions with her mother and offers an example of how a show balances supernatural powers with emotional vulnerabilities more familiar to many women.

Television's first characterization of a profiler, that of Samantha Waters in *Profiler* (1996–2000; producers Kim Moses and Ian Sander and story editor Bob Lowry) offers a similar blend of power and vulnerability. *Profiler* is a detective series in which an FBI Special Forces team of men and women hunts down serial murderers all over the country. The Violent Crimes Task Force based in Atlanta includes police experts specializing in cutting-edge computing and surveillance technologies, as well as medical doctors with expertise in forensic anatomy and psychology. *Profiler*'s blend of nineteenth-century Gothic conventions and twentieth-century high-tech gadgets updates the classic pattern of a horror story (a male villain threatening a woman victim) by making the protectors a diverse group of men and women, including female medical experts. Viewers' attention is focused on the forensic psychologist who profiles the murderers by reviewing physical evidence and using supernatural revelations to get into the mind of the killer.

The continuing plotline about Dr. Samantha Waters illustrates how she is endangered by a male predator, a criminal known as Jack. Jack killed her husband and terrorizes her friends, family, and colleagues. Sam is both the stalked and the stalker, a blended characterization that represented an innovation for modern television dramas, according to the producers, but a plot device that has since been adopted by other series. Her imaginative reconstructions of various crimes contribute to the FBI effort because she visualizes and articulates details of motive, method, and opportunity that complement more technical methods of fingerprint analysis, DNA testing, and computerized criminal records. Sam's mental imagery is both blessing and curse, for it provides her with a livelihood in solving weekly cases that come before the team, but it is also the reason she remains haunted by graphic depictions of her husband's dying moments.[47]

Sam's ability to "visualize" a crime causes her to experience each killer's emotions and to sense his/her motivation and rationale. She expresses herself according to a language and method that can be summed up by the cliché "feminine intuition." Like Grace Alvarez, the female forensic pathologist on the crime team, Sam speaks authoritatively about what the crime scene details indicate. Many situations Sam faces evoke choices confronted by ordinary women: how to be a competent professional and still be respected as a woman; how to balance work with family; how to maintain a friendship during periods of stress that test both parties; how to express emotions in the workplace; how to conduct a romance with a colleague and still be professional; how to collaborate successfully with colleagues of different genders, races, ethnicities, and levels of professional expertise; and how to protect one's privacy in a world in which technology enhances the powers of each computer user, whether George (the team's hacker), the arch-villain Jack (who has panoptic vision), or anyone else with a computer connection.

The characterization of a woman used and abused by technology is a mass media construction of gender and science that remains within the conservative dimensions of the Gothic thriller, punishing women for stepping out of domestic roles. On the one hand, the forensic pathologist Dr. Grace Alvarez and the profiler Dr. Samantha Waters represent the highest level of scientific expertise, but, during many episodes, they face discrimination from colleagues and friends of victims as they practice their jobs. In the initial shows depicting Samantha's joining the team, her telekinetic abilities are viewed as hocus-pocus by some male colleagues who question her credentials until her visions about the murders are proved accurate. Her practice of mental imagery also draws criticism from the local police detectives who are forced to collaborate with the FBI team on cases from around the United States.

In each episode of the first seasons of *Profiler*, the team resolves the crime of that week, while Jack is ever elusive. Again and again they come close to finding him, but he escapes. His computer lurking bespeaks a creepy virtual mysterious presence as he witnesses FBI conversations and flaunts an evil intelligence that frustrates Sam and threatens her and her daughter. Grace and Sam are on occasion represented as frightened in their own homes after loved ones have been attacked, especially Grace after learning that she is pregnant. At one point, all Violent Crimes Task Force members retreat to the underground team headquarters, where they camp out with family members because Jack's threats to Sam include everyone who works with her. Sam remains the calmest during a period in which everyone she knows shares her reality: that Jack can strike violently at any moment means that all lives are constrained by his lurking presence.

Despite Sam's precarious position as a stalking victim, her insight and intellect empower her to fight back, while her powerful sexuality marks her as a target. She is generally depicted as a polished professional, clothed in an elegant, tailored, restrained wardrobe composed of neutral colors emphasizing her sleekness and complementing her carefully tousled blonde hair and large vulnerable blue eyes. Sam, whose name, as Susan Squier suggested, can be deciphered as Sexual Attraction plus Magnetism, remains a powerful sexual object even as she demonstrates her talents as a hunter of sexual predators. She can live at home with her daughter Chloe and her close friend Angel only because her FBI boss puts her under the protection of the bureau. Yet Sam appears no more vulnerable than her colleagues who after Jack's attacks are also in danger, reflecting a social reality of our time, or at least our television era, which has given birth to *The X-Files* (1993–2002), as well as many dramas depicting supernatural processes resolving crimes (for example, *Strange Luck*, 1995–96) and shows investigating the aftermath of a mystery such as *Lost* (2004–10) and *FlashForward* (2009–).

Saving Grace (2007–10) describes the supernatural forces assisting a female investigator with its characterization of Earl, an angel who guides law officer Grace Hanadarko (Holly Hunter). Set in Oklahoma, *Saving Grace* has it both ways: Grace both represents the law and also transgresses social convention as a Major Crimes police detective who has a wild life and "a tender side" contemplating the divine. Grace works with a former boyfriend and has a tempestuous relationship with a married man, but she is a loving aunt to 22 nieces and nephews. In addition to her male colleagues, Grace works with Rhetta Rodriguez, a female criminalist (played by Laura San Giacomo) whose faith is stronger than hers. Rhetta wears glasses and a lab coat but over a low-cut dress; she believes in Grace's visions of Earl after she tests Grace's evidence and sees that Earl leaves behind saliva without a genetic trace. Written by Nancy Miller, *Saving Grace* considers issues familiar to women of a certain age while representing crime investigations and Grace's journey to redemption.

Females with authoritative positions in police departments or hospitals generally appear as odd women. Kyra Sedgwick's portrayal of Deputy Police Chief Brenda Leigh Johnson in *The Closer* (2005–) fits in the category of alpha female characters in police dramas. Johnson treasures her idiosyncrasies: wearing feminine sweaters or highly stylized suits, leaving her hair long and loose, preferring "comfort" food to healthy options, and emphasizing her Southern accent when interrogating suspects, most of whom have no idea who they are up against. Johnson does not hesitate to lie to trick criminals into confessing. She says that lying is a logical, if seemingly unethical, procedure, and that since criminals lie, deceiving them is a necessary police tool to unmask their lies. Helen Mirren's Jane Tennyson in *Prime Suspect* (1991–2006) presents a different style—no nonsense, cut-to-the-chase, succinct—but, like Chief Johnson, Deputy Inspector Tennyson also has more culturally sensitive interactions with witnesses and suspects than her male counterparts do. Brenda Johnson and Jane Tennyson lead police units dominated by men and rely on being tough and sensible. These detectives do not shrink from using any approach to solve the crime, using both feminine wiles and masculine authority. Yet Johnson and Tennyson are so focused on work that they are rather disorganized in their personal lives, which are complicated by their past romantic relationships with professional colleagues.

CSI's lead female role belongs to Catherine Willow (Marg Helgenberger), who works as a senior forensics specialist. Catherine's past work as an exotic dancer in Las Vegas and her complicated family relationships offset her professional competence and logical way of proceeding through a case. During the course of the series, she discovers who her real father is and has continuing anxieties about her teenage daughter Lindsey. Contributors to the Internet Movie Database entry on Catherine recognize how issues of being female and feminine "haunt" this character and her relations with her supervisor Gil Grissom (William Peterson):

> Catherine, while well-liked and highly successful at her job, seems to be trailed by bad luck in her personal life. Grissom is known to have criticized her for having a personal life at all, as drama seems to find her despite her best intentions. Her dates seem to end up jeopardizing investigations, or involved in them. Her daughter was kidnapped as a warning to her, and soon after her safe return, her father was killed in her arms by the kidnapper. Her recent dating life is next to nil, though she shares an unresolved, and ultimately tragic, flirtatious relationship with her co-worker, Warrick Brown.
>
> While not vain in the strictest sense, Catherine has a dancer's strong sense of beauty and style to go with her natural good looks. . . . In recent episodes, Catherine is shown to be transferring her maternal tendencies to the team, attempting to steer Grissom through his fiancée's departure, and helping Warrick through drug dependency and a murder charge.[48]

As viewers understand, television dramas focusing on science and technology establish women as competent and authoritative, while allowing more feminine characteristics or events to undermine positive qualities.

Joan Haran et al. report in *Screening Women* that many television dramas depict a battle of sexes and include gender stereotypes that might both reinforce and reverse expectations of "masculine" rationality and "feminine" emotionality, as if winking at convention.[49] Many times the actresses playing these roles are far more attractive and glamorous versions of professionals than the ordinary people in these jobs, ratcheting up expectations of what a criminal pathologist or investigator should look like. A professional woman hoping to find solutions to managing a busy career and active family life would be hard-pressed to find fictional protagonists who succeed at home and work, for they are more likely to reveal strains and stresses of marriages and motherhood or the reasons women do not have such family attachments. A preponderance of female characters are single, sometimes with dead or estranged parents, siblings, or children. More realistic portrayals of women in these roles could offer a greater diversity of characters representing various ethnicities, social classes, ages, appearance, and family status. A variety of characters and situations could encourage more creative plots that reach beyond the difficulties that women experience in trying "to make it in a man's world."

Female crime-fighters appear valued in contemporary television, but largely for their intuition, sentimentality, or peculiarly feminine way of pursuing truth. Despite the plethora of characters and shows, stereotypes about women's different ways of committing and solving crimes persist and are largely replicated rather than reversed. The next chapter discusses narratives about female doctors and caregivers who blend masculine professional skills and feminine emotional qualities within plots emphasizing the significance of motherhood as a heroic trait.

Mothers
and Medicine

M edical treatment of mothers and newborns has improved in many ways as a result of modern reproductive and lifesaving technologies such as fetal heart monitoring, ultrasound, in vitro fertilization, and drug therapy for premature infants. However, anthropologists who study cultural rituals of birth find it troubling that the management of pregnancy and childbirth in the United States is imbued with military rhetoric and that obstetricians have adopted "the model of the assembly-line production of goods as its base metaphor for hospital birth."[1] In addition, technical improvements have not prevented an increase in the infant mortality rate in lower socioeconomic groups in the United States, nor have they offset the rising costs of health care, which limit access to prenatal care for many mothers.[2] Despite access to innovative technologies, doctors, patients, and even some insurance executives recognize that medical practice in the United States far too often calculates costs and benefits as more valuable than caring for patients' overall health.[3]

Post-Romantic narratives about medical theory and practice consider human dimensions of technological interventions such as those mentioned above. Nineteenth- and twentieth-century realist literature and films describe intersections of gender and medicine, identify physicians' and caregivers' "natural" and "instinctive" practices, and sympathize with the challenges faced by female physicians. Fictional narratives considered in this chapter describe gendered sentimental attitudes and practices related to pregnancy, childbirth, and children's diseases and detail the ways in which humanistic contributions, identified largely with women, improve medical care. These texts sacralize maternity and privilege the authority of parents and physicians. Their narratives reflect and reinforce the influence of the nineteenth-century popular health movement, positivism, and progressive politics that encouraged women's medical education. That the nineteenth-century popular health adage "every man his own physician" has a counterpart in today's image of "Dr. Mom" recognizes shifting cultural views of gender and medicine.[4]

Viewing women as spiritual guides for husbands and children, and emphasizing good health as benefitting from sentiment on one hand and common sense on the other, fictions and films discussed here reveal disparate ideological associations. Representations of gender and medicine include not only pronouncements celebrating maternal love but also portrayals of sympathetic women doctors that point to these feminine attributes as efficacious in medicine. The narrative texts considered here recommend parental faith, patient persistence, and physician integrity as key factors in effective medical practice, as these attributes supplement innovative procedures and technical mechanisms. Zola's novel Fécondité idealizes motherhood for the sake of nationalism, while the film Lorenzo's Oil describes maternal persistence as encouraging medical research. Novels and stories about female doctors point to gendered characteristics that affect women's practice of medicine. Imbricated in different historical, social, and cultural contexts, these narratives agree that feminine influence and ideals can transform medicine.

"Scientific Motherhood": Zola's Cure for Society

Zola's representations of motherhood link scientific theory and social values. One of his last novels, Fécondité (1899; translated in 1900 as Fruitfulness), glorifies motherhood as a secular religion that brings progress to society. In this novel, the first of his projected quartet The Four Gospels, Zola proposes that by acting on their innate desire to procreate, women might solve the depopulation problem in France, provide economic prosperity to their families, and redeem individuals from the inevitable effects of egotism. This solution to the falling birthrate—recommending that families have more children—is founded on Zola's acceptance of the mysterious power of female fertility as a positive natural force more powerful than science.

The dramatic consequences of the depopulation crisis in nineteenth-century France, including the decreasing fertility rate and the high infant mortality rate, persuaded Zola to employ an amended version of his naturalist program to solve a pressing national problem. Influenced by the historian Jules Michelet's theories about women, and elated by his own experiences as a middle-aged father, Zola depicts the good mother in Fécondité as the ideal role model for French society—ideal because she provides domestic harmony and peace without making demands. Bearing children becomes a political gesture for parents who create an improved national state. In Zola's view, when mothers nurture children, the bonds of a happy family are extended to other citizens and the state, for greater numbers of children mean more soldiers to defend France, a significant concern for the country after the Franco-Prussian War (1870–71).

In "Dépopulation," an essay published in an 1896 issue of *Figaro*, Zola admits that he was haunted for ten years about writing a book documenting the crisis, a novel that he thought of titling *Le Déchet*, a French word meaning loss with the sense of "criminal waste."[5] Agreeing with contemporary political scientists who argued that a declining birthrate signified the diminishing political status of the French nation, he claims, "The future belongs to fecund nations."[6] Zola acknowledges that the problem was severe, that it was not a natural phenomenon, and that couples voluntarily chose to restrict the number of children they would raise.[7]

Among the possible causes for the decreasing fertility rate that he notes in "Dépopulation" are alcoholism, the great migration of people to urban areas, and the high cost of living that encourages the "egotistical calculus" of limiting family size. Today, historians of demography theorize that family limitation practices in nineteenth-century Europe effectively reduced the birthrate; that marital and non-marital fertility declined; and that in cases in which women did become pregnant, the practice of "infanticide by neglect" became common.[8] The decreasing population alarmed some citizens of France—the European nation most severely affected—to such an extent that they formed the National Alliance for the Growth of the French Population. Like the other one hundred or so members who joined the league, Zola hoped that active discussion of the cause of depopulation would increase the rate at which women bore children.[9]

Zola approved the league's resolution to pass legislation that would relieve the economic burdens faced by fathers, but he asserts in his essay that social values and morality cannot be effectively legislated. Therefore, he claims, the job of encouraging families to have more children falls also on "moralists, writers, and poets" (14: 787), who must set the right tone. He points to how Schopenhauer's and Wagner's negative attitudes toward healthy sexuality and toward children encourage the depopulation problem. Schopenhauer's philosophical pessimism claims that "to give life to a human being is a crime" (14: 787), and Wagner's aesthetic exaltation of virginity, present a perverse and abnormal way of life that young women naively admire. In Zola's view, popular writers encourage people to believe that it is better to have a love affair than a satisfying marriage, for novels describe the many favorable aspects of passionate love while demeaning the bourgeois virtues of domesticity. Even worse, he writes, are novels presenting androgynous men and women as ideals, for "[i]t is certain that, if literature truly has an influence on manners, [then] nothing would make the depopulation problem worse than all those literary and artistic works that exalt the infecund woman while scorning the strong and powerful male" (14: 788).

According to Zola, what has been missing from literature is the depiction of a loving mother fulfilled in her relationship with her strong, equally loving husband. This ideal female character would ardently desire to bear his children, preferably in a more congenial environment than Paris, and she would inspire others to give up their pessimistic views. As Dr. Boutan in *Fécondité* says, "Manners and customs, our notions of what is moral and what is not, our very conceptions of the beautiful in life—all must be changed. If France is becoming depopulated, it is because she so chooses. It is simply necessary then for her to choose so no longer. But what a task—a whole world to create anew" (19). Zola argues that people would accept large families as politically and socially correct if an aesthetically attractive representation of motherhood were available.[10]

Zola hoped that by describing large, happy, and prosperous families, his inspirational narrative of motherhood would provide an incentive for a woman to become pregnant. Realizing that a large family can sometimes seem comic to those who observe it, he argues in his essay that authors should convince young, pretty women to be proud of their fertility. Zola asserts that people will change their behavior if beautiful examples are set before them: "one will suffer, one will fight, one will end indeed by accommodating oneself to the new social ideal in order to be strong, in order to be beautiful" (14: 787). He claims that a positive representation of motherhood can persuade families to find personal fulfillment while effecting a cure for France's ills. Writing a novel of domestic harmony instead of the tragic story of infant mortality that he originally intended in his notes for *Le Déchet*, Zola presents in *Fécondité* "a patriotic story" in which "abundant motherhood becomes the force to bind the nation together and to enable it to fulfill its national and international destiny."[11]

In *La Femme* and *L'Amour,* guides on love and marriage written to teach men how to treat their wives, Michelet encourages women to accept their feminine role and admonishes men to treat their female companions with a tenderness befitting the weak. For him, woman should stand on a pedestal as a goddess of purity inspiring man to do good. In *La Femme* (1859), he advises his male readers, "La femme est une religion,"[12] ("Woman is a religion") and "La pureté c'est la femme même" (123) ("Purity is the essence of woman"). As the "douce médiateur entre la nature et l'homme, entre le père et l'enfant" (148) ("sweet mediator between nature and man, between father and child"), she creates harmony in the family. Her remarkable powers of fecundity and nurturing enable her to be connected with nature and share in the expression of universal love by procreating. Man creates woman and initiates a transformation from girl to woman by erasing her past.[13] As noted in the previous chapter, Michelet counseled that a husband should take care to make his wife submissive by absorbing her sexual energy into pregnancy and child-rearing.[14] Woman's uncontrolled sexuality, symbolized by her menstruation, would thus be managed by motherhood.[15]

In Zola's earlier novels, there are only brief glimpses of maternity as a positive natural force that redeems humanity. The last novel of his *Rougon-Macquart* series, *Doctor Pascal* (1893), ends with a portrait of Clotilde nursing her child, a serene image based on Michelet's vision of motherhood as society's hope for the future. Clotilde's son was fathered by her uncle, Pascal Rougon; their baby embodies the parents' sexual transgression and has an unknown future. Many marriages in this earlier series demonstrate how husbands fail to tame wives. Liberal women are dangerously promiscuous, and conservatives excessively authoritarian. Nana, the prostitute who symbolizes Second Empire decadence, neglects her son; he eventually dies of a childhood illness (*Nana* 1880). Bourgeois women such as Lise Macquart in *La Ventre de Paris* (1874) and Félicité Rougon in *Doctor Pascal* manipulate their children to satisfy their greed. The series as a whole traces the gradual decline of the Rougons and Macquarts that resulted from their madness, greed, and penchant for alcohol, all inherited from Adélaide Fouque. In this series, no marriages are happy, and the few relationships that satisfy both partners are adulterous and result in the death of at least one partner.

The *Rougon-Macquart* novels indicate that maternal sympathy, while welcome, does not compensate for social problems. In *Germinal* (1885), Catherine's mother is a strong woman who suffers to protect her children, but she cannot combat her social and economic circumstances. Yet maternal love does partially ameliorate even the worst situations, for even female criminals occasionally display love for their children. Although bearing children and caring for them remain the most important feminine pursuits because maternal love creates harmony in the world, few women in the *Rougon-Macquart* novels enjoy this privilege.

Zola's novels point out that efforts to improve the human condition are bound to fail unless they employ the scientific method. In his "Letter to young people," he argues that youth should improve on the world of their parents by working hard and pledging faith in science, for the scientific method, as described by Claude Bernard, "seeks causes, wishes to explain them, and act on them."[16] The *Rougon-Macquart* novels argue that social problems faced by workers in politics, industry, banking, agriculture, and mining could be solved by application of the scientific method, while *Fécondité* endorses a political program consonant with naturalist doctrine, advocating sensible principles of health that focus on woman's fertility.

Linking maternal love and scientific principles in *Fécondité*, Zola produces an aesthetically satisfying poem to serve as the basis of a secular faith. His view that female fertility is a balm for society is developed from Michelet's doctrine of femininity, but Zola resists capitulating to the fear of female sexuality demonstrated in the historian's work. In notes for the novel, Zola remarks that the world will be a healthier place if we learn to admire the fecund woman as a cult figure.[17] The novel describes a national problem, the demise of the family in France, proposing an ideal of motherhood and illustrating examples of good mothers who embrace maternity.

The spectrum of mothers in *Fécondité* is based on Zola's observations and extensive reading of scientific sources. Although some women are selfish, others deny their "natural" feelings as mothers in order to survive in a harsh world. Subplots reveal many unhappy circumstances: a mother and a daughter are victims of unsanitary abortions; trusting women permit doctors to perform unnecessary sterilizations; working-class women are forced to part from infants because of the high expenses of child-rearing; women waiting for a convenient time to have children risk being unable to conceive; and mothers limiting the size of their families find that their children might not survive them. While many women are unable to enact Michelet's theory of the ideal mother, Marianne Froment is the exception and the dynamic focus in the novel. She raises her twelve children according to the healthy practices endorsed by the family physician.

The large Froment family, numbered at the novel's end as more than 158 children, grandchildren, and great-grandchildren, attests to the common sense of the parents and their willingness to accept the "natural" roles of husband and wife. Marianne, whose name evokes the Virgin Mary and the French revolutionary representation of Liberty, embodies the virtuous woman who sublimates desire in raising her family.[18] Like Michelet, Zola praises women who have sex for procreative purposes, believing that the fertility of women will save France.[19] He depicts Marianne's maternity in *Fécondité* as a positive natural force that generates love and fertility, and he thereby conflates two myths—that of the good mother and that of the good earth.

In recounting Marianne's and her husband Mathieu's responses to the birth of their fourth child, Zola's novel connects expansive rhetorical passages detailing the glories of having children, didactic information concerning scientific care of a child, and matter-of-fact descriptions of family life. Daily ritual includes bathing the child, weighing him in order to check on his progress, and breastfeeding him, activities requiring both parents and a servant:

How pretty he looked in the water his pink skin shining in the sunlight! And how well-behaved he was, for it was wonderful to see how quickly he ceased wailing and gave signs of satisfaction when he felt the all-enveloping caress of the warm water. Never had father and mother possessed such a little treasure.

"And now," said Mathieu, when Zoé had helped him to wipe the boy with a fine cloth, "and now we will weigh Master Gervais."

This was a complicated operation, which was rendered the more difficult by the extreme repugnance that the child displayed. He struggled and wriggled on the platform of the weighing scales to such a degree that it was impossible to arrive at his correct weight, in order to ascertain how much this had increased since the previous occasion. As a rule, the increase varied from six to seven ounces a week. The father generally lost patience over the operation, and the mother had to intervene. (106–7)

After noting the baby's weight, Marianne feeds him while her husband watches with nearly religious adoration: Mathieu "came back and lingered near the bed. The sun's rays poured over it, and life blazed there in a florescence of health and beauty. There is no more glorious blossoming, no more sacred symbol of living eternity than an infant at its mother's breast" (108).

Other scenes of breastfeeding figure prominently in the novel. Although technology assists parents, parental love remains the dominant power in the most successful families. In one case, a woman who had given birth to her third illegitimate child is persuaded to nurse the infant even though she already declared that she will send him to a wet-nurse as she has sent her other babies. After breastfeeding her son, Norine, a reformed prostitute, undergoes a radical transformation as she begins to bond with the baby, the only child she will keep:

The poor, pale, puny infant had weighed but little the first time he took the breast. But every morning afterwards he had been weighed afresh, and on the wall at the foot of the bed had been hung the diagram indicating the daily difference of weight. At first Norine had taken little interest in the matter, but as the line gradually ascended, plainly indicating how much the child was profiting, she gave it more and more attention. All at once, as the result of an indisposition, the line had dipped down; and since then she had always feverishly awaited the weighing, eager to see if the line would once more ascend. Then, a continuous rise having set in, she laughed with delight. That little line, which ever ascended, told her that her child was saved, and that all the weight and strength he acquired was derived from her—from her milk, her blood, her flesh. She was completing the appointed work; and motherliness, at last awakened within her, was blossoming in a florescence of love. (224)

The chart measures Norine's love and her baby's weight, illustrating how science and maternal affection combine to improve individual lives. Although

Norine can barely afford to support herself, her maternal affection for her baby encourages her to set up a home with her sister, who has been sterilized by an unscrupulous doctor. Together the women create a family, saving themselves and the child from wretched lives. Zola's message is blunt: fertility generates love, and love nurtures families. Connecting human fertility and marital and parental love to the fruitfulness of nature, *Fécondité* proposes that fertility promises progress. Science and technology are useful adjuncts that can enable healthy environments, but loving mothers are also important in determining the outcome of family life.

Fécondité contrasts the unhealthy temptations of urban life with the simple pleasures of living in the country to encourage close-knit families. Some families living in Paris seek social success, but they undermine their own efforts because they do not cultivate their greatest resource: their ability to procreate in the way that nature teaches them. The strongest example of negative motherhood in *Fécondité* is Constance, Marianne's cousin, who egoistically raises one son in order to pass on an unencumbered inheritance. Although her husband spouts Malthusian principles and approves of limiting sexual relations with Constance, he indulges in extramarital affairs and impregnates his young mistresses. Constance's misery after her beloved only son dies portrays the chaos engendered by an unfulfilled woman, for her grief turns her into a liar and a murderer when she realizes too late that her excessive contraceptive practices prevent her from enjoying a family. Her husband's dissolute lifestyle and her selfishness could have been controlled within the guidelines outlined by Michelet and Zola if the couple had respected the power of fertility.

Mathieu Froment achieves success by harnessing the fertility of the earth, reclaiming worthless marshland.[20] Unlike the bleak picture of agricultural life presented in *La Terre*, the earth is a generous mother to the Froment family. Mathieu's transformation of the marsh into a fertile field proves that the proper application of labor and love produces miracles. His success in growing wheat on previously fallow property is described not as a great scientific feat but as a project to inseminate nature that requires respect for the earth. Farming and procreating amidst the gentle beneficence of nature, the Froments are productive and hope for an even better future for their offspring. *Fécondité* teaches that motherhood makes a woman complete because she becomes more beautiful and closer to nature by exuding love and procreating. To be prosperous, man should inseminate nature in both of its guises, woman and earth.

While Michelet directed his works about women and love to the male reader to persuade husbands to control their wives, Zola aimed his novel at women, for he believed that the population problem could be solved by encouraging women to believe that pregnancy and motherhood are aesthetically satisfying experiences. Numerous examples of motherhood serve as a background for

Marianne's successful life as a pantheistic goddess, a pseudo-socialist political emblem of the proper kind of farm wife, and a modern woman who raises her children according to her best judgment of scientific principles. This fictional presentation of the good mother avoids the issue of equal political rights for women while also detailing a powerful domestic vision of how a wife-and-mother inspires her family.

The image of a wise mother who relies upon love and scientific method in raising her children connects interests in motherhood and science as positive, reciprocal forces that improve individuals and societies. But the emphasis on the state's role in encouraging births of future soldiers resembles policies endorsed by eugenicists and the Nazi state, along with the plotline of *Dracula* noted in the previous chapter. Harnessing woman's procreative capacity as central to national interests constrains individual and family for state benefit, but encouraging procreation does not necessarily promote positive social and political outcomes and often restricts woman's choices to pursue educational and career pathways.

Stereotypes of Women Doctors

Zola praised the new mother whose fertility might keep France a world power, but American authors interested in gender displayed more interest in exploring the lives of women who entered the world of work. Responding to stereotypes of women physicians and to cultural arguments concerning the propriety of women working outside the home, William Dean Howells's *Dr. Breen's Practice* (1881), Elizabeth Stuart Phelps's *Dr. Zay* (1882), Sarah Orne Jewett's *A Country Doctor* (1884), and Charlotte Perkins Gilman's "Mr. Peebles' Heart" (1914) and "Dr. Clair's Place" (1915) imagine how medicine is best served by feminine virtues. Sex roles and stereotypes in these narratives illustrate configurations of sexuality, science, and technology, inviting readers to consider the New Woman doctor who faced cultural prohibitions concerning her work.

Like Child's story "Hilda Silfverling" and Zola's *Fécondité*, these American realist narratives perform cultural work. The fictions of Howells, Phelps, Jewett, and Gilman invite readers to accept, reject, or negotiate characters' choices regarding whether women should practice medicine, while also acknowledging the ways in which a female doctor's partner, family, and society benefit from her interventions. Medical doctors are characterized as helping individuals and society in ways that are consonant with woman's traditional role as caregiver. Thus, *Dr. Breen's Practice, Dr. Zay, A Country Doctor,* and Gilman's stories illustrate what some historians consider to be a golden age of women's participation in U.S. medicine.

From 1848, when the New England Female Medical College, the first women's medical college, was founded, until 1910, when the Carnegie Foundation published Abraham Flexner's report on medical education in the United States, women's medical colleges and female students' matriculation in coeducational medical schools flourished.[21] During this period, Sue Wells points out, "women entered a large, loose profession in relatively ample numbers, participated in its work as it developed scientifically, formed their own institutions, [and] were accepted into the male institutions as scientific medicine achieved its greatest triumphs." This era ended with Flexner's recommendations to promote uniform standards for medical education for college graduates. The reconfiguration of medical schools into graduate programs limited the participation of women, who "then were both marginalized and dispersed."[22]

Writing their fictions in the 1880s, before women's medical colleges were put out of business, Howells, Phelps, Jewett, and Gilman acknowledge the ways in which female physicians were affected by conflicting ideologies promoting and constraining their participation in medicine. Rosemary Pringle reports that many women

chose medicine because they regarded independent, self-supporting careers as a positive alternative to marriage and not as a necessary fall back in the event they failed to marry. . . . Some married women also embraced the ideology of financial independence and self-reliance. At a time when salaried jobs for married women were almost impossible to obtain, there were great hopes that medicine would offer more flexibility and permit women to combine family and career.[23]

These fictions about women doctors illustrate their struggles to combine personal and professional responsibilities and to be accepted as competent caregivers in ways that still resonate with readers.[24]

Recognizing the ethical power of realism to convey social problems and solutions, Howells acknowledges, "Realism is nothing more and nothing less than the truthful depiction of the material."[25] Phelps's memoir *Chapters from a Life* similarly defines moral realism as an effort both "to tell the truth about the world [she] live[d] in" and to write "with ethical purpose."[26] Jewett also accepts that fiction ought to have a "point of view" and that in selecting material, an author should develop a moral perspective. Gilman's short stories are moral parables exploring how sex role constraints can be overturned by innovations often related to science and technology. *Dr. Breen's Practice, Dr. Zay, The Country Doctor,* and Gilman's stories dramatize real-life dilemmas by illustrating unconventional women surrounded by admirers and critics. Narrators resist sermonizing about the propriety of women working outside the home in favor of creating scenes that invite readers in as direct observers of how the protagonists' work helps others. These narratives do not offer elaborate plots, preferring instead to document how various characters judge women doctors and to incorporate extended dialogues among those commenting on the talents and shortcomings of female doctors. Narrators also guide readers' interpretations to ensure that female doctors emerge as sympathetic innovators.

Protagonists sacrifice personal relationships to pursue medical careers.[27] The first American novel about a woman physician, *Dr. Breen's Practice,* has an ironic title, for Grace is most often referred to as Miss Breen by the women who board at her mother's seaside resort on the coast of Massachusetts south of Boston. Many guests are convinced that this form of address is more polite than "doctor" in that it acknowledges that she is a woman. The confusion over Grace's title signals her ambivalence about being a physician. Grace decided to attend medical school after being jilted by a lover. After graduation, she begins her career by treating her friend Mrs. Louise Maynard, who is estranged from her husband and staying at the Breen resort. Mrs. Maynard tries to convince Grace that she is wrong about everything, although Grace pays her bills and provides her with free medical care. When Grace asks Louise to stop complaining about her marital troubles to other guests because such talk encourages criticism, Louise laughs and tells Grace, "[Y]ou defy public opinion a good deal more than I do, every minute . . . [by] being a doctor."

Other characters also criticize Grace for becoming a doctor or for practicing homeopathy. Some guests do not understand why Grace went to medical school at all. As Mrs. Scott suggests, "But they say Miss Breen wasn't obliged to do it for a living" (64). Dr. Mulbridge, the town's allopathic physician, refuses to consult Grace when he treats Mrs. Maynard, who appears to have contracted pneumonia, and he demands that Grace agree to act as a nurse on the case and not as a doctor (55).[28] Dr. Mulbridge's mother approves this plan, telling her son, "If one half the bold things that are running about the country had masters it would be the best thing" (115).

Fewer characters offer favorable opinions of Grace's work. Grace's mother is supportive, although she believes that her daughter is wasting her time caring for the passive-aggressive Mrs. Maynard. The feminist Miss Gleason, a resort guest, offers unqualified, public praise about Grace's actions, whether Grace is caring for Mrs. Maynard or turning the case over to Dr. Mulbridge; but Howells represents Miss Gleason as a "heroine worshipper" who admires Grace unconditionally and not objectively (28). Mrs. Breen confirms that Miss Gleason "is a fool" (98). According to the narrator, Miss Gleason's feminist politics make her oblivious to what happens around her; for example, she is unaware of romantic intrigues brewing and is incapable of understanding Grace's feelings and preferences.

Readers enter a social world that prefers to regard Grace as a marriageable young woman rather than respect her status as a doctor. Resort guests prefer to speculate about romance and fashion, differing on whether Mrs. Maynard will get a divorce and which man Grace might marry. Readers know more than the guests do because readers can observe the comfortable intimacy between Grace and Walter Libby that contrasts with her strained meetings with Dr. Mulbridge. Confessing he loves Grace, Mr. Libby reveals he understands her professional predicament: "You were always thinking, because you had studied a man's profession, that no one would think of you as a woman, as if that could make any difference to a man that had the soul of a man in him!" (90). There is little doubt which man Grace prefers, even though her confusion about her career delays her decision about marriage.

Grace refuses Mr. Libby's first proposal, but she almost instantly regrets this response and admits to her mother she does like him. Meanwhile, Miss Gleason promotes Dr. Mulbridge's suit, proclaiming that "the perfect mastery of the man-physician constitutes the highest usefulness of the woman-physician. The advancement of women must be as women" (102). Grace appears tentative because it is impossible for her to live up to Miss Gleason's ideal of a female physician. Nor can Grace follow her mother's advice to cast off the annoying Mrs. Maynard.

Contrasting Grace's lack of professional experience and submissiveness with Dr. Mulbridge's confidence, Mrs. Maynard reminds her friend, "You're not fit to be a doctor. You're too nervous, and you're too conscientious," and she advises Grace that "what you want to do is to get married. You would be a good wife, and you would be a good mother" (121–22). The tables turn, however, for after Mr. Maynard shows up and lets Dr. Breen know that he will "take care" of his wife, Mrs. Maynard's domination of Grace comes to an end (109).

Grace is then free to do as she pleases, which means choosing a husband who suits her and her career choice. Walter Libby treats Grace as a peer, but Dr. Mulbridge courts her by asserting his power and authority over women: "He saw that rude moral force alone seemed to have a charm with his lady patients,—women who had been bred to ease and wealth, and who had cultivated, if not disciplined, minds" (111). Dr. Mulbridge wants to convince Grace to marry him and give up her medical practice to become part of his, but Grace wants to become more independent, not less, by marrying.

Muddling through her confusion about men and medicine, Dr. Grace Breen determines that she must do as she wishes—not what Miss Gleason, her mother, Mrs. Maynard, or Dr. Mulbridge sees fit. Grace tells Mr. Libby she loves him, affirming, "Nothing is easy that men have to do" (145). After marrying, Grace continues to practice medicine; she cares for the children of her husband's mill workers because he has asked her to do so. The novel ends by emphasizing Grace's happiness in her marriage: she "trusts [her husband's] sense with the same completeness that she trusts his love. On the other hand, when it is felt that she ought to have done for the sake of woman what she could not do for herself, she is regarded as sacrificed in her marriage" (158). Dr. Grace Breen attains respectability in marriage and practices medicine in a way she finds comfortable.

Howells was midway through serializing his novel in the *Atlantic Monthly* when he received a manuscript of the second American novel about a female physician, Elizabeth Stuart Phelps's *Dr. Zay*.[29] As the journal's editor, he decided to publish *Dr. Zay* after *Dr. Breen's Practice* concluded, and he invited readers to compare the fictions. While Howells's novel focuses on a woman physician who establishes a professional practice after marrying, *Dr. Zay* considers how an already successful female doctor contemplates marriage.

Aware that approximately two thousand female physicians practiced in the late-nineteenth-century United States,[30] Phelps begins her novel from the patient's point of view. The novel details the perspective of a young man of society, the wealthy, indolent Waldo Yorke, who comes to know a female physician in rural Maine. Waldo surprises his mother when he tells her that he will leave their Boston home to execute his recently deceased uncle's estate in Maine. Whatever the reader learns about the title character, Dr. Zaidee Atalanta Lloyd (Zay), is filtered through the comments of other characters and the hazy perceptions of Waldo, an effete, narrow-minded Bostonian lawyer who, at the beginning of the book, is without a law practice. On his second day in Maine, Waldo has a carriage accident, loses consciousness, and awakens to realize he has serious injuries and is being treated by a young woman who he assumes is his nurse. Until Waldo's health improves, all those around him withhold the shocking information that his doctor is a woman. Waldo quizzes Zay about her experience and expertise, at first distrusting her advice and prescriptions as possibly misguided or naive.

Mrs. Butterwell, who is landlady to both the doctor and her patient, tells Waldo that Dr. Zay is wealthy, which surprises him: "Was it possible that this young woman had practice enough to keep two horses? He knew nothing of the natural history of doctresses. He had thought of them chiefly as a species of a higher nurse,—poor women, who wore unbecoming clothes, took the horse-cars, and probably dropped their 'g's,' or said, 'Is that so?'" (63). Asking Zay why she became a doctor, Waldo is surprised to learn her the depth of her sacrifices to cope with what she describes as a "terrible . . . need of a woman by a woman, in country towns" (75).

The narrative plot describes how Waldo learns to trust Zay's authority as he becomes more sympathetic toward Zay as a person, more understanding of her life choices, more personally interested in her, and more mature about his own career. Mrs. Butterwell explicates the doctor's virtues to the bedridden Waldo, testifying to Dr. Zay's important role in the community and the challenges of practicing medicine in a rural location:

> "She will be worked half out of her wits," proceeded Mrs. Butterwell. . . . "East Sherman has the scarlet fever. . . . Doctor will be up and down day and night, now, you'll see. She has no more consideration for herself than a seraphim. She'll *be* one, if she don't mind. The poorer they are, the more nobody else goes near 'em, the more they get of *her*. . . . She has such a spirit! You'd expect it, if she wasn't smart. When a woman ain't good for anything else she falls back on her spirit! You don't look for it when she's got bigger fish to fry. But there! There's more *woman* to our doctor than to the rest of us, just as there's more brains. Seems to me as if there was love enough invested in her for half the world to live on the interest, and never know they hadn't touched the principal. If she didn't give so much, she'd be rich on her own account before now." (85–86)

Mrs. Butterwell appreciates Dr. Zay's superior feminine and medical attributes, explaining that the doctor's homeopathic medical knowledge sustains the community.[31]

Nonfictional accounts of women doctors in the mid- and late nineteenth century also elaborate Victorian values characterizing woman as the sensitive angel of the house.[32] Historian Regina Markell Morantz-Sanchez notes that in the 1850s, Elizabeth Blackwell and others "always used the concern about the potential compromise of female delicacy generated by male treatment as an argument in favor of training women in medicine."[33] Women physicians in the 1880s differentiated their treatments from those done in masculine style, claiming that women "had more patience and insight" and arguing that women "practiced a more nurturing, milder, and more holistic brand of therapeutics" (211, 210). Educators urged their students, in the words of Dean Clara Marshall of the Woman's Medical College of Pennsylvania, to "reach patients and cure them too, by a scientific use of your humanity" (210).

Waldo witnesses the close relationships Dr. Zay has with her patients and her strong idealism when he accompanies her during rounds. In one case, he must sit idly by when a worker named Jim is nearly drowned in a mill accident (142), while Dr. Zay and a number of healthy men on the scene work hard to ensure that Jim will cheat death. After Jim is saved, Dr. Zay wastes not a minute in arranging for a minister to marry him to her patient Molly, the woman he recently impregnated (146). Dr. Zay imposes her values concerning the sanctity of marriage and motherhood on Molly and Jim as a natural extension of her authority as a physician.

The doctor believes that a vulnerable, unwed, expectant mother like Molly will find affection, social approval, and financial stability only by marrying the father of her baby. Although Dr. Zay fears that marriage would constrain her own life and would conflict with the demands of her practice, Phelps has other plans for the doctor and connects the professional story of Dr. Zay with the romantic plot Yorke initiates. The novel thereby optimistically blends career and personal growth for both parties in a romantic relationship.

Although at first Waldo does not enjoy Dr. Zay's being "in charge," he learns to admire her authoritative confidence as a doctor and her other, more feminine virtues. After leaving Zay's care, Waldo eventually gains power as architect of their sentimental attachment. Mrs. Butterwell's observation that Dr. Zay is a perfect doctor who knows nothing of men and Zay's claim that she must sacrifice sympathetic relations to practice her scientific profession encourage Waldo's attentions. While the first part of the novel develops how Waldo's views on professional development are enlarged, the second part concentrates on his enlightening Dr. Zay regarding the value of sentimental attachments.[34]

Dr. Zay acknowledges to Waldo that she recognizes it is a natural mode of human behavior to marry and have a family but that she must resist such personal indulgences because of her professional position and because she has not seen many true marriages. After Waldo proposes for the second time, Zay tells him:

> You have been so unfortunate as to become interested in a new kind of woman. The trouble is that a happy marriage with such a woman demands a new type of man. By and by you would chafe under this transitional position. . . . You would need me when I was called somewhere urgently. You would reflect, and react, and waver, and then it would seem to you that you were neglected, that you were wronged. You would think of the other men, whose wives were always punctual at dinner in long dresses, and could play to them in the evening, and accept invitations, and always be on hand, like the kitten. I should not blame you. (244)

Zay admits that she had almost engaged in a Boston marriage, a living arrangement with another woman that might have fulfilled her need for intimacy, but she is married to her work.

Since Waldo cannot logically convince Zay, whose scientific training gives her the upper hand, over time he uses sentiment to persuade her to marry him. Zay objects that an equitable marital arrangement is rarely achieved and that she doubts whether even he, who has managed to say things she had not expected any man to say to her, can live up to what he describes. Instead of giving up his pursuit of her, Waldo celebrates the miracle of their love and argues that he loves all of her: "the strong-minded doctor" and "the sweet-hearted woman" (254).

Medicine appears a suitably feminine project in Phelps's novel as women appear natural healers. At the same time, the novel revises the roles assigned to men and women in marriage, celebrating two lovers who revise conventional sex roles to achieve a potentially happy marriage. The cultural history of neurasthenia supports Phelps's portrait of Waldo as an effeminate man who takes on feminist as well as feminine attributes. According to Jackson Lears, the contradictory demands of Victorian values concerning gender-appropriate behavior created "problematic expectations":[35] "The tendency to define autonomy as male and dependence as female made ambivalence especially severe among those for whom gender identity was most problematic: women who sought 'masculine' careers in public life, men who nurtured 'feminine' aspirations toward literature, art, or the increasingly 'feminized' ministry" (221). The schizophrenic demands of culture, Lears argues, permits an escape into neurasthenia that invalids could use to justify both autonomy and dependence.

Phelps describes Waldo's neurasthenia (his masculine invalidism) as a counterpoint to her characterization of the feminine aspects of science. The novel reverses gender roles and depicts how a female physician and a male patient converse. Because Waldo sees his resignation to his illness as courageous, he is taken aback to hear Dr. Zay reply that "he had received a nervous strain," using a term more often applied to women. The demystification of neurasthenia as a typically masculine propensity develops a romance that reverses sex stereotypes.

The narrative takes the occasion of Waldo's lengthy convalescence as an opportunity for a good deal of interaction between him and Zay. The contrast between the hardworking, socially activist Zay and the neurasthenic Waldo could hardly be greater at the beginning of the novel, but their differences encourage their mutual attraction. It is only when Waldo observes how attentive Zay is to her work, to her patients and their health, that he realizes how significant an occupation can be. By discarding his preexisting ideas and admitting that women can achieve professional authority even in nontraditional fields, Waldo works harder at his profession, law, and becomes a sympathetic companion for Dr. Zay.

Waldo and Zay enter a relationship defined according to their terms. Resisting stereotypical roles, each develops a sense of self combining attributes of both genders, for Waldo's experience as an invalid has raised his consciousness about what it means to be socialized as feminine. Like Grace Breen's assuming the role of assertive lover and giving up a nascent independent medical practice to marry, Zay moves toward Waldo, agreeing that she must also change if they are to have a relationship. Phelps's novel offers a more radical solution than Howells's in suggesting that Zay might move to Boston to set up practice, while Jewett's novel both describes a heroine whose temperament resembles

Dr. Zay's and also details the experiences of a young woman determined to go to medical school regardless of what people think.

Jewett's father was a country doctor, and for a time she also considered becoming one.[36] As a young child she accompanied her father on his rounds to see patients on surrounding farms,[37] and these visits to patients provided a foundation for the relationship of the orphaned Nan Prince and her guardian Dr. Leslie in *A Country Doctor*. Familiarity with a doctor's life also helps to explain why Jewett might have chosen the female physician as the subject of her first novel, even though Howells and Phelps had just published their books. Like *Dr. Zay*, Jewett's novel is set in rural Maine. It begins by describing how Nan's mother Addy contemplates suicide as she struggles to get home to her own mother, walking and then crawling to the family farm while carrying the young Nan in her arms. Addy begs Dr. Leslie to watch over Nan and then dies within hours of making this request. Addy's mother raises the girl and lets her visit Dr. Leslie, but Mrs. Thacher resists the entreaties of Nan's father's family to adopt or support her granddaughter because the Princes' treatment of Addy was partly responsible for her daughter's decline. Two years after taking Nan in, Mrs. Thacher dies, and the girl goes to live with Dr. Leslie and his housekeeper Marilla.

Hoping to guide her, the doctor takes her on his rounds and asks her, "'What are you going to do when you grow up, Nan?' to which she answered gravely, as if it were the one great question of her life, 'I should like best to be a doctor'" (202).[38] Information about Nan's family background emerges from dialogues between Dr. Leslie and his peers. The doctor's conversation with a college classmate, a ship captain, reveals that Nan's father was a ship's surgeon and that her mother worked in Dunport as a dressmaker. Addy offended her soon-to-be husband's sister, and the women feud even after Addy becomes her brother's wife. Addy is described as "ambitious" and "impatient" (209), and Dr. Leslie thinks she could have been consumptive and insane, for he heard she had been drinking and begging in the streets in her last days before returning to her family home in Oldfields.

Dr. Leslie and Nan agree that medical school and practice suit Nan's abilities. He unwaveringly supports Nan's decision to become a doctor:

> "I want you to be a good woman, and I want you to be all the use you can," he said. "It seems to me like stealing for men and women to live in the world and do nothing to make it better. You have thought a great deal about this, and so have I, and now we will do the best we can at making a good doctor of you. I don't care whether people think it is a proper education for women or not. It seems to me that it is more than proper for you, and God has given you a fitness for it which it is shame to waste. And if you ever hesitate and regret what you have said, you

won't have done yourself any harm by learning how to take care of your own health and other people's." (261–62)

The doctor expresses the most liberal attitudes in the novel toward women training as physicians, whereas other adults who attempt to influence Nan, including Dr. Leslie's friend Mrs. Graham, differ on whether being a physician is respectable for a woman. But no one shakes Nan from the belief that she was born to do something important, for she has all her mother's ambition along with her father's medical talent and interest in doing good.

Taking a break from medical school, Nan visits her father's sister in the city and learns firsthand of her aunt's bitterness toward her mother, who was blamed for stealing Jack Prince away from his family. Nan's aunt, Miss Prince, thinks highly of Nan's gentle nature and courtesy, nurtured by her grandmother, Dr. Leslie, and by Mrs. Graham in turn, but her aunt objects to Nan's professional plans. Miss Prince tells her that medical school is a ridiculous notion Dr. Leslie has mistakenly encouraged. Miss Prince presses Nan to marry George Gerry, the son of Miss Prince's own former beau.

Although Nan likes George, their relationship does not flourish because George is uncomfortable with her skills. During a boating party, as George and Nan seek refreshments for the young people taking the excursion, he witnesses Nan's medical abilities as he observes her tending to an injured farmer who has dislocated his shoulder:

> Nan pulled the spectators into the doorway of the kitchen, and quickly stooped and unbuttoned her right boot, and then planted her foot on the damaged shoulder and caught up the hand and gave a quick pull, the secret of which nobody understood; but there was an unpleasant cluck as the bone went back into its socket, and a yell from the sufferer, who scrambled to his feet. (316)

Her heroism confuses George, who "somehow wished it had been he who could play the doctor" (317). Unlike Waldo Yorke and Walter Libby, who admire the abilities of the women they love, George is troubled by Nan's expertise.

Other Dunport residents are also disturbed by Nan's ambition to become a physician. The aging Mrs. Fraley, the reigning social arbiter, criticizes Nan for insisting she will be a doctor. Responding to Nan's argument that boys and girls with talents should be equally encouraged ("I don't see why it should be a shame and dishonor to a girl who is trying to do the same thing and be of equal use in the world"), Mrs. Fraley tells her:

> "My dear, it is quite unnatural you see, . . . Here you are less than twenty-five years old, and I shall hear of your being married next thing,—at least I hope

I shall,—and you will laugh at this nonsense. A woman's place is at home. Of course, I know there have been some women physicians who have attained eminence, and some artists, and all that. But I would rather see a daughter of mine take a more retired place." (327–28)

Nan patiently listens to such criticism, but she lets nothing, not even George's proposal of marriage and her aunt's intimidation, dissuade her from following her life's ambition. At the end of the novel, Nan anticipates completing medical school and practicing medicine in Oldfields.

Charlotte Perkins Gilman's stories about female physicians similarly highlight their wisdom and independence. In "Mr. Peebles's Heart," Dr. Joan Bascom develops an unusual prescription for her brother-in-law, Mr. Arthur Peebles, when she suggests that "for his health" he should sell his store and take the proceeds to travel without his wife, her sister Emma (275). Although Emma worries about what people think of such a plan, Dr. Joan proposes it to her sister only after buying the store and establishing vacation plans for Arthur. When all arrangements are in place, Emma cannot oppose what her sister and husband support.

Joan also prescribes a more enlarged life for Emma, and during the husband's absence she stays with her sister, whose children are grown and married. Freeing Arthur from his business so that he can explore his interests, Dr. Joan introduces Emma to independence during Arthur's two-year trip abroad and encourages her sister to learn about art and music.[39] Dr. Joan's medical prescription improves the store's business when she hires a more adept manager, encourages the healthy development of husband and wife, saves her sister's marriage, and turns a profit for the doctor. Like Zay, Joan effects social engineering through her "prescriptions."

The first-person narrator of "Dr. Clair's Place" attributes scientific expertise to Dr. Willy Clair, a female physician who has established a Southern California mountain spa where men and women can relax and reinvigorate their minds. The narrator is a former spa guest and at the story's outset serves as an "associate" who helps others learn to be happy. The facility is less medical than a sanatorium and more stimulating than a friend's country place might be; Dr. Clair's place is a calm, peaceful retreat where patients, friends, and associates can interact for everyone's good. The story's ending is idyllic: the narrator explains that she now makes a living "by knitting and teaching it to others. And out of the waste and wreck of my life—which is of no small consequence to me, I can myself serve to help new-comers. I am an Associate—even I! And I am so Happy!" (303).

Dr. Breen's Practice, Dr. Zay, A Country Doctor, and Gilman's stories describe intersections of medicine and femininity that reconfigure readers' ideas of appropriate roles for women by making it appear "natural" in these fictional worlds for women to become physicians, exercise authority over others' lives, and serve as role models. Narrators present doctors (and mothers) as well-intended, thoughtful caregivers who encounter unfair criticism from those who deem medicine an inappropriate profession for women. The New Woman and the New Woman doctor appear as competent, caring, and rational in resolving individual and social problems.

These fictions also broadly engage readers by reconfiguring sex role stereotypes to suggest that women should be more assertive than social conventions allow. Gilman's stories and novels by Howells, Phelps, and Jewett demonstrate how women pursue education, work as physicians, and, in some cases, marry according to what might seem unconventional paths. While sketching different personal prospects for women physicians, the authors suggest that it is the inevitable lot of competent professional women to cope with harsh critics who believe that women's roles should be more limited. Their fictions observe dilemmas for women seeking professional roles and establish possibilities for feminine and feminist interventions in medicine that promote positive social change. In our own day, film performs such cultural work, as the next section and chapter explore.

Science and Parental Love in *Lorenzo's Oil*

The critically acclaimed 1992 film *Lorenzo's Oil*, directed by George Miller and starring Susan Sarandon and Nick Nolte, was not a box-office hit, perhaps because the subject of terminal illness kept away viewers more interested in happy endings or blockbuster special effects. Yet the film has achieved a cult status as indicated by numerous high ratings on the Internet Movie Database, references to it in Internet chat-room discussions concerning rare diseases, and Web sites about it.[40] From the perspective of science studies, the film deserves attention as a political manifesto for families affected by orphan diseases and as a depiction of female medical heroism. Influenced by cultural responses to medicine, illness, and death, *Lorenzo's Oil* adapts conventions of biographical films describing a hero's scientific discovery by delineating how Lorenzo Odone's parents, who were not physicians, contributed to scientific research.[41]

Based on a true story, *Lorenzo's Oil* melds family documentary and scientific history within a fictionalized narrative to reveal how the collaboration of doctors and those affected by a disease results in scientific progress. As a medical case study, the film links Lorenzo and his parents with tenacity and persistence, connecting these traits with their travel in Africa and their interest in crossing cultural boundaries. Miller stages Augusto and Michaela Odones's struggle to understand their son Lorenzo's adrenoleukodystrophy as a heroic battle in which the family's weapons include cultural adaptability, willingness to synthesize information from unfamiliar technical disciplines, parental love, and patient fortitude.

Lorenzo's Oil opens with an epigraph emphasizing heroism, a quotation from a Swahili warrior's song: "Life has meaning only in the struggle / Triumph or defeat is in the hands of the Gods." The credits unroll over opening shots set in the visually stunning Comoros Islands depicting a healthy five-year-old Lorenzo whose social, linguistic, and cultural skills provide evidence of his intelligence and maturity. The prologue records Lorenzo's July 1983 leave-taking of his African friends, particularly Omouri, a farewell marked by their exchange of homemade gifts (a kite to Omouri and his sword to Lorenzo). The kite Lorenzo made for his friend depicts the Odone family; his explanation of the figures reveals his family history, encoded in his name "Lorenzo Michael Murphy Odone," son of an Irish-American mother who is a linguist (Michaela Murphy Odone) and an Italian father who works as an international economist with the World Bank (Augusto Odone).

The film follows the chronology of Lorenzo's illness, diagnosis, and therapies. Three months after returning from Africa with his parents to their home in Washington, DC, Lorenzo exhibits behavior that puts his well-educated, culturally savvy parents at odds with schoolteachers and administrators who suggest assigning the boy to special education. Lorenzo's physical abilities dramatically degenerate in late 1983 when he falls first from his bicycle and later from a chair while taking an ornament off the Christmas tree. Puzzled by his inexplicable physical and mental lapses, Lorenzo's parents and doctors arrange to have him intensively tested in a hospital. The Easter (April) 1984 diagnosis of adrenoleukodystrophy (ALD) is tragic news to the Odones, for the physician indicates that Lorenzo's decline will be rapid, inexorable, and painful. The doctor delivers this diagnosis, explaining that myelin surrounding Lorenzo's nerves is eroding and that there is no therapy known to prevent or forestall degeneration.

The dates of onset and diagnosis (Christmas and Easter) relate the progression of Lorenzo's disease to the family's Catholic faith. The settings of Lorenzo's school and the hospital where he is diagnosed appear in the film as cathedrals. The camera frames his parents' conversations with authority figures in these settings against the backgrounds of soaring ceilings. The library where Augusto (Nick Nolte) first looks up the medical research on ALD is a large space with a high ceiling resembling a church. Michaela (Susan Sarandon) prays in a cathedral during a mass, tearfully but silently imploring God to save her son. Augusto flees the cathedral-like library, where he has been reading in medical journals about the painful fate awaiting his son, to go scream in a library stairwell where he is wracked by sobbing. As Anne Hudson Jones argues, "Even while these scenes reinforce Lorenzo's identity as substitute Christ, other scenes in the cathedral sequence prepare for the substitution that soon comes of scientific research for religious faith."[42] During their son's illness, the Odones move from despair to optimistic hope and determined curiosity to learn all they can about this disease and what they can do to fight it. The sacralized settings of the library and hospital highlight the Odones' resistance to their son's illness. Instead, they choose an active course: putting faith in science by prodding individuals and institutions to develop a therapy that might treat Lorenzo.

In May 1984, shortly after Lorenzo's diagnosis, his parents enroll him in a clinical trial at the Johns Hopkins University in Baltimore to test the effect of a low-fat diet on ALD patients. The trial's director, Dr. Gus Nikolais, makes it clear that the study's diet might not prove a therapy for Lorenzo; however, its results could lead to the development of a more sophisticated understanding of ALD, only recognized as a disease in the 1970s. Augusto and Michaela know already that ALD is a genetic disorder, but they learn from Dr. Nikolais that it is a sex-linked disorder transmitted via mothers who pass on the genetic defect to their sons. Augusto asks Dr. Nikolais about the biochemical processes of ALD, but Michaela seems stricken as she contemplates that her genes have caused Lorenzo's illness. Dr. Nikolais patiently answers Augusto's questions and tries to comfort Michaela by telling her that "you have nothing to blame yourself for." Nikolais's office is another seemingly sacred space, for the backdrop to the conversation between doctor and parents is dominated by a large, semicircular, translucent window revealing no view, only light. Lorenzo's parents—Augusto by breaking down during Nikolais's explanation and Michaela by maintaining stoicism—assert their primary concern as their son's health, not the doctor's opinion of them.

The Odones recognize that their interests and the doctor's do not coincide. Their experience in the Comoros has shown them that acquiring information about another culture and appreciating its different values and conventions can be challenging, worthwhile processes, and they adapt these lessons to battling Lorenzo's illness in constructing medicine as a foreign culture. Having bridged cultural differences of the West and Africa, they refuse to be intimidated by medical experts or resign themselves to Lorenzo's predicted fate. Instead, they collaborate with each other, with researchers, and with anyone else who will partner in creating new knowledge and establishing more effective therapies as part of winning the war against ALD.

Cultural sensitivity and empowerment through education bind the family and structure their days. Lorenzo's parents interrogate doctors who recommend only the most conservative therapies and who guard against experimental or innovative approaches, but the Odones establish their own rules, for example, deciding when Lorenzo's other relatives might visit, at first limiting such opportunities and then having a large birthday party to celebrate his sixth birthday in May 1984. When the low-fat diet required by Dr. Nikolais's study does not appear to control the level of fats in Lorenzo's bloodstream, his parents are perplexed and begin to investigate other means to alleviate their son's degenerative illness, going so far as to have him embark on a radically experimental three-week course of chemotherapy in Boston in June 1984. But until they figure out why the recommended diet does not work, Augusto is reluctant for Lorenzo to stop following it, for he refuses to be unscientific in his objections to standard scientific practices.

The Odones' willingness to challenge existing medical research puts them at odds with medical professionals and parents, notably Ellard and Loretta Muscatine, the couple leading the parents' foundation. The Muscatines' experiences with their sons with ALD and their witnessing of the devastating effects of ALD on many other families make them submissive; in their view, parents cannot change the course of the disease and should unquestioningly support the doctors who are working to understand it and create possible therapies. Michaela and Augusto attend one parents' foundation conference in July 1984 but become frustrated by what they see as a misplaced focus on caring for parents rather than for children. When Michaela asks the participants to discuss whether Dr. Nikolais's diet benefits the boys enrolled in the research study, the Muscatines and the nutritionist state that such information is anecdotal and that parents should simply follow the directives of Dr. Nikolais and other experts. Although Michaela stops arguing her case at the conference, the Odones do not change their focus on children, seeking Lorenzo's improvement by any means necessary. Caring for him at home, they valiantly speak first of his recovery and later of prolonging and enhancing his life. They envision him as a warrior against the disease. At bedtime in August 1984, they tell him the Italian story of the night of the shooting stars to encourage him to have hope; having heard it many times, he knows its triumphant end. The camera frames the family in a window as they fix their gaze on stars beyond, affirming their courage and their recognition of the mysteries of nature.

Later, Michaela and Augusto's persistence provokes new medical research. They subsidize and reconfigure standard medical procedures related to clinical trials, to funding of research, and to experimental protocols that will help their son and other afflicted boys. They review medical research, raise funds to support collaborative conferences and scientific research, and serve as home caregivers because they believe that their continuing involvement on all fronts can help them better understand the disease and that consistently nurturing Lorenzo's mind will help him recover from the disease.

Michaela and Augusto learn biochemistry and begin constructing alternative hypotheses of etiology and treatment to prod researchers to speed up scientific discoveries. Augusto's "simple-minded" approach to the understanding ALD encourages him to use commonplace methods of visualization to describe it, including the image of a kitchen sink with its faucets and drains to represent the inputs and outputs of Lorenzo's blood. The Odones puzzle over "the paradox" of why the low-fat diet appears to increase the levels of fat in his system, and Michaela assiduously looks through the medical research about biosynthesis of fats, finding in October 1984 a Polish study on rats that demonstrates fatty acid manipulation as a possible mechanism in ALD.

Recognizing that scientific researchers are isolated from each other by national and disciplinary boundaries, the Odones convince Dr. Nikolais to help establish an international conference on ALD. The ALD parents' foundation would also sponsor the international symposium bringing together researchers from around the world, but only if Michaela links it with the parents' conference to be held in nine months. Instead, the Odones proceed quickly, conscious that every minute delays the possibility of helping Lorenzo, and they find funding and arrange for the event to take place in five weeks. Michaela insists that a *Washington Post* reporter meet Lorenzo, which results in publication of an article about the symposium, but by the date of the meeting, Lorenzo can no longer speak clearly, and Michaela finds it difficult to determine what he wants.

The November 10, 1984, symposium developed by the Odones was the first devoted to ALD and related biochemical processes, and it is represented in the film as taking place in another cathedral-like setting. Although not professional scientists, the Odones insist on participating in the meeting, at which they help piece together what might be a promising therapy. Dr. Nikolais reports on the paradox of the low-fat diet resulting in higher fat levels. A Japanese scientist asks about inhibiting biosynthesis by fatty acid manipulation, and in response to this inquiry Michaela distributes findings of the Polish rat study. An American researcher remarks he has used oleic acid (olive oil) in ALD cells to affect fat levels, but he questions whether it will work in human beings. The scientists suggest that it might be hard to find the right chemical, for commercial applications of the oil are limited and indicate that scientists should do more research before testing human subjects ("Science has its own time"). Unwilling to wait, Michaela immediately calls various chemical companies to find pure oleic acid that would be safe for Lorenzo. After Petrochem Labs in Cleveland sends the Odones a bottle, Augusto and Dr. Nikolais come to a tense agreement on November 21, 1984, that Lorenzo can ingest the oil. One month later, Lorenzo's blood levels reveal a decrease in fats, but his physical condition continues to degenerate, and he begins to experience convulsions. The oleic acid has its limits; over the course of a few weeks, his blood levels plateau.

Lorenzo's tenacity to endure despite his pain is honored by parents, who unstintingly care for him and seek to learn more about ALD from medical research. They represent his interests to physicians, nurses who assist in caring for him, and researchers who are working on solutions. Medical authorities and the general public's submissive reliance on the professional wisdom of research scientists and doctors are regarded as suspect within Miller's film, for the source of strength and nurturing deemed most significant for the patient is the force of parental love, especially the love of a mother for her child. Michaela embraces Lorenzo as he suffers terrible fits; this mother and child imitate the configuration of the *Pietà* in these moments, for the doctor has indicated Lorenzo might understand that his involuntary spasms are temporary. In one scene, after Lorenzo has been brought to the hospital because the severity of his convulsions indicate that extreme measures might be needed, Michaela holds Lorenzo on her lap and tells him that he can let go and "fly to baby Jesus" if it is too hard for him to go on. Although she has been accused of hanging on to Lorenzo beyond the bounds of any reasonable hope, a sobbing Michaela assures her son that "Mommy and Papi will be okay without you." When the doctor suggests that placement in hospice might be better than home care, Augusto acknowledges Lorenzo's perseverance by saying, "It would not honor Lorenzo." Although the Muscatines characterize a shorter illness and quicker death as "a blessing," the Odones refuse to accept Lorenzo's imminent death; instead, they work to stop his degeneration and improve his condition.

Michaela never loses sight of this goal, as she prays, fights, and studies on his behalf. Her life, her home, and her attitude toward the world focus on Lorenzo. She becomes more resilient and less inclined to accept death after she sees her son weather several crises, although each stage of the disease brings new challenges in caring for him. She earns the title of "mother tiger" from her sister Deirdre for dismissing everyone who diminishes hopes for her son. She fires two nurses and asks Deirdre to move out because they all are unwilling to follow Michaela's regimen for Lorenzo, which includes speaking and reading to him as if he were a normal boy.

Augusto concentrates on research that might help his son, bringing home copies of relevant studies for Michaela to analyze as she manages Lorenzo's home care. Augusto spends long hours in the National Institutes of Health Library in Washington trying to figure out why the oleic acid appears to be of limited benefit in that Lorenzo's levels of very-long-chain fatty acids (VLCFAs) plateau in early 1985. Augusto tinkers with paper-clip chains as models to figure out the paradox of the VLCFAs input and output, finally concluding, after a dream in which Lorenzo appears holding both chains, that they are "the same bloody enzyme." Building on existing knowledge about high levels of saturated VLCFAs that are the "hallmark" of ALD, Augusto offers a new twist on the hypothesis of the disease and suggests that a dietary therapy introducing certain fats, notably purified versions of olive and rapeseed oils, would decrease the levels of VLCFAs and would fight the degenerative effects of the disease. Since monounsaturated fatty acids inhibit the synthesis of saturated VLCFAs and reduce their accumulation in cells from ALD patients, Augusto argues that a diet rich in monounsaturated fats could decrease the saturated VLCFAs, which are toxic at high levels. Although impressed by Augusto's theorizing, Dr. Nikolais remains cautious about publicizing the therapy until it is adequately tested.

The Odones proceed with courage. With the same efficiency she demonstrated in locating the oleic acid, Michaela finds a chemist willing to synthesize erucic acid to mix with the oleic acid. Don Suddaby accepts the project six months before his retirement (he plays himself in the film) and succeeds in synthesizing erucic acid in September 1985, seventeen months after Lorenzo was initially diagnosed with ALD. The Odones conduct their own home-study, first allowing Deirdre (Michaela's sister, who is also a carrier) to be the guinea pig testing the combination of oleic and erucic acids before administering this new therapy to Lorenzo. Over a short period, the Odones and the doctors observe that Lorenzo's blood levels improve and that his physiological condition stops deteriorating. Another advance represented in the film concerns Lorenzo's ability to communicate via blinking and raising a little finger, demonstrating that his mother's faithful efforts to minister to his mental capacities have positive outcomes.

The Odones understand that their sacrifice for their son might more significantly benefit other children whose illnesses could be diagnosed and treated earlier than Lorenzo's was. The final conflict represented in the film between the family and the medical establishment depicts the Odones' discussions with Lorenzo's doctor about releasing information about the new therapy to the public. Although the Odones are convinced of the efficacy of the blend of acids they now call "Lorenzo's oil," Dr. Nikolais and the Muscatines resist publicizing the Odones' discovery as a solution for all patients until more tests and studies determine its effectiveness. Augusto and Michaela privately share the oil with another family whose son's symptoms also decrease, but they can't subvert existing protocols.

Near the end of the film, at an ALD parents' foundation meeting, other ALD parents begin to complain that the American medical establishment prevents them from accessing what the Odones represent as a moderately successful treatment for ALD. Angry mothers and fathers shout at Dr. Nikolais and the Muscatines, as Michaela did at her first foundation meeting. This time a number of parents vociferously demand action, and the meeting erupts in a chaos of voices. One parent claims that the U.S. government made it difficult for persons with AIDS to obtain AZT until AIDS activists succeeded in changing policies, promoting research, and calling for therapies. Although the ALD parents' foundation board defers to the medical doctors, these angry parents of children with ALD take up the Odones' call for more research. Parents confront medical researchers and recommend that therapies be quickly investigated and approved, for new therapies might save current patients if treatments are affordable and efficaciously administered. Following the example of AIDS activists whose public demonstrations had an impact, ALD parents hope to induce the medical establishment to produce effective research and therapies.

Representing parents who try anything to help their afflicted son, *Lorenzo's Oil* demonstrates that patients and relatives should undertake scientific investigation and explore the efficacy of new treatments that might not yet be approved by the medical establishment. *Lorenzo's Oil* incorporates the history of AIDS as an object lesson in medical activism, alluding to racial categories in referencing Omouri's talents as caregiver to demonstrate the cultural representations of orphan diseases, specifically ALD.

Lorenzo's Oil sketches the plight of families with boys with ALD as a version of the AIDS narrative, recommending that heroic measures support further investigations into etiologies and therapies. ALD is described as "orphan disease," according to Dr. Nikolais: "You see, ours is what is known as an orphan disease. Too small to be noticed, too small to be funded, especially with the iron hand of Reaganomics." Lorenzo and other ALD sufferers share certain symptoms with full-blown AIDS patients (progressive loss of bodily functions, tendency to become depressed and angry, infections, critical need for nursing). ALD is a sex-linked disorder, inherited like hemophilia, a disease culturally associated with AIDS. The film commends AIDS activists and the Odones for rebelling by necessity and enabling a new medical discourse that acknowledges the rights of patients and families to direct the progress of medical research.

Shifts in the cultural imaginary indicate that HIV/AIDS was the dominant cultural metaphor of the late twentieth and early twenty-first centuries.[43] Enumerating the various aesthetic endeavors inspired by AIDS, Richard Goldstein argues that the influence of AIDS on high art and popular culture can be productively distinguished: "Popular culture gave voice to the fear and rage of the majority, while the arts helped dispel stigma by deconstructing it."[44] In the early 1980s, AIDS activists fought medical authorities, including the government bureaucracy, individual and corporate caregivers, insurance companies, and the pharmaceutical industry, dramatically using performances and exhibitions to which the popular media gave voice.[45]

According to *Lorenzo's Oil,* the Odones and other parents of ALD children recognize that in seeking alternative therapies, they have been directly inspired by the precedents set by AIDS activists. An interviewer agrees that "the Odones see themselves . . . as doing what the doctors couldn't do[:] . . . exerting pressure on the medical world to speed up research, much as AIDS activists have done." Carefully noting that "we have never fought the medical establishment," Michaela claimed, "During the '80s, there were only AIDS activists and the Odones out there."[46] The historical record bears out Mrs. Odone's recollection. The formerly complicated, lengthy process of approving experimental drug therapies in the United States was revised because of the interventions of AIDS activists, who recognized that unregulated, unapproved drugs could supplement accepted therapies endorsed by physicians.

Surveying AIDS activism, the cultural critic Paula Treichler explains, "A remarkable development in the evolution of the AIDS epidemic is the crusade of AIDS activists for the testing and release of experimental drugs by the U.S. Food and Drug Administration (FDA) and for participation in the design and implementation of clinical drug trials."[47] Her analysis of AIDS activism notes strategies designed to battle government, media, and social apathy, specifically their "commitments to civil disobedience, self-empowerment, technological expertise, and action outside the law" (78–79). Activist strategies listed by Treichler incorporate the American ideological privileging of dissent as a necessary phase of political improvement that is often identified with a marginalized social group working to battle injustice.

Popular culture narratives represent persons with AIDS as either "isolated sufferers" or those lucky enough to have or to create a loving family.[48] Whether the person with AIDS (PWA) is depicted as a marginalized figure living in opposition to dominant social values or as a member of a supportive family that resists ignorance and social bigotry, the representation of the PWA demonstrates the significance of sentiment and its relation to medical care. Dramatic conflicts in popular AIDS narratives such as Jonathan Demme's film *Philadelphia* pit the enlightened against the prejudiced, those who accept the disease as a biological fact versus those who see AIDS as a sign of moral decay. Fictional and journalistic narratives describing persons with AIDS are frequently built on assumptions about sexuality, disease, and drug use that involve questions of fate and choice and that are inflected with stereotypes about race, class, and gender.

Lorenzo's Oil consciously blends elements of tragedy and of heroic epics into its allusions, building on ideas about disease as a sign of God's testing of humanity and humanity's understanding of fate.[49] The redemption narrative of Lorenzo as a substitute Christ in the film demonstrates that representing another disease as being similar to AIDS can provide a transcendent experience for subjects and observers, patients and caregivers, and can make possible wider social sympathy for all affected. The deaths of vulnerable, aged parents and fragile children (particularly orphans) in realistic fiction similarly serve as signs that their social worlds are out of joint and that their families pay the price.[50]

Lorenzo's Oil alludes to cultural prejudices against race and persons with AIDs as a means of defining, and investing pathos in, Lorenzo's dilemma and the tragic circumstances faced by children who suffer from ALD and similar conditions. The film's representation of the Odones' experiences in Africa and their friendship with Omouri reinforce associations of AIDS and ALD, connecting medical narrow-mindedness with racism. While Mr. and Mrs. Odone demonstrate remarkable willpower and patience in fighting battles with Lorenzo's physicians to open the minds of scientists to new theories of and treatments for ALD, the boy's improving health is also associated with the arrival of Omouri, who has been invited by Michaela to come to his friend Lorenzo's aid. Augusto at first disapproves of having Omouri visit, questioning the wisdom of inviting this black, Muslim friend who does not speak English to live in a "racist culture," but his fears are not realized. Some American nurses employed by the family had difficulty accepting that Lorenzo's mind might still be intact despite his physical degeneration, but Omouri immediately sings to the boy when they are reunited, making their relationship a bridge between two cultures.

Living with the Odones, Omouri demonstrates his generous affection for their son by becoming one of Lorenzo's primary caregivers. Director Miller invests the African and the image of Africa with stereotypical attributes of exoticism and primitivism as a means of pointing out the benefits of incorporating African healing techniques, all the while showing the insufficiencies of traditional Western medicine. Omouri's chanting and spiritual presence correspond with the Odones' wish to surround their son with healthy interactions. A gifted nurse to Lorenzo and a healing presence in the extended family who welcomes Deirdre's return, Omouri reveals to Michaela a short time after he moves in, after the combination of oleic and erucic acids is administered, that he has been able to disconnect a suction machine assisting Lorenzo's breathing because the boy has regained the ability to breathe on his own, an improvement that astonishes Lorenzo's doctors.

On May 30, 2008, one day after his thirtieth birthday, Lorenzo Odone died from aspirative pneumonia with his father and his friend Omouri Hassane at his side.[51] His parents' faith and diligence to improve his environment by stimulating his mind, and their discovery of the oil, lengthened his lifespan far beyond what doctors had predicted at the onset of his disease. His mother's death on June 10, 2000, was reported in a *New York Times* obituary that affirms the efficacy of the Odones' treatment of olive and rapeseed oil and the power of Michaela's care.[52] Reading to Lorenzo and encouraging him to communicate by moving his eyelids and fingers, his parents and other caregivers hoped for his improvement and the possibility that myelin might be reintroduced to reverse his physical degeneration.[53] The last frames of the film show how Lorenzo used a computer to communicate and indicate that other children improved by following the dietary therapy first recommended by his parents.

Despite these claims, doctors wondered whether Lorenzo's progress could be duplicated in others. For some years, "Lorenzo's oil," the combination of oleic and erucic acids first pointed out as a possible therapy by Augusto Odone, was not sufficiently described in medical studies as being clearly efficacious for most ALD patients, just as Lorenzo's doctors had warned.[54] A ray of hope appeared in the late 1990s when European and American researchers agreed to investigate the oil's benefits by pooling their collective data. In October 2002, news media reported that a ten-year study found that other boys also benefitted from a diet including Lorenzo's oil. The study found that if young boys take the oil early and follow a low-fat diet, their symptoms could be delayed.[55] By fall 2002 Dr. Moser cautiously affirmed that the oil could prevent degeneration, at least for a prolonged period, in a number of boys with ALD: "It's not an absolute preventive. It reduces the chance of developing the symptoms, but . . . [t]he need to pursue other treatments remains critical."[56]

Developments at the time of this writing confirm that continuing research is likely to yield more promising results for ALD patients. On November 5, 2009, Gina Kolata reported in the *New York Times* that gene therapy developed for two ALD children was successful and their illnesses did not progress after the therapy.[57] Hollywood's version of Lorenzo's medical case history becomes more realistic as science progresses and as social forces promote the development of medical research on orphan diseases.

The fictions and film discussed in this chapter identify gendered interventions in medicine, particularly those depending on motherly contributions, as effective, persistent attempts to offer care despite the reluctance and resistance of those identified with traditional social conventions and established interests. These narratives represent science and technology as accessible in productive, socially beneficial ways to both women and men.

Babe Scientist

SCIENCE AND SEX

Films and fictions about gender, science, and technology appearing in the past two decades acknowledge the ambivalence concerning women in STEM, illustrating aspects of cultural debates about the participation of women in U.S. scientific fields and adapting conventions about women in science.[1] Taking stereotypes related to appearance as an example, audience reactions to characterizations vary. A female teenager in the United States blogged, "Though movies are slowly getting more intelligent women, who actually know science and mathematics, they are still usually portrayed as unattractive dorks who have the social skills of a rock."[2] Attractive female scientists seem to resist the stereotype of a female nerd who requires a makeover, but some viewers are offended if female scientists appear as glamorous model types. One focus group participant interviewed by the UK Resource Centre for Women in Science, Engineering and Technology pointed to the lack of realism in one British docudrama (*If . . . Cloning Could Cure*): "I'd like to know, is anybody aware of any female scientists who can afford vintage Jimmy Choos because it's unrealistic, especially given the pay levels in this country."[3]

Although opinions differ about what the cinematic role models who inspire women in science should look like, many films default to depicting female scientists as unusually attractive. "Babe Scientist," an Internet Movie Database keyword, bears traces of historical associations of male scientists studying feminized nature in emphasizing the scientist as sexual object.[4] Like the association of pink with tools, the term "babe scientist" incorporates femininity where it might seem unexpected and conveys cultural ambivalence about women working in science, a domain stereotypically associated with men.

Some films tagged as including a "babe scientist" incorporate this character into a makeover plot transforming her from nerdy intellectual to brainy beauty.

In literature, female scientists, like the female doctors discussed in the previous chapter, act and think in socially unconventional ways. In Zola's *Doctor Pascal*, Clotilde is the doctor's niece, research assistant, and defender; she also becomes his lover and the mother of his child. Christa Wolf's story "Self-Experiment" (1990) describes what happens after a female research scientist takes a drug that changes her into a man. She realizes that "[m]an and woman live on different planets" (211), for almost everyone the scientist encounters treats the male version of this person differently from the way the female version was treated.[5] The protagonist of Charis Cussins's "Confessions of a Bioterrorist" (1999) appears in the beginning of the story as Mary, an ordinary wife and mother who works on assisted reproduction of hybrids in her position as research scientist at a zoo.[6] By the end of the fiction she has crossed the species line and is about to give birth to a bonobo, after impregnating herself with a bonobo embryo.

Peter Høeg's novel *Smilla's Sense of Snow* illustrates cross-cultural interaction in Smilla Jasperson's appreciation for her mother's native Greenland landscape and culture as it combines with her scientific expertise concerning ice.[7] Smilla draws on her knowledge of cultural practices and physical aspects of climate to solve the mystery of her neighbor Isaiah's murder. The film (Dir. Bille August, 1997) and novel make Smilla's scientific background an important component of her character in detailing her rebellion and cautious suspicion.[8] These texts linger on Smilla's cultural marginality as part-Greenlander in Denmark and on her status as the odd woman in science, as she questions what she knows about herself and about other women: "Deep inside I know that trying to figure things out leads to blindness, that the desire to understand has a built-in brutality that erases what you seek to comprehend. Only experience is sensitive. But maybe I'm both weak *and* brutal. I've never been able to resist trying" (247).

Smilla's uncertainty and loneliness propel her into an affair with the mechanic who lives in the apartment below hers. Her quest to figure out why government scientists were involved with Isaiah and who is responsible for the boy's death leads her to stow away on a ship that has been implicated in the murder plot and that, as it turns out, is going to Greenland. By the end of the novel, she figures out the motive for killing Isaiah, who was infected with a parasite as part of a government conspiracy linking politics, business, and science. But solving the crime does not resolve what will happen to Smilla, who realizes that understanding is always provisional and contingent: "Tell us, they'll say to me. So we will understand and be able to resolve things. They'll be mistaken. It's only the things you don't understand that you can resolve. There will be no resolution" (469). Smilla's sense that ambiguity is inevitable sums up the position of female scientists, who sometimes succeed by leveraging their different situations.

Documenting the Lives of Women Scientists

Evelyn Fox Keller explains how real-life geneticist Barbara McClintock responded to research results in ways different from those of her male peers, partly because she was isolated from the mostly male scientific community of population geneticists.[9] The resistance to McClintock's research and her willingness to listen to others rather than fight with them allowed her to learn more from her colleagues than they learned from her. Keller's chapter "A Different Language" explains how McClintock was unable to articulate her ideas using a language commonly accepted by other scientists; instead, she developed an "alternative scientific practice," one that "values sympathy for the object being studied," what Keller calls "a feeling for the organism."[10] Keller describes "seeing in science" in this way: "Based on vision, our most public and our most private sense, it gives rise to a kind of knowledge that requires more than a shared practice to be communicable: it requires a shared subjectivity. . . . Inevitably, 'seeing' entails a form of subjectivity, an act of imagination, a way of looking that is necessarily in part determined by some private perspective" (149–50).

Highlighting different perspectives of women in science to provide role models for girls and enhance public understanding of science, producers of the 1995 PBS documentary series *Discovering Women* interview six notable women who succeeded in scientific disciplines. Each show profiles an exemplary individual from a scientific field; a wide range of scientific fields are represented, including archaeology, neuroscience, physics, and biochemistry. The subjects reveal that despite achieving success in their research fields, they must work harder than male colleagues to attain the same goals. Personally and professionally dedicated to science, these women overcame a variety of obstacles, including economic constraints, discrimination, and social stereotypes. Their biographies inspire others to attempt and persist in scientific careers, for these narratives demonstrate pathways and strategies.[11]

Some critics of *Discovering Women* wonder if too much attention is given to the personal lives of the women rather than to their professional careers, but others recognize that balancing home responsibilities, personal interests, and work is an issue for many prospective scientists. Students particularly appreciate hearing how private and professional interests combine.[12] The series humanizes scientific endeavors by putting human faces on practices and theories that seem esoteric to most TV viewers. Presenting notable women with significant STEM

expertise reconfigures gender stereotypes by countering assumptions and prejudices with facts.

The subjects of the six-part documentary represent a variety of historical,
regional, and ethnic experiences, although the majority of the women are white
(one is Latina and one African American) and middle-aged. They range in age
from the almost-thirty Misha Mahowald, a computational neuroscientist working out biological processes that resemble functional processes of computers,
to sixtyish archaeologist Patty Jo Watson, who refined techniques to determine
functions of agricultural artifacts and inspired a number of female students
to study archaeology. All six women attest to witnessing or experiencing gender discrimination: thirty-something physicist Melissa Franklin, now tenured
at Harvard, talks about her disappointment at not receiving an appointment
she wanted at her alma mater in Canada, near her family; the physics depart-
mental search committee's decision to hire her was not approved by those in
higher positions and therefore did not become an actual offer. Misha Mahowald notes that during her undergraduate and graduate studies, other computer
scientists and engineers, most of whom were men, treated her questions with
suspicion; she describes how even silence works against her: "If you keep silent
as a women, people assume you're a fool."

All six subjects credit their interest in scientific careers to working closely
on research with mentors during their undergraduate years and/or depending
on advice offered by mentoring colleagues. The geophysicist Marcia McNutt,
a fortyish widow at the time of filming and the mother of two daughters, tells
about how she was attracted to studying plate tectonics because she took an
undergraduate course taught by a male University of Colorado professor who
instructed his students in reasoning about science and scientific method in
creative ways. Raised in a housing project in Boston, African-American bio-
chemist Lynda Jordan cites her positive Upward Bound experience with a male
"coach," an experience which proved to her that someone cared about her education. She chose to teach at her alma mater, a historically black university
without the cutting-edge resources necessary for her work on human enzymes
important in birth and reproduction. Jordan describes in the documentary
how her graduate research notebooks were stolen at MIT and how she would
not have persevered to obtain her Ph.D. there if the astronaut Ron McNair had
not encouraged her to maintain courage in the face of adversity.

The female scientists are filmed teaching and advising college students,
talking with high school students, and training graduate students so that they
might attract other women and minorities into science. Lydia Villa-Komaroff
mentors Latino and Latina students in her home state of New Mexico because
she wants to encourage them to earn university degrees. Although Villa-Komaroff's research on brain development is demanding and at a delicate stage, she

maintains a close mentoring relationship with a female high school student in Boston who wants to become a doctor. Lynda Jordan has to raise most of the money to fund her research lab, but she also takes the time to facilitate discussions about graduate school and career prospects with her undergraduate science students, and she trains them to do the sensitive procedures necessary for her experiments. Patty Jo Watson is called a "living inspiration" by one of her graduate students for providing research opportunities and training for young women.

Viewers see the subjects interacting with parents, siblings, spouses, children, or friends. For example, Marcia McNutt and her parents discuss her competitive nature and her desire to do it all—to have a family and to take part in long research field trips away from home—and she speaks candidly about her husband's unexpected death when he was in his forties. She worked out a domestic arrangement with a live-in housekeeper/nanny who is also a single mother, and she later lets the camera observe how she and a male colleague begin a romantic relationship. All six subjects speak about having children: some are mothers, some want to be, and others have parental relationships with children other than their own. Villa-Komaroff and her husband attest to their affectionate relationships with nieces and nephews and tell about their difficult, painful decision not to have children so that they could continue with their separate research projects on pediatric medicine. After Watson tells us that she took her family along with her on research trips as long as she could, her college student daughter talks about Watson's work with admiration but reveals that it was irritating at times to have to deal with a mother who often took professional field trips.

What remains most salient in the six parts of *Discovering Women* is that these highly accomplished scientists articulate their intellectual development as scientific thinkers as being inextricably bound with their individual interests and personalities. Some characteristics reveal what might be thought of as traditionally feminine behaviors, others masculine; but each woman sees that her essential character traits enhance her scientific capabilities and abilities. Jordan and Villa-Komaroff regard their labs as communities they must nurture, revealing both administrative pragmatism and human sentiment. When shown her mother's new kitchen gadget, Melissa Franklin takes it apart and explains its workings on-camera, demonstrating her tendency to get into the inner workings of a mechanism, a trait that has motivated her intense passion to acquire her intimate knowledge of the Fermilab particle detector. This scene has a counterpart, as we see Marcia McNutt building a play car for her caregiver's daughter, understandably taking up irregular household responsibilities that better suit her demanding work schedule.

We also see Franklin fixing the accelerator and McNutt analyzing soundings from a vessel, each agonizing over the general public's lack of understanding for her scientific research. Franklin is disappointed when the Texas supercollider project loses funding, and McNutt has a tense episode when her Lake Mead research is almost put to a halt by Nevada citizens worried about environmental effects. Learning about scientists' life histories, and hearing narratives about their research and why science is important to them, the audience sympathizes with the expert who is a woman, recognizing the human face of science.

Female Scientists in Recent Films

Although some critics have discussed how individual scientists are portrayed in film, few have analyzed the ways in which narrative plots establish contexts for audience evaluation of characters.[13] I focus here on fictional films portraying female scientists who are glamorous, professionally successful, and pursuing romances. As Mary Ann Doane explains, "In a patriarchal society, to desexualize the female body is ultimately to deny its very existence" (19). Thus, the female scientist's sexiness and glamour increase her cultural capital. Viewers might think that such traits conflict with scientific expertise and make her less of a scientist, or they could reflect that a woman must be a truly great scientist to get away with explicit expressions of sexuality. But perhaps the formula linking glamour and expertise is faulty, perhaps scientists are sometimes sexy and sometimes not, and perhaps de-linking these categories as oppositional or related liberates us from categories and stereotypes. As Doane explains, "it is only through a disengagement of women from the roles and gestures of a naturalized femininity that traditional ways of conceptualizing sexual difference can be overthrown" (182).

The discussion of films in this chapter considers how the romance plot blends courtship and scientific work. The films are from different genres, including action-adventure, science fiction, and thriller (*Twister, Contact, The Saint*), that incorporate romance plots as secondary to the main action of showing how science benefits society and comedies (*IQ, Kettle of Fish, Laurel Canyon*) that make romance a vehicle for commentary on women's participation in science. I also include a film that defies easy categorization, Sally Potter's *Yes*, in which a romance between a scientist and a doctor crosses cultural boundaries.

Characterizations of female scientists in a number of films produced in the last twenty years reflect and refract cultural values about women in science. Films emphasize women's appearance in and motivation to do science, as well as their peer interactions and status in science. Sidney Perkowitz's book

Hollywood Science notes how popular science fiction films portray science and scientists enthusiastically if somewhat inaccurately. In his chapter "Scientists as Heroes, Nerds, and Villains," Perkowitz points to the props used to signify characters' scientific expertise (lab coat, "stodgy" eyeglasses, wild hair) as visual elements also identifying female scientists (168–69).[14] Perkowitz acknowledges traces of "monastic aspects" of science as identified by historians of science, traces that persist in science and that in some ways account for the low numbers of women in some scientific fields, particularly computing, physics, and engineering.[15]

Films illustrate the low proportions of female scientists by including few female characters and constraining most female scientists to limited, secondary roles. Eva Flicker and Jocelyn Steinke separately inventoried films to calculate how many female scientists appear in films. Flicker's survey of 60 films produced between 1929 and 2003 counted 11 female scientists, or 18% of the scientists portrayed in these films. Steinke's survey of films produced between 1991 and 2001 calculated 23 female scientists in 74 science-related films, or 31% of the scientists represented in the films.[16]

Flicker argues that the female scientist is usually incorporated into a film "to develop suspense," for the woman has feminine traits of intuition and emotion and takes part in love affairs, elements that conflict with "the rational scientific system of their male colleagues."[17] Sex-typed traits of female scientists are often prominent in films, for these women appear more emotionally sensitive, socially marginalized, and interested in social good than their male peers, as in, for example, *Inspector Gadget* (Dir. David Kellogg, 1999). Cinematic female scientists rarely appear as selfish, dangerous, and ambitious, unlike the many male variations of Victor Frankenstein. The female scientist is often more serious than her peers, and if she is mousy, she is quite often destined to be transformed into a more sensuous woman. The transformation plot performs a makeover that enables a female scientist to access her true, inner beauty, previously ignored. Eventually her attractiveness matches her intelligence, thereby normalizing her, that is, making her more traditionally feminine, as in, for example, *Love Potion Number 9* (Dir. Dale Launer, 1992).[18]

Although "relational tension" between a female scientist and a male protagonist drives many film romances, outcomes of science and romance converge when one partner is a female scientist. (Films focusing on male scientists usually do not incorporate a romance, perhaps because romance appears a woman's genre, devised for women about women.)[19] Cinematic plots and the mise-en-scène of many romances about female scientists point to how gender stereotypes and sexual discrimination affect women's careers in science. Comedies incline to optimistic endings, sketching the theory and practice of science as a conjoined quest for scientific achievement and romantic resolution, whereas dramas end without resolving conflicts between doing science and having a personal life. In this way, films reference debates about the representation and advancement of women in U.S. scientific fields. Plots and characterizations allude to both cognitive and non-cognitive (social/cultural) factors affecting different performance outcomes for men and women, yet without aligning with one side or the other in the debate that makes "women in science" a controversial topic in the United States, as noted in chapter 1.[20]

Testimonials supplement social science studies of scientific organizations. Seeking to convince those who might doubt that STEM climates are chilly to women, many women working in science, mathematics, engineering, computing, and information technology who contributed to the 2006 collection *She's Such a Geek* testify to the barriers and facilitators they have encountered in their careers.[21] Their accounts mention dismissive attitudes, demeaning peer comments, unfair employer decisions, and the high price of STEM careers for parents. Some authors point to stereotypes embedded in films and television they saw when they were young. Editor Annalee Newitz mentions that all 1970s and 80s productions apparently include what she calls "the 'girl takes off her glasses' myth: Women are viewed as either smart or sexually appealing" (221).

Eva Flicker argues that a number of recent films create a new, more positive character type: "Since the 1990s, [we're seeing] the powerful, competent, utterly qualified, and feminine woman scientist—the uniting of an intellectual and erotic person."[22] Although they offer more balanced and realistic depictions of female scientists, these movies resist taking sides in the women-in-science debate. The films analyzed below, and many others, allude to discrimination with as much as force as they depict essential or innate differences between men and women. Thus, films acknowledge both cognitive and non-cognitive factors affecting different performance outcomes for men and women in science, creating fictional narratives with mixed cultural messages.

Romantic narratives share generic conventions that include characters conversing about personal and social identities and values.[23] Such discussions often, but not exclusively, occur between the romantic partners. As Nell Minow defines it, "A romance film, whatever the genre, will have two people who are destined to be together but are kept apart by some force for most of the movie."[24] When romances include female scientists, the conflict between "boy and girl" has resonance beyond masculine and feminine, for the films become commentaries on how and why women work in science.[25]

Exploring issues of motivation and persistence, Keller's description of McClintock's marginality in science found her isolation to be key to her independence and eventual success. For Keller, McClintock's story "demonstrates the capacity of science to overcome its own characteristic kind of myopia, reminding us that limitations do not reinforce themselves indefinitely."[26] This vision of science as a meritocracy also pervades the biopic *Madame Curie* (Dir. Mervyn LeRoy, 1943), a film that considers Marie Curie's passion for science as exceptional and intertwined with her partnership with Pierre; it sets the standard for romances about scientific women.

Hugh Crawford's analysis of *Madame Curie* recognizes that "Marie succeeds in a world traditionally marked as masculine, and at the end of the film delivers a triumphant hymn to science while standing in what had been the exclusive haunts of male scientists."[27] Marie's exceptional status derives both from her astounding success and from her atypical, for science, gender. Crawford points to how Marie's femininity is marked by her poetic discourse, arguing that "LeRoy clearly exploits such stereotypes to build his traditional love story, even though his strategy subverts his science story."[28] Focusing on Marie and Pierre's courtship and marriage enables the exceptional woman to be ordinary, as Madame Curie avoids much criticism by taking up domestic roles familiar to many women: fiancée, wife, mother, and widow.

Mining the same romantic vein and incorporating similar gender stereotypes as *Madame Curie,* movies from the past two decades more lightheartedly employ romantic plots involving exceptionally attractive and intelligent female scientists. Stereotypes about the female as the inevitable, somewhat disruptive focus of male attention surface in *Roxanne* (Dir. Fred Schepisi, 1987). Daryl Hannah plays Roxanne Kowalski to Steve Martin's long-nosed C. D. Bales in this update of Edmond Rostand's play *Cyrano de Bergerac* (1897). The film's action is set in a Northwestern town full of eccentric characters, some wishing to pursue Roxanne, who is gorgeous and intelligent and occasionally wears nerdy glasses.[29] That Roxanne works as an astronomer helps develop a small subplot about her discovery of a comet; however, her education and career are represented in a folksy, comfortable way rather than by piling on technical details that would set her at odds with the community. Bales's clever wit (as well as his nose) make him the center of this story, a hero overcoming a challenge, while Roxanne's unusual profession (for a woman) and her beauty mark her as a worthy love object.

A more recent comic film, *The Life Aquatic with Steve Zissou* (Dir. Wes Anderson, 2004), characterizes Steve's estranged wife Eleanor as "the brains" of his oceanographic exploration team. Anderson parodies the conventions associated with female scientists by making Eleanor (Anjelica Huston) more compassionate, competent, ethical, and elegant than the goofy Steve (Bill Murray). He appears to spend most of his time smoking marijuana, drinking alcohol, hitting on women, and "borrowing" equipment from his nemesis, while Eleanor instructs her husband's crew to stay out of unprotected waters to avoid pirates and manages the financing for the team's documentary films. Cool in a crisis and more strategic than Steve, she finds the kidnapped hostage from his ship (*The Belafonte*) and organizes the plan to rescue the hostage from the pirates. Her role in this adventure brings her back into Steve's work, allows him to finish his documentary, and enables their reconciliation.

As my emphasis on exceptionality demonstrates, the general theme in romance films featuring a female scientist is that she is a fish out of water, a cliché explicitly invoked in *Kettle of Fish*. The female scientist, particularly in a romance plot, appears marginalized in the lab and the world of scientific research, exhibiting a quirky understanding of social conventions and human behavior. Her characterization emphasizes competence, ethics, and an inclination to sacrifice personal interests (romance, family, hobbies, etc.) to science. Her innate aptitudes, family history, social stereotypes, and social dynamics in scientific organizations sometimes help and at other times hinder performance outcomes.

The female scientist in a romance has some personal vulnerability based on her physical or emotional health. For example, in *The Saint* (Dir. Phillip Noyce, 1997), Dr. Emma Russell suffers from a heart problem. Jo Harding in *Twister* (Dir. Jan de Bont, 1996) has lost her father to a tornado and wants to develop better ways of spotting violent storms to protect other families. In *IQ* (Dir. Fred Schepisi, 1994), Catherine Boyd pursues mathematics in tribute to her deceased father who discovered and named a comet. *Contact*'s (Dir. Robert Zemeckis, 1997) Ellie Arroway learns about astronomy from her father and pursues a career in it after his death. The female biologist in *Yes* has no family other than her elderly, dying aunt and an emotionally distant husband. Such vulnerabilities mark these protagonists as feminine, even as they overcome professional hurdles.

IQ and *Contact*

Both *IQ* (1994) and *Contact* (1997) focus the audience's attention on attractive, intelligent female scientists who work in male-dominated fields—mathematics and radio astronomy, respectively—and whose research makes personal, social, and scientific attainments possible. In these romantic plots, the female scientists' partners, who are not scientists, offer complementary skills and emotional support, although each story reconfigures and resists gender stereotypes. *IQ*'s 1950s romantic plot matches an unlikely couple: the math doctoral candidate Catherine Boyd (Meg Ryan), who plans to marry an appropriately intellectual man to father her children, and automobile mechanic Ed Walters (Tim Robbins).

After Ed meets and instantaneously falls in love with Catherine, he applies what he learns about the randomness of the universe and the space-time continuum to describe to his fellow mechanics how he feels about her. Catherine is about to leave her uncle Albert Einstein's Princeton home to marry her pompous fiancé, psychologist James Moreland, who is called "Rat Man" by Einstein and his buddies; however, the aging scientists decide to manage Catherine's love life. They agree to work together to convince her that Ed is a brilliant, intuitive scientist, albeit without a degree, and therefore worthy of her affections. Rearranging Catherine's future because they love her, and sensing that she is disinclined to assert her professional or romantic desires without some outside support, Einstein, Kurt Godel, Boris Podolsky, and Nathan Liebknecht, and Ed, want Catherine to learn that she is an intelligent scientist in her own right.

The film begins with a violinist, presumably Einstein, playing the children's tune "Twinkle, Twinkle Little Star," also known in English as the ABC song and "Baa Baa Black Sheep." The song identifies the movie's basic themes: the fascination with the universe shared by Ed and Catherine, the basic schooling in science that Catherine has had and that Ed has missed, and their common status as outsiders in science (here illustrated as an all-male Princeton University in the 1950s).[30] Ed is an amateur aficionado of science, and Catherine is interested more in recently published scientific research than in domestic matters, making her an unusual woman in the fictional world of the film.

Ed and Catherine flirt at the garage where her fiancé James's failing car conks out, after which Ed suggests that the car, like James a British import, has "premature injection." Catherine pretends not to recognize the joke, but James does not understand it. Despite his advanced degrees in psychology and his university positions as professor and director of a human behavior lab, he is immune to sexual innuendo and perhaps sex. This assumption is later confirmed when James rebukes Catherine for suggesting, at a professional dinner and in front of the chair of James's department no less, that James and Catherine might honeymoon at the Hawaiian resort called Million Kisses on Your Skin. James stops Catherine from privately snuggling with him at his chairman's house after dinner and speaks baby talk to her as he informs her that he accepted a position at Stanford and bought a house for them to live in after they marry. Viewers understand that Catherine's relationship with James is not sexually satisfying for her, and she appears dominated in that he determines their future without any input from her.

IQ depicts Catherine as the lone female in the world of science, here identified as white, upper-class, elite, competitive, and male. Shots of the idyllic, green Princeton campus dotted with flowering trees, and of imposing Richardsonian university buildings and prim wood-frame town residences, provide lush backgrounds for the characters' interactions. Catherine works out calculations in her notebook and helps out with the administration of Princeton's Institute for Advanced Study, but the film does not show her in class or meetings with advisors or peers. Indeed, she has no peers, for no other women are depicted as primary or secondary characters, much less as scientists, in the film. As Catherine is encouraged by her uncle Albert and his friends, it becomes apparent that her mathematical talent is a genetic gift, one she has trouble managing until she meets Ed. Each cinematic frame of Catherine focuses on her as a demurely dressed young woman whose blonde beauty is set against the greasy outfits of the mechanics or the sober, tailored business suits of visitors to the Institute. Her stylized suits and pastel dresses with feminine decorative touches mark her as different from the men at the Institute and identify her exceptionality in the world of science.

Only in scenes where Catherine appears in town with Ed—when he is dressed in casual, modern clothes and not in his mechanic's coveralls or in his purported role as Einstein's scientific collaborator—does Catherine's clothing look right for the context. Her fiancé James's wardrobe is too fussy, as is his manner, but Ed's 1950s unconstructed jackets with tabs fit right in with Catherine's modernized pinafore dresses. Costume complements the film's plot by identifying Ed as a critical ally for Catherine, a friend and a love interest who assists in her transformation from Einstein's niece and James's fiancée into a full-fledged scientist.

After Catherine discovers that she has identified a flaw in a proof actually written by Einstein but presented to her as the intuitively brilliant work of Ed, she begins to appreciate her aptitude for mathematics and to recognize Ed's scientific performance as a hoax. This discovery gives her confidence and brings her out of Einstein's shadow, although for some time afterwards, Catherine distrusts Ed. The final scenes acknowledge that Catherine's interest in science links with her desire to remain close to her father. She eventually realizes that she loves Ed because he is like her in loving science for its own sake, despite his lack of a degree. Catherine's life with him promises to build on their common interest in science, allowing her to continue in the profession as opposed to limiting her horizons to passive domestic work in marriage, which marrying James would have done.

Both *IQ* and *Contact* imagine the female scientist as practicing in a nontraditional field out of a personal need to reconnect with her deceased father. Catherine Boyd and Ellie Arroway succeed in science by constructing lives without fathers and working in fields dominated by men. Both films reference the theme of life as a journey akin to scientific exploration, illustrating how science enables personal maturation as well as cultural advancement. In *IQ*, Einstein discusses his compass with Ed and Catherine, saying it is always with him as an inspiration for his theories. In *Contact*, Ellie Arroway's friend Palmer Joss gives her a compass from a Cracker Jacks box, and she hangs on to the toy compass even after she has discarded his phone number.

Ellie's intuitive sense that there must be intelligent extraterrestrial life impels her to listen for signs of activity on her radio telescope, an older technology. Her father's ideas about space—that it would be an awful waste of space if no one else were out there and that small moves enable big discoveries—inspire Ellie (Jodie Foster) throughout her career. As a child amateur radio operator, Ellie tries at different times to contact her deceased parents and later transfers her wish for that miracle to her study of radio astronomy, which offers her the opportunity to contact extraterrestrials. Carl Sagan's novel describes Ellie's gender as a central problem in finding respect for her research, and it acknowledges the difficulty of being a woman in the male-dominated and hostile field of physics. The film represents Ellie's marginality as based on her pursuit of "little green men" rather than on her gender, although few female scientists are represented.

Ellie's conflicts and alliances in the film are based on individual responses to the search for extraterrestrial life. Her former supervisor, David Drumlin (Tom Skerritt), visits her SETI (Search for Extraterrestrial Intelligence) project in Arecibo, only to pull funding on it, arguing that he does so to protect her career, which is in danger of being destroyed by her pursuit of aliens. Encouraged by her collaborator Kent Clark to seek private funding after their government grants evaporate, Ellie tries to convince wealthy billionaire S. R. Hadden to subsidize time for her SETI project at the Very Large Array in New Mexico. In the boardroom where Ellie makes her plea, she looks small until the camera zeroes in on her face as she reacts to the spokesperson's comment that her project seems more like science fiction than science:

> Science fiction. You're right, it's crazy. In fact, it's even worse than that, it's nuts. You wanna hear something really nutty? I heard of a couple guys who wanna build something called an airplane, you know you get people to go in, and fly around like birds, it's ridiculous, right?! And what about breaking the sound barrier, or rockets to the moon? Atomic energy, or a mission to Mars? Science fiction, right? Look, all I'm asking is for you to just have the tiniest bit of vision. You know, to just sit back for one minute and look at the big picture. To take a chance on something that just might end up being the most profoundly impactful moment for humanity, for the history . . . of history.

This impassioned speech convinces Hadden, who has watched proceedings on a video link, to provide funding for Ellie's SETI project, while viewers also understand that Ellie's unusual, intense commitment to pursue scientific knowledge motivates her unconventional behavior.

After four years in New Mexico, Ellie hears a signal that comes to be known as the Message, but she has to fight to keep her team involved in the project to build the Machine directed by the Message. Scientists and politicians, most of them males, seek to control the response to the Message, but presidential aide Rachel Constantine offers a compromise that provides roles for both Drumlin and Ellie. Ellie's previous run-ins with Drumlin seem trivial compared to his taking over aspects of her project and later positioning himself to travel as the sole occupant of the Machine when it goes into space.

The romantic plot of *Contact* develops Ellie's femininity and sexuality in her affair with the religious figure Palmer Joss (Matthew McConaughey). After having sex with Palmer in Arecibo, where they bond over their shared aversion to Drumlin, Ellie avoids seeing Palmer for four years. She runs into him again while she is competing to use the Machine to take the journey to meet the extraterrestrials and he is a presidential advisor tasked with approving who will take the first ride. After a protester bombs the Machine and kills Drumlin, the chosen candidate for the mission, Ellie finds herself tapped by S. R. Hadden to take a trip in the duplicate Machine he has secretly funded.[31] Palmer meets with Ellie in Japan shortly before she takes off in the Machine; he admits to her he chose Drumlin for the first Machine ride to protect Ellie from harm, and he openly reveals his love for her. In turn, she lets Palmer know that she is fearful but committed to the mission. The scene reconfigures stereotypes of male and female heroism to show how Palmer becomes comfortable with waiting for Ellie to return from her exploration: he is more emotionally engaged in the relationship, while she focuses on work.

During her trip in the duplicate Machine, Ellie meets extraterrestrial life in the form of her father, although she thinks she has no evidence proving this encounter: "I had an experience I can't prove and can't explain, but everything that I know . . . tells me that it was real." Palmer supports her through the congressional hearings during which she gives her testimony. After her congressional appearance, he helps her confront the massive crush of press outside the Capitol. In a final scene Congressman Kitz (James Woods) and presidential science advisor Constantine (Angela Bassett) discuss what is not known to Ellie: that the confidential investigation report notes that 18 minutes of static appear on the videotape she recorded. This fact is never revealed to Ellie or the public. *Contact* distinguishes between politically motivated scientists and passionate scientists, offering Drumlin and Ellie as examples of the differing types, but these characters are only loosely associated with stereotypical masculine and feminine features. Drumlin seems selfish, ambitious, and hypocritical, while Ellie resists domestic and romantic entanglements as she searches for truth by any means.

Ellie's prioritizing of truth aligns her with Palmer. Within the romantic plot, Palmer and Ellie reverse stereotypical roles concerning who pursues whom. He wants to work on the relationship whereas she prefers to go to work.[32] Yet she is attracted to him: when Ellie plans to attend a presidential dinner, she asks the female science advisor where to find "a really great dress." In Ellie and Palmer's final scene together, when they leave the Capitol after the congressional hearing, Ellie is dressed in a sober, brown coat without accessories or ornaments. In contrast, Palmer has a flowing red scarf wrapped around his neck as he tells the world that he and Ellie have the same goal, "the pursuit of truth."

Just as Ed supports Catherine's scientific work in *IQ*, Palmer protects Ellie's, whatever she believes. *Contact* ends with Ellie teaching schoolchildren what she and Palmer believe: that the universe is vast and that individuals must find their own way in exploring it. Except for Ellie's scenes with her father and those with Palmer, she appears as a lonely, small figure standing or seated in crowded labs, boardrooms, or hearing rooms. In these techno-scientific settings she seems in opposition to all around her. When she is in the wormhole, she is a solitary figure in a large space. After wide, establishing shots in these scenes, the camera swoops down on her to emphasize her loneliness and integrity. Ellie appears isolated in a number of scenes in Puerto Rico and New Mexico, and later she is shown meditating as she sits alone on a canyon wall. In contrast, medium shots of Ellie with the schoolchildren at the end of the film frame her as an authority by having the camera look up to her and having her appear in the same frame with a group, signaling that her authority and integrity are not threatened or threatening and that science welcomes diversity. *Contact* resists ending with a marriage; however, the film concludes with an opportunity for Ellie to exhibit femininity and scientific aptitude in the same moment in teaching and inspiring young children.

Twister and *The Saint*

The films *Twister* and *The Saint* offer romantic plots within adventures in which the female scientists are heroic figures battling natural forces and international gangs to pursue scientific truth, help others, and establish mutually supportive romantic relationships. In these films, the female scientist is a feminist adventurer challenging establishment conventions while retaining femininity in her emotions and her interest in helping others. Her romantic partner combines feminine and masculine traits to complement the female scientist's knowledge and passion.

At the outset of *Twister*, a tornado sweeps over a farm and kills young Jo Harding's father as Jo, her mother, and their dog huddle in the storm cellar. The loss of her father inspires Jo to become a tornado hunter. She works to develop better storm warning systems to save those who might be in the storms' paths. The present-day action of the film begins when Jo (Helen Hunt) reencounters her estranged husband Bill (Bill Paxton), who was formerly a collaborator on her team. Bill reappears with his fiancée Melissa (Jami Gertz) to demand that Jo sign divorce papers he sent her months ago, for he wants to get on with his life as a weatherman and marry Melissa. Jo delays signing the papers; because she has to run after a tornado with her team, Bill and Melissa trail the team to retrieve the documents. But Bill quickly reenters his old life as tornado hunter; he begins driving Jo and using his talent to figure out where the tornado might go. While Jo appears knowledgeable about twisters, Bill has an intuition about storms that makes him as clever as any Ph.D.

Although the film does not explain why Jo and Bill have separated, their on-screen bickering and Bill's conversations with Melissa offer clues. Jo's knowledge and Bill's intuition about storms are rarely in conflict, but her hardheaded charging forward into the path of danger worries Bill. Bill's fiancée, a woman dressed in white who works as a reproductive therapist, provides a distinct contrast with Jo's strong, assertive, capable personality. Although Melissa tries to meet her own professional obligations while off on this field trip with her fiancé and answers phone calls from her patients worried about their sexuality and fertility, her calm, soothing manner is shattered after she drives through a tornado. When Bill finds himself in the position of holding Jo back from plunging into extremely dangerous situations that would likely kill her if he did not intervene, he tells his estranged wife, in a conversation Melissa overhears on the radio, "Things go wrong. You can't explain it, you can't predict it. Killing yourself won't bring your dad back. I'm sorry that he died, but that was a long time ago. You gotta move on. Stop living in the past, and look what you got right in front of you." After Jo asks, "What are you talking about?" Bill does not hesitate to tell her: "Me, Jo." Bill respects her authority to lead the team while she respects his telling her that putting herself in danger will not save anyone and that he is not her enemy for protecting her.

Bill and Jo revive their romance and Melissa departs, but the focus of the film remains on the twisters that are portrayed in the film by spectacular special effects. The large, unpredictable storms threaten the tornado hunters and those they seek to protect. Jo's scientific team has a number of strengths—collaboration, quickness, intuition, integrity, ingenuity—that will help the tornado hunters map the inside of a twister. When Bill comes back to the team, he is thrilled to see the launching of his invention, "Dorothy," which is designed to release sensors into a tornado in order to map it. He is disturbed to find that a competing team of tornado hunters, managed by Jonas Miller and funded by corporations, has copied his idea.

The oppositions between Jonas Miller's team and Jo's team, and the conflict between romantic rivals Jo and Melissa, are represented in subplots that offset the backstory of Jo's scientific motivation to warn families of a tornado's approach. Each plot stresses characteristics associated with feminine collaboration as having moral ascendancy. While the teams compete to chase down a storm, Jonas cannot believe that Jo and Bill are sincere in warning him to get out of the way of the twister. Jonas suspects they are lying to get ahead of him and he ignores their advice, a misperception and a choice that cause his death. Jo and Melissa never face off about Bill; instead, Melissa retreats. Understanding that Bill and Jo are meant for each other, Melissa gives Bill up after seeing his excitement in chasing the storms and overhearing Bill and Jo talk about their marriage. Melissa's refusal to blame Bill or Jo and her willingness to leave them tornado hunting together seems logical given the huge destruction caused by the storms.

After Jo's Aunt Meg is nearly killed and her home completely destroyed, Jo and Bill rescue her from the wreckage. Jo appears inclined to stay with her injured aunt, but Meg refuses to give up or to let her niece do so:

> MEG: Jo, it could have happened to somebody else. You, you go stop it.
> JO: I don't know how.
> MEG: Well, I think you do. You've been chasing these things since you were a little kid. It's what you do. Go. Do it.

Leaving Meg to recover in the hospital, Jo and Bill risk their lives by positioning themselves in the tornado's path in order to insert "Dorothy" into the storm. They release the sensors in the eye of the storm and struggle to find a safe place on the farm to hide from it. Jo's team of tornado hunters reunites in celebration after the farm family survives despite devastation to their property. In *Twister*, successful science converges with caring for others and protecting society from nature's violence.

Reconfiguring elements of the Saint narrative established in various fictions, films, and television shows, the 1997 film version of *The Saint* creates a female lead (Elisabeth Shue) to complement the modern-day Saint, Simon Templar (Val Kilmer), who in this rendition is an international thief eager to make millions by stealing technologies and scientific formulas.[33] American chemistry professor Emma Russell's successful breakthrough with cold fusion makes her a target for the Russian politician and mobster Ivan Tretiak. Tretiak hires Simon to steal Emma's formula while she is working in Oxford. Emma's guest appearance in an Oxford laboratory littered with chemical beakers shows her to be a sexy scientist, dressed in a lab coat, knee socks, and high heels, a scientist who is capable of flirting with a member of the audience seconds before facilitating a question-and-answer session with other scientists and students about the controversial possibility of cold fusion.

In her responses to questions in the session, Emma avoids directly explaining the process of cold fusion; instead she speaks indirectly of the technology's promise. She asks her audience to trust her, to believe she has transformed chemicals into energy. But Emma does not perform any chemistry that viewers observe; instead, we see her most often as Simon's romantic partner and ally in intrigue. The romance plot in *The Saint* centers on questions of trust and transformation, as Simon adopts pseudonyms of Catholic saints and masquerades in various costumes to supplement his use of many communication and surveillance technologies.[34] Simon's mastery of disguise and his ability to determine the attitudes and emotions of those he spies on enable him to approach Dr. Russell, a target Tretiak describes as too difficult for his henchmen to reach.

In contrast with the Russians who shoot first and ask questions later, Simon figures out what makes Emma tick after he enters her Oxford apartment and finds her journal, a photo of her as a child posing with her long-haired father, and scattered Post-It notes about her work attached to different walls and pieces of furniture. Emma's love of Percy Shelley and poetry, her preference for artistic men, and her incipient romantic passion are obvious to Simon, who decides to adopt the name Thomas More as a means of wooing her. The persona of a heroic saint, Simon figures, will attract Emma, who plans to do social good by donating her cold fusion formula to the world. What Simon does not predict is that Emma's vulnerability (both her heart condition and her romantic leanings) as well as her directness and sincerity will attract and transform him. Although Simon manages to steal Emma's formula, which she has written on notes kept inside her bra, he also wants to protect her. He must convince her to trust him so that he can get her away from the Russian police and save her from Tretiak's men. Simon realizes Emma must finish the formula to help block Tretiak's coup.

Tretiak has stashed away all available heating oil in Moscow in an attempt to take over the government from Premier Karpov. After a Russian scientist has trouble finishing the cold fusion formula stolen from Emma, Tretiak decides to demonstrate the likely-to-fail formula to prove Karpov has wasted government funds. Emma and Simon manage to sneak her into the American Embassy in Moscow to work on the missing parts of the cold fusion formula. Simon then smuggles Emma's corrected formula to the Russian scientist who agrees to cooperate. Outside the embassy, addressing the crowd, Tretiak denounces Karpov's supposed decision to fund cold fusion because he believes that the formula will fail, but the Russian scientist uses Emma's completed formula to demonstrate that cold fusion creates energy. This proof motivates Tretiak's military supporters to align with Karpov, and Tretiak and his mob are imprisoned.

Emma and Simon's adventure through Moscow and the successful comple-
tion of her formula enable vast oil reserves to revert to the Russian people.
Emma and Simon pursue their romance; although the British Secret Service
suspects their involvement, they can never trap the always disguised Simon.
Because their relationship distracts Emma from her nervous heart condition,
she no longer needs medication. After returning to England, Emma gives away
the cold fusion formula. Simon goes along with this plan and donates millions
to the foundation supporting cold fusion research. Trust leads to transformation. His turnaround, his shift from international thief to saint, occurs because
of his relationship with Emma, and, in turn, she gains health and happiness.

The Science of Attraction

Three films from the early 2000s portray a female scientist's research interest in human sexual behavior. Female scientists in *Laurel Canyon, Kettle of
Fish,* and *Yes* work as research biologists. Each woman is a fish out of water,
becoming involved in a romance that begins in an odd way. Each protagonist
appears competent at research but not so competent with life, although each
takes off her glasses (or goggles) and finds romance. These women are vulnerable because although they succeed in science, they struggle to find romance.
Each film concludes with the female scientist understanding her romantic
desire and poised to fulfill it.

In *Kettle of Fish* (Dir. Claudia Myers, 2006), Ginger (Gina Gershon) is an
English biologist transplanted to Manhattan. Her apartment search results in
her meeting the late-blooming jazz musician Mel (Matthew Modine), who
agrees to sublet his apartment to Ginger while he tests a live-in relationship
with his latest girlfriend. After Mel's girlfriend throws him out, he sneaks back
into his old apartment and persuades Ginger to share his place with him.
Because her research on frogs takes up most of her time and she only sleeps in
the apartment, Ginger agrees to let him back if he sleeps on the couch and she
takes the bedroom. Mel and Ginger become good friends even as Mel chases
Diana, a young bride neglected by her entrepreneurial husband. Although Mel
resists Ginger's interviewing him to record his comments about love, she persuades Mel to let her study his fish Daphne. When Ginger moves Daphne the
fish to live in her lab next to one of her other research subjects, a frog named
Casanova, the animals appear attracted to one another.

Ginger's biological research focuses on sexual attraction, "long-term pair
bonding," but she is no more adept in romance than the bumbling Mel. The
romantic plot in *Kettle of Fish* illustrates how the biologist and the jazz musician move backwards along the path to romance. First, Ginger and Mel live

together, adjusting to each other's habits. Then Mel helps Ginger set up her own apartment by moving in her stuff and hanging up curtains and pictures. It is only when they are no longer sharing an apartment that they share their first, passionate kiss. They fight as friends, and then they fall in love.

The relationship between Ginger and Mel is one of several romances in the film. Daphne and Casanova, Diana and her husband Bruce, and Mel's friend Freddie and his wife appear respectively as examples of love at first sight, mismatched partners, and love over the long haul, situations that apply at different times in the narrative to Ginger and Mel. Diana becomes disillusioned with her marriage and succumbs to Mel, trying to seduce him. Although Mel has sought to woo her for weeks, he ultimately rejects Diana's proposition because he realizes that his relationship with Ginger is more satisfying than any brief sexual encounter.

Kettle of Fish includes many scenes depicting Ginger in the lab, where we observe her "professional" interactions. Her supervisor periodically asks colleagues how Ginger is getting on with her work, suggesting that he has his doubts about this foreign woman, likely because of her quirky behavior in the lab: getting close to her frog subjects and chasing after the escaping Casanova on her hands and knees. Ginger is the only scientist the film puts in this humiliating position, although Mel crawled back into his apartment and also crawls around the lab helping Ginger look for the frog. Ginger must assert her authority in the lab as head of the long-term pair bonding project; for example, she demands that her male assistant continue working after hours, even though he has a date, to show he is serious about science. The film suggests that her grouchiness on this occasion stems from problems in her relationship with Mel. There is a certain humor in Ginger setting up a barrier for her assistant's romance so that she and he can observe sexual attraction in animals, indicating that Ginger fits the stereotype of a brainy scientist too absorbed in technical work to recognize what is obvious to the layperson.

Ginger's love life takes up about the same amount of on-camera time as her research. Another scientist in the lab becomes infatuated with her and manages to date her before she concludes she would rather have a relationship with Mel. As a scientist, Ginger is able to be as eccentric a woman as Mel is a man, for his reluctance to mature and enjoy domesticity provides some common ground between them. Their characters invert stereotypes of femininity and masculinity: Ginger's wit and liveliness align with logic and rationality, while Mel is a dreamer who prefers not to be hemmed in by women or work and whose life is organized by his personal relationships rather than any professional ambitions. According to classical Hollywood film conventions about couples, opposites attract while eccentrics deserve each other.

Films about female scientists demonstrate how fragile emotional attachments are and how they depend on a variety of circumstances to flourish. For example, in Lisa Cholodenko's 2002 film *Laurel Canyon*, Alex (Kate Beckinsale), a research biologist, is engaged to medical school classmate Sam (Christian Bale), the son of famous, successful rock-and-roll record producer Jane (Frances McDormand). Alex and Sam intend to live in Jane's Laurel Canyon home while she lives in her Malibu beach house. Instead, the couple find out as they move into the Laurel Canyon house that Jane will also stay and work there. Jane has taken up with Ian (Alessandro Nivola), the lead singer of the band whose album she is producing, and she has given her former boyfriend Bobby the beach house while he "gets on his feet." Because Jane and her new boyfriend Ian are distracted by their romance, the record's required hit-single develops slowly; instead of working, Jane and Ian spend much of their time drinking, smoking marijuana, hosting pool parties, and swimming naked in the pool. Sam avoids being around his mother, spending his time at the psychiatric hospital where he does his residency and befriending a female resident from Israel. While Sam works, a clash of cultures is taking place in the Laurel Canyon home between the straitlaced, overachieving Alex, who graduated at the top of Sam's and her medical school class, and the rock-and-rollers in the house. Raised in the northeastern United States in a family obsessed with success, Alex becomes distracted from her dissertation on genomics while living at her mother-in-law's because she becomes fascinated with Jane and Ian.

The crux of the film has Alex loosening up in what at first seems to be a positive way: she learns more about popular music, enjoys a more relaxed lifestyle, and takes breaks from writing her dissertation. Then Alex stops working altogether and wonders about her engagement to Sam. When Jane confronts her son about his resentment and admits that she was not a responsible mother in the past,[35] Sam reveals that he is less than content living in the household. This admission comes after Sam finds Jane, Ian, and Alex in Ian's hotel room, just after Jane has refused her boyfriend Ian's invitation to engage in sex with him and Alex. Jane's freewheeling disposition is still evident: she tells Ian that he is free to pursue Alex if he wishes but that Jane cannot participate. Although Ian wants Jane and wants to watch Jane and Alex together, Jane's refusal puts an end to the ménage, and Ian gives up. Jane refuses to cross an ethical line and hurt her son by engaging in sex with Alex, despite Ian's protestations that Sam and Alex are due to break up anyway.

After Sam finds his fiancée, his mother, and her boyfriend in the hotel room, he storms out. Alex chases after Sam and defends her actions, protesting that she wants to marry him and that her flirting with Ian and Jane means nothing. At the end of the film, Alex and Ian agree to be friendly without having sex, while Sara pursues Sam, who appears overwhelmed and indecisive about whether to pursue his new passion for Sara or to reinvigorate his relationship with Alex. The scientists (Sam, Alex, and Sara) seem more confused about their sexuality than the non-scientists. Studying the reproduction of the fruit fly, as Alex does, and treating difficult psychiatric cases, as Sam and Sara do, does little to enhance their capacities to understand what and whom they desire in this story. Jane's attitude (anything goes as long as someone is not damaged by it) and her ability to set aside pleasure because of her concern for others indicates that she is more mature than the others. She thus rises above Sam's criticism of her as developmentally impaired and becomes an example of maturity that he may or may not follow. In not trusting their own feelings and failing to respect personal ties, the scientists in this film are less admirable than the intuitive, comfortable-in-her-own-skin record producer.

Pursuing desire over hate is the message of *Yes* (2004), which British director Sally Potter wrote as a response to post-9/11 attitudes about Muslims, Arabs, and immigration. As she explains in the foreword to the film's published script,

> Perhaps YES is ultimately about the commonality beyond our political and cultural differences. It is also about the very small and the very large; from the micro-world of molecular science to the enormity of war; the giant clash of fundamentalisms, Eastern and Western. And in between those two worlds— somewhere on the middle of the scale of the very small to the very large—lies the human body with its desires, frailties, strengths, and ultimately, its mortality.[36]

Potter's film is consciously literary: the title is the last word of James Joyce's *Ulysses*—from Molly Bloom's monologue—and the film's dialogue appears in verse—iambic pentameter. Appearances by house cleaners functioning as a Greek chorus in commenting on the action and acknowledging their professional interest in washing away dirt and restoring order mediate for the viewer. The main characters of *Yes* are iconically named She and He, although other characters have assigned names.

The film's settings—London, Beirut, Belfast, and Havana—provide rich texture for the story as urban histories of violence evoke a range of emotions related to characterizations of major and minor figures. She is a married Irish-American biologist in England, and He, a Lebanese expatriate surgeon, works as a cook in London. Potter illustrates the sterility of She's marriage by filming the stark-white modernist decor of her home in cool, blue light, and she contrasts marital emptiness with She's passionate relationship with He, conducted in warm natural light in a lush park, an expensive restaurant, his well-furnished apartment, and a brightly painted Havana hotel. Their infatuation, which provides them escape from their constrained professional and personal lives, begins quickly. After She learns of her husband Anthony's adulterous liaisons, He flirts with the rather despondent She while He is serving as a waiter at a formal embassy dinner.

Their clandestine affair allows them to reflect on the politics of hate and the place of science in a world dominated by clashing faiths. Although both are scientists, She and He differ on whether science or faith should dominate one's outlook. In her job as a molecular biologist, She outlines a position on the beginning of life in a corporate boardroom:

> I understand that you've invited me
> To make a case that life begins at three
> Hours; or at one, or two, or maybe four,
> As if there is a moment when we can be sure
> That we are human. You'll want evidence.
> Material. Not big ideas, nor common sense,
> But what is measureable, what you can see.
> And not just once, but many times, repeatedly.
> For this is science and that's what we do.
> But wait a minute. Is this really true?
> Could "objectivity" be just a point of view?
> We interpret what we see; and can see
> What we expect, in embryology. (8)

She understands science both as a means to truth and as a methodology with its own interpretive lens.

Surprised to learn that her lover was trained as a surgeon, She asks why He no longer works in science and learns that he walked out of a Beirut hospital after one of his surgical patients was shot for being on the wrong side of politics. He tells She,

> They'd killed a man and murdered an idea—
> That doctors answer to a human need
> Without a thought of colour, or of creed—
> And then had the effrontery to claim
> That they had done it in my people's name.
> It's something that you wouldn't understand. (25)

Her Belfast background makes her familiar with violence; however, she has not known misfortune as an expatriate, whereas his Arab background makes him suspect. He loses his job at the restaurant for defending himself in a fight with other kitchen workers. She and He share an aversion to political dictatorship and violence, but their main connection is a sensual one.

Keeping the focus on the political as it mixes with the personal, *Yes* illustrates dimensions of She's scientific research only to acknowledge that her work on embryos is controversial and important. Her work allows her to have integrity, according to her husband, whose profession in politics seems contaminated in comparison. Yet the film treats science as only seemingly superior in pursuit of knowledge, for science, in not being mystical, fails to inspire the soul according to He. She's research in the sterile lab seems as cold to her as her marital home, where She and her husband are not often together.

She and He quarrel, not directly about science or religion but vaguely about politics. He feels overwhelmed by his desire for her and his "fall from grace" in pursuing this beautiful woman from an imperialist nation (52). She becomes incensed that he reduces her to being an object of sexual temptation, and they separate. He returns to Beirut to find it a city in rubble, and She goes to her favorite aunt, who is on her deathbed in Belfast. Overcome with emotion after her Belfast aunt dies, She calls He and begs him to meet her in Havana, a destination inspired by her communist aunt's saying "In Cuba" just before expiring: Cuba was a place the aunt wanted to visit to see the results of Castro's revolution.

In Havana, speaking directly to God via video camera, She acknowledges in her mind her turn from God to science and back again:

> I know I've strayed so far I don't belong
> In any church of yours. I've sung the song
> Of science. Yes, I've sung it every day.
> But, I could argue, that is how I pray . . .
> For twenty years—god, can it be?
> I've cut, dissected: carefully
> And with respect. Each living cell
> A source of wonder, as I tried to see . . .
> To penetrate your mystery,
> The point is, God, you never lie.
> But you have secrets. So have I. (71)[37]

After She begs, "Oh God . . . can you forgive me, For not—for not believing in you," She hears a shout from a woman outside that a man approaches (72). *Yes*'s final scenes are of He and She on a Cuban beach where the word "YES" is traced in the sand and of She's cleaner reminding us "[t]hat 'no' does not exist. There's only 'Yes.'" The film frame merges a shot of the lovers' kiss with the image of a dividing cell. The poetic rendering of a romance involving a female scientist complements the other films discussed in this chapter and provides a glimpse at the female scientist's motivations, intuitions, and reasoning. Potter's movie demonstrates shared motivations of science and religion as pursuing truth and fulfilling desire.

Recent films and television shows include other portraits of women scientists, but many narratives tend to reproduce, rather than resist, stereotypes associated with women in science. Stylistic conventions of dramas and thrillers differ appreciably from those of romantic comedies, yet films incorporating female scientists as characters frequently reference how passions for science and for romance converge. Although success in science may or may not provide similar success in personal relationships, film romances idealize men who support women's professional ambitions and personal desires.

The increased frequency of cinematic representations of women as scientists establishes a professional norm. Incorporating female scientists as characters across genres in some ways naturalizes the participation of women in scientific fields. However, conventions associating the odd, marginalized female scientist with unusual behavioral traits or emotional vulnerability, or connecting her scientific abilities with a kooky or a glamorous appearance, make these women exceptional as scientists and as women, thereby only slightly raising the consciousness of film audiences about gender equity in STEM.

Gender Matters in *Intuition*

Allegra Goodman's novel *Intuition* (2006) focuses on a case of scientific misconduct in a cancer lab. Cautious and careful female researcher Marion Mendelssohn directs the lab in collaboration with the male, personable, publicity-minded medical doctor Sandy Glass. Goodman reported in an interview that she wrote about a senior female research scientist at the request of her oncologist sister because there were no novels about female scientists of this rank.[38] This stated intention and the title's allusion to the cliché "feminine intuition" point to the significance of gender in the novel. Goodman highlights gendered aspects in the novel's setting in descriptions of the Mendelssohn-Glass lab and its personnel as well as in those of its parent institute. *Intuition* notes social stereotypes that identify science as masculine and sketches various characters' perceptions of women doing science. Major female characters in the novel reveal their experiences of gender bias and discrimination. Most significantly, the conclusion of the novel references how female scientists might overcome these barriers by enabling professional opportunities for other women.

Social hierarchies within science are apparent from details about the location and management of the Mendelssohn-Glass lab. In 1985 this fictional lab was part of the Philpott Institute, which the novel describes as "famous, but . . . full of old instruments" (4).[39] Overshadowed by Harvard, the Philpott is located in the former home of the Cambridge Manual Training School for boys (37), a location connecting science with discipline (rather than knowledge) and with science's roots as an institution enforcing gender and class restrictions. According to the narrator, the institute's management understands technicians as a "scientific servant class" (4), for post-docs and technicians serve at the pleasure of Marion and Sandy, who manage both research projects and social outings for their small group. Stiff competition for federal funding demands that the Mendelssohn-Glass lab produce results quickly and efficiently. Reprimanded by the lab directors for continuing what appear to be failed experiments, post-doc Cliff Banneker considers post-docs as "overeducated . . . scientific sharecroppers" who "slaved all day" and "kept repeating their experiments" (20). Most female scientists in the novel are junior researchers or technicians, while most men are senior researchers (Marion is an exception). Being female is invoked as a hurdle in the career paths of Marion, the head tech Nanette, and the senior post-doc Robin.

Characters experience what Robert Merton's analysis of the Matthew effect describes—the cumulative advantage of many small advantages pertaining to the male scientist—and what Margaret Rossiter describes as the Matilda effect—the cumulative results of many small disadvantages for each female scientist. The professional challenges female scientists face in the novel include acting on their motivations, maintaining productivity in their fields, and managing personal relationships while doing science. Marion's career should be stellar because of her aptitude, as her husband Jacob, who was a child prodigy in science, reflects, but her rewards have not matched her potential. Although others say that "her papers were repetitive, descriptive, and nothing more" (19), the authorial reader shares Jacob's view that Marion deserves a better position than the one she holds at the financially struggling Philpott. Enough hints are dropped about her competitor, Art Ginsburg, to convince us that if the world of science in the novel were just and equitable, then Marion's talents would be better appreciated, and she would work at Harvard instead of the Philpott.

Highlighting sexism in science, Goodman compares Marion with another female scientist whose accomplishments were not appropriately recognized. Marion's early work involved "elegant crystallography," the same application that Rosalind Franklin used when she took photos in the 1950s illustrating the double-helix structure of DNA. However, Franklin's achievement was not recognized: a fellow scientist, Maurice Wilkins surreptitiously showed her photos to Watson and Crick, who were applauded for their discoveries and went on to receive the Nobel Prize.[40] Sandy recognizes that Marion's work has a "myopic brilliance" but also that Marion is "stubborn," traits that might make her end up as Rosalind Franklin and not Watson or Crick (74).

At the outset of the novel, Marion Mendelssohn and Sandy Glass appear as complementary collaborators whose personality traits are connected with gendered stereotypes. Disagreements between the lab codirectors illustrate their predominating tendencies as akin to stereotypical traits of masculinity and femininity. Sandy accuses Marion of being too tentative, but Marion fears that Sandy will "go off half cocked" if he hears Cliff's preliminary, promising results (31), so she keeps this information from him while confiding in her husband.

Descriptions of Marion's and Sandy's families also reveal gender differences pertinent to women in science. Sandy's family includes his English professor wife and three daughters with humanistic interests, who see their father's formidable medical talents as intimidating. None of Sandy's daughters is attracted to studying medicine, a discipline which Sandy appears to own; instead, Louisa is a graduate student in the history of science, Charlotte studies art history, and Kate prefers poetry.

In contrast, Marion's family aids and abets her scientific work: her husband Jacob teaches biology and her son is interested in math and science. Jacob Mendelssohn was "in his eighteenth year, when he gave up being a genius . . . gave his heart to Marion, and more than that, he laid his formidable mind at her feet. . . . She was only a girl, but he believed she would make radical discoveries" (30). Jacob's decision to leave the frenetic world of scientific research to teach science owes much to his understanding that he does not generate enough new ideas. He appreciates that Marion's brilliance justifies his putting his career second to hers. In contrast, Sandy refuses to be second to anyone, although his ambition and Marion's caution mean they are good collaborators for a time.

Jacob's enthusiasm for Marion's talent and prospects is matched by his reservations concerning Sandy. Jacob thinks of Sandy as "a terrific publicist . . . a great fund-raiser" who can "charm money from N.I.H." (31); he contrasts Sandy and Marion and finds his wife a superior scientist in that she prefers knowledge to attention: "True, Sandy was excited by discovery. . . . But Sandy was not Marion. Sandy's work was not about giving of himself, but about building up himself, his ego, his persona" (32). Jacob acknowledges that "Sandy would go off rampaging for bold new results, sometimes forgetting what might be small and diffident, and difficult to describe—the truth" (32). Sandy's key to success as a medical doctor, that he appears supremely confident advising terminal patients, turns out to be hindrance in research, where confidence alone doesn't produce good results.

Senior post-doc Robin Decker distinguishes the different styles and prospects afforded to female and male scientists. Her career has suffered from favoritism in that her progress has been slowed to accommodate others. Her graduate advisor, John Uppington, pushed through a male candidate before allowing Robin to finish her degree a year later (89). At the novel's opening, we are told that in the Mendelssohn-Glass lab Robin spends "five years working on what had once been considered a dazzling project, an analysis of frozen samples of blood, collected over the years from cancer patients who died of various forms of the disease" (7). She looks for "a common marker, a significant tag" (7). Presented with the dead blood project by Glass, Robin must work out the disorganized documentation and any possible results by herself, a difficult task that might have been easier with good collaboration or more careful supervision by him. Glass chose Robin for this project because of her beauty and his high expectations for her, but Marion regards Robin's research as "spinning her wheels for five years" (100).

As post-docs for Marion and Sandy, Robin and Cliff enter a romantic relationship that develops as a result of their spending so much time in the lab and at lab social functions. Indeed, the post-docs appear to spend all their waking moments with each other in one way or another, so it seems inevitable that Robin and Cliff develop a romance. After Marion observes them kissing in the supply closet one night, she refuses to speak to them, for she remembers the similar beginning of her romance with Jacob. Robin's passion for science is not matched in Cliff until he has what others consider to be excellent results in experimenting with R-7, a chemical to destroy cancerous tumors. That Cliff ends up in science as the best available option for him appears insulting to Robin, who feels her talents—diligence, hard work, patience, and scientific motivation—are superior to his. Cliff thinks Robin is jealous. Finding him unbelievably arrogant about the apparent success of R-7, she prefers to break up with him rather than endure his posturing about his results.

Reported at the outset of the narrative, Cliff's results indicate that R-7 might be a significant factor in eliminating tumors. Marion and Sandy consequently "draft" other post-docs "to join a war effort," "a brutal, jingoistic marshaling of resources for R-7," as observed by Robin, whose own project is laid aside as she is enlisted to verify that R-7 is successful (89). Such verification proves impossible for her, and Robin is unable to defend herself against criticism for not confirming such important results for the lab. In front of other post-docs, Cliff criticizes Robin: "It's not my fault you can't get the same results I did. Don't blame me for your mistakes" (119). His arrogance stems from his seemingly superior results and former status as her boyfriend; Robin responds by slapping him.

Cliff's self-importance recurs in the narrative as Marion tries to be a mentor, telling Robin that "you can't just blame Cliff" but repressing what she really thinks: "blaming ex-boyfriends for one's failures was not the behavior of a scientist" (137). Because of her relationship with and estrangement from Cliff, Robin's abilities are discounted by her superiors and her peers. Her initial failure to duplicate Cliff's work seems to reflect her inabilities because Marion believes Robin is a jealous ex-girlfriend and not a careful scientist. Marion's caution about pursuing scientific truth as carefully as possible decreases as she begins to defer to Sandy's authority. Pushed by her collaborator, Marion authorizes the publication of results from Cliff's work in order to justify the lab's research. Instead of following through on Robin's intuitive doubting of Cliff's results, and believing that Robin diligently tried to confirm what would be a big discovery for the lab, Marion takes Cliff's side and counsels Robin to go work as a teaching assistant for Jacob at his university.

Although Marion defers to Sandy, Jacob cannot submit to Sandy's ambition and remains convinced that Marion should follow her patient, plodding way to achieve genuine scientific results. Jacob crosses a line when he works to undermine his wife's "castle in the air" (139): he hints to Robin, because Marion will not listen to him, that there might be a problem with Cliff's data, that "the results seem almost too good" (144). Following up on Jacob's hint, Robin finds messy recordkeeping and confronts Cliff about his gassing some mice, which she presumes he destroyed as counterevidence of R-7's value as a tumor reducer (158). Robin warns Marion that there might be a problem with Cliff's data, but Marion continues to believe that Cliff and Robin are at odds because of the broken romance. Outside of the lab, Jacob understands that the disciplined Robin searches for truth whereas Cliff is a disorganized, overconfident researcher (196), but it takes Marion some time to discover this difference.

Robin spends more time at the university where she assists Jacob as she persists in her accusations about the R-7 experiments, accusations that go forward to the Office of Research Integrity at N.I.H. Some of her friends from the Mendelssohn-Glass lab consequently refuse to speak to her, but the institute's senior lab technician, Nanette, stands by Robin. Nanette views the lab's authorities as motivated by power and sexism: "I love to watch chronic overachieving S.O.B.s scramble. The people who never give their underlings the time of day. Little words like please or thank you. All the type As killing their post docs and ignoring their wives for the sake of science, fighting tooth and nail to get ahead" (254). Robin makes herself unwelcome at the Mendelssohn-Glass lab because her persistent assertion that Cliff might have reported only his most favorable results of R-7 punctures the status of the lab and its researchers.

The lab's work is called into question in an informal hearing by Office of Research Integrity in Science (O.R.I.S.) government investigators and then by a congressional hearing followed by an appeal to the O.R.I.S. board.[41] At the congressional hearing, after Representative Redfield accuses Marion and Sandy of scientific fraud, the argument takes a turn. The congressman's unfortunate comparison of the Mendelssohn-Glass lab researchers to Nazi scientists allows Sandy to respond to Redfield in a way that revises the terms of his analogy. Sandy affirms his Jewishness and announces he is insulted by Red-field's remark, which Sandy identifies as anti-Semitic; Sandy's outrage gains more favorable media coverage for the lab. Over time Sandy's pugnaciousness and Marion's caution come into conflict to greater degrees as the lab mounts a defense of its data and research publication. Sandy remains confident about the data and Cliff's methods, but Marion anxiously veers between doubt and hope: "how would she know if [Cliff] adjusted or revised the numbers, or sacrificed mice without telling anyone? . . . The postdocs answered to Marion, but she depended on them for the truth of their answers" (309).

Although Marion and Sandy's appeal of the original O.R.I.S. decision prom-ises to clear the lab, Marion wants to return the N.I.H. grant money. Sandy talks her out of returning the money, but Marion does retract the *Nature* paper, regardless of Cliff's objections, because of what she terms "flawed results" (322). Marion also refuses to work with Cliff. After Sandy tells Marion the outcome of the appeal ("We got the judgment against O.R.I.S., a rebuke to Redfield's subcommittee, a call to reform ethics oversight at N.I.H. We got everything" [327]), Marion feels relieved, and Cliff feels "spared" (328). Robin is stunned, but she appreciates the ironies of her situation when her new employer, Art Ginsburg, Marion's nemesis, tells Robin that "sometimes the truth has to be enough" (330).[42]

Female collective action such as the support Nanette offers Robin reappears at the end of the novel when Marion compensates for her earlier inattention to Robin by providing her former post-doc with the opportunity to ask a ques-tion in response to Marion's presentation at a major conference. The likenesses between Marion and Robin are never more apparent as we realize they both experienced discrimination in science and were harmed by it: Marion by being denied a Harvard position (19) and Robin by her major advisor and then in Marion's lab. Goodman suggests that only by working with truth-minded, rather than success-minded, colleagues will women experience and create a more equitable environment in science. Robin's confidence in asking the ques-tion at the professional conference indicates that she will persist in science despite its inequities.

Femininity, Feminism,
and Technology

Technologies can enable social empowerment, allowing women to resist social constraints and increase individual opportunities, but the intersection of gender and technology is not always positive or progressive and can be regarded, according to Elisabeth Sundin, as "mutually constituting and limiting."[1] Asking "Was the female experience of technological change significantly different from the male experience?" Ruth Schwartz Cowan outlines "four areas where one might look at how [the experiences differ]: with respect to women's bodies and their functions, in work outside the home, in domestic labor, and in the ideological realm."[2] Judy Wajcman asserts, "Masculinity and femininity are produced in relation to each other and what is masculine, according to the ideology of sexual difference, must be the negation of the feminine" (158). Wajcman notices longstanding assumptions and associations of technology and "manliness,"[3] for "the ideology of masculinity . . . has this intimate bond with technology" (141). Sexuality, control, combat, and heroism are recurring images in technological rhetoric, and there is a "continuing male monopoly of weapons and mechanical tools" (150).

Women have often been on the leading edge of developing and using technologies, although their work is not always credited. Autumn Stanley collected information about many domestic, agricultural, and scientific technologies that women inventors created, including the digging stick (the precursor of modern agricultural tools), the cotton gin, the McCormick reaper, and the radioimmunoassay test.[4] Richard Menke reports historical references to male and female telegraphers in various British fictions, including those by R. M. Ballantyne and Anthony Trollope.[5] Menke explains that women were attractive employees in late-nineteenth-century telegraph offices: "Employing women and paying them lower wages supported the great goal of cheaper telegrams" (182). Arguing that "[t]he omission of women from the history of computer science perpetuates misconceptions of women as uninterested or incapable in this field," Jennifer Light considers the case of 200 young female mathematicians who worked as ENIAC calculators for the United States during World War II.[6]

Women's achievements in technology are also shortchanged by attempts to understand their work according to masculine models or by diminishment of their contributions as merely a result of collaborations with relatives. Ruth Oldenziel surveyed publications by and about women engineers in the period 1870–1945 in the United States, concluding that women engineers largely adopted an assimilationist strategy in a male-dominated profession.[7] Contrasting one female civil engineer and women's activist with a female industrial engineer who worked alongside her husband, Oldenziel describes how "American women engineers ignored the kind of bridges Nora Blatch [the first woman to earn a degree in civil engineering] tried to build between women in the technical field and those working in the women's movement. They instead honored the model Nora Blatch's contemporary Lillian Gilbreth (1878–1972) offered. Gilbreth . . . received her technical knowledge and her legitimacy in engineering through her husband . . ." (149–50). After her husband's death in 1924, Lillian Gilbreth worked as a consultant for, among other areas, time-motion studies and consumer products; "she considered herself an expert in human psychology, industrial management, efficiency models, business consultation, and home economics (her personal expertise by rearing twelve children)."[8]

Tensions between domesticity and technology appear in biographical accounts of exceptional female engineers, particularly in renderings based on Gilbreth family life. The book *Cheaper by the Dozen* (1950), written by two Gilbreth children, and its cinematic adaptation (Dir. Walter Lang, 1950) illustrate the career of Frank Gilbreth Sr. who appears in this narrative as a management engineer raising a large family of twelve children and testing techniques that made his efficiency methods well-known. In their first book, Frank Jr. and Ernestine describe the household as "a sort of school for scientific management."[9] In the 1950 film, Frank Gilbreth Sr. prohibits his daughters from using cosmetics, dating boys, and learning about contraception. Lilian Gilbreth appears in the film as a moderating force of domestic wisdom, although generally deferring to her husband: "Throughout his life, Lillian Gilbreth remained, in her eyes, the junior partner."[10] Tested in the Gilbreth's home research and development lab, their timesaving methods appear in print and film narratives as beneficial for both industry and household.[11] The Gilbreths seem happier, more efficient, and more productive as a result of their incorporating scientific efficiencies, although the presence of domestic servants in the family's home is clearly a factor.

In the sequel to *Cheaper by the Dozen,* the 1952 film *Belles on Their Toes,* directed by Henry Levin and with a script by Henry and Phoebe Ephron, Lillian struggles to manage the family without her husband's income. She confronts sexist attitudes in her work as an industrial engineer and guides her daughters through courtship and marriage. The Gilbreth books, and to a lesser extent the films, identify Lillian's kitchen design as enabling domestic efficiency of the Gilbreth household, but technological improvements were not timesavers for all women.

Although improved domestic technologies were marketed in the early twentieth century, these appliances in actuality increased women's hours of housework. Cowan's *More Work for Mother* documents that time diaries produced by rural and urban housewives in the United States in this period show that the use of technologies such as the refrigerator, washer, and vacuum cleaner did not decrease the amount of time women spent on housework. Rising standards of hygiene and increased maternal involvement in childcare, both promoted in advertising, prompted many housewives to elevate their standards; increase their range of activities to include decorating, beauty rituals, and hands-on childcare; and spend more time on housework.[12]

The interaction of gender and technology also appears in art and media, which document and shape women's engagement with technology, as Julie Wosk considers in her study of visual representations of women and machines.[13] This chapter details narrative representations of women's use of domestic and industrial technologies, analyzing their claims for feminine empowerment and romantic satisfaction while identifying costs and constraints for women. Charlotte Perkins Gilman's fictions promote women's use of technology for professional and personal success, while films starring Katharine Hepburn acknowledge compromises that women effect. More recent cinematic depictions of women developing and accessing information and robotic technologies demonstrate the persistence of gender stereotypes and feminist attempts to maintain authority over technology.

Work for Women in Gilman's Fictions

Charlotte Perkins Gilman's best-known story, "The Yellow Wallpaper" (1890), explores a female narrator's descent into madness, an outcome of a troubling medical therapy that includes no work, complete bed rest, and isolation from her husband and child.[14] The story exhibits Gothic conventions in conveying suspicions of patriarchal medicine and acknowledging the bleakness of a woman's life without work.[15] Other writers of the period also regarded women's labor prospects as limited. For example, Henry James's Maggie Verver in *The Golden Bowl* (1904) and Isabel Archer in *The Portrait of a Lady* (1881), because of social position, do not consider establishing careers. For many of Edith Wharton's heroines, a wedding, ideally to a European noble, secures a woman's future. But after Lily Bart's value as a bride in *The House of Mirth* (1905) tanks on the marriage market (she loses social status after allowing her friend's husband to trade stocks on her behalf), she is unable to maintain any paid employment. Kate Chopin's *The Awakening* (1899) acknowledges Edna Pontellier's chafing at restrictions placed on her sexual desire and artistic creativity as she becomes dissatisfied with her life as a New Orleans wife and mother. The locales are different—New York and New England, Europe, the American South—but the fictions agree in indicting a repressive society that limits women's lives to marriage and children.

Gilman's other works more often explore how paid employment improves women, families, and society.[16] Her fictions become case studies of how women apply management and technical skills to create entrepreneurial opportunities in the workforce and attain equal partnership in marriage and family.[17] Gilman takes up the problem faced by talented women excessively burdened with household duties and family responsibilities and limited by social conventions to few, lower-paying, careers. These women develop ingenious reconfigurations of domestic arrangements, often incorporating innovative technologies. Designed to inspire readers to action, her texts offer specific solutions to the problem of work for women.[18]

Gilman's novella *What Diantha Did* (1909–10) describes the heroine's path from underpaid schoolteacher to successful entrepreneur. Twenty-one-year-old Diantha Bell applies her original ideas about the professionalization of housekeeping to create businesses devoted to cleaning houses and delivering cooked food.[19] She figures out what housewives need and how her skills might fill these needs, deciding to develop a cafeteria and food delivery and housecleaning operations. These initiatives benefit employees (by raising domestic servants' self-esteem and professionalism) and customers (by relieving housewives of the burdens of cooking and cleaning). Diantha's businesses quickly expand to include a restaurant and a hotel as she manages to earn enough money to support her marrying a man burdened with the support of his five sisters. Her husband Ross doubts Diantha's schemes while courting her, and he endures her financial success in the early years of their marriage; however, after he travels abroad and hears her praises sung, he recognizes the social value of Diantha's achievements and finally also praises her.[20]

Gilman's lessons are clear: take inventory of resources and skills, develop and deploy entrepreneurial strategies, persist regardless of criticism, and engage in satisfying work performed out of one's own home. Readers are encouraged to follow the examples of Diantha, who shares her cost accounting with her father, and of the widowed Mrs. Morrison, the heroine of "Three Thanksgivings" (1909), who takes stock of her assets, including a spacious home replete with furnishings for large gatherings, the efficient assistance of a housekeeper, and her own gift for entertaining.

Mrs. Morrison decides to turn her large home into a women's club for her town. This scheme results from her detached, logical analysis of her frightening options after her husband's death: marrying the "pompous, sturdy and immovable" Peter Butts or living as a welcome, but unneeded, severely constrained dependent in her daughter's or her son's home (108).[21] Instead of taking her children's advice, Mrs. Morrison relies on her own judgment to keep her home and engages her best talents to serve her community. Her clubhouse provides an outlet for her female neighbors who were previously "starving for companionship, for occasional stimulus and pleasure" (114). That the club turns a profit allows Mrs. Morrison to pay her mortgage by working instead of resorting to an uncongenial marriage.

The young Dacia Boone in Gilman's "Girls and Land" is not in demand in the marriage market and turns to business instead. Consulting with her kindly stepfather, Dacia builds a successful "road-making business" and later builds and coordinates, in partnership with him and Olaf Pederson, a young immigrant, a network of "Working Girls' Clubs" on the West Coast. Dacia's stepfather proudly describes her virtues in non-stereotypical terms, telling her, "I'm mighty glad that I inherited you. You see, I can work and I'm honest, but you've got the brain. You can push" (293). Dacia Boone eventually marries, agreeing to "partner" in life as well as in business with the hardworking Olaf.

Other stories by Gilman celebrate young women's resourcefulness by focusing on their development of communities. Collective solutions respond to social problems faced by women. Several narratives look at the cooperative technical efforts of women who form networks to support them and their families. "Five Girls" (1894), written in imitation of Louisa May Alcott, sketches how five schoolmates (artists and architects) continue their friendship into adulthood after they agree to one friend's plan that they build and live in "a beautiful 'model tenement' affair, artistic and hygenic and esthetic and everything else; with central kitchens and all those things; and studios and rooms for ourselves, and a hall to exhibit in and so on. Then we could have suites of apartments for families and let them; and bye and bye, if we are families, we can occupy these ourselves and let the others" (85).

"Bee Wise" (1913) describes a community of that name and its sister town called "Herways," which are constituted on principles of cooperation and encouragement of work for women by "some dozen or twenty" women of different training who graduated from the same college class (227). The names of towns are inspired by the biblical proverb "Go to the ant, thou sluggard, consider her ways and be wise."[22] The female college graduates work hard to make their endeavor succeed, and their project benefits enormously from the $10 million gift donated by one of their number, Margery, who wants to "set a new example to the world—a place of woman's work and world-work too" on property that includes "an upland valley" and "a little port" in California that she received from her uncle (229). The scheme, as "the Manager" details, "is a plain business offer. What I propose to do is to develop that little port, open a few industries and so on, build a reservoir up above and regulate the water supply—use it for power—have great gardens and vineyards. Oh, girls— it's California! We can make a little Eden! And as to Motherhood . . . there's no better place for babies!" (229). The two communities function together as a utopia first peopled by the founders, then expanding to include men and families. After the towns have "filled their normal limits," the founders extend their model, "beginning another rational paradise in another beautiful valley, safer and surer for the experience behind them," and spreading their ideas to "every part of the world" (233, 234).

These narratives neatly resolve characters' dilemmas of balancing work and family by elaborating successful entrepreneurial innovations of products and procedures. Gilman hoped her stories would motivate women to pursue professional opportunities while encouraging men, children, and other women to support female professionals in the workforce and at home. In "Mrs. Merrill's Duties" the narrator describes how one woman's responsibilities to self, family, household, and society change over time although her passion for scientific research remains consistent. The well-educated Grace Leroy works as scientific researcher in a laboratory after graduating from college. But after a period of assisting Dr. Hammerton, "a great chemist and physicist," she must leave her position to help her mother and father by first managing their household and then traveling with her mother who is ill (277).

After her mother dies, Grace manages her father's house and cares for her younger brothers and sisters because her father will not hear of hiring a housekeeper. Grace leaves one set of family responsibilities for another when she marries Mr. Merrill. Despite her "high promise in 'the scientific imagination'" (277) and a secret "aching want" to pursue her laboratory work (280), Grace devotes herself in the first years of her marriage to her husband and then to her children, foregoing any kind of intellectual stimulation; as the narrator points out in criticizing this arrangement, "There is such a thing as being too good" (281).

Grace becomes exhausted by fulfilling the continuous obligations required to care for her family and home and forgoes work while her children are small.

After they grow up, she begins to work daily in her laboratory. Despite having little time and many interruptions due to social obligations, her persistent scientific efforts eventually pay off:

> With long waiting, with careful use of summer months when her too devoted friends were out of town, she managed in another five years, to really accomplish something. From her little laboratory, working alone and under all distractions, she finally sent out a new formula; not for an explosive of deadly power, but for a safe and simple sedative, something which induced natural sleep, with no ill results.
>
> It was no patented secret. She gave it to the world with the true scientific spirit, and her joy was like that of motherhood. She had at last achieved! She had done something—something of real service to thousands upon thousands. And back of this first little hill, so long in winning, mountain upon mountain, range on range, rose hopefully tempting before her. (282)

Grace's work results in a genuine achievement that brings her personal satisfaction as well as public renown. Her friends brag about this 46-year-old woman whose devotion to family is matched by her scientific accomplishments. When new burdens (a widowed, ill sister asks to live with her, and even more invitations arrive from her admiring friends) threaten Grace's work, her mentor, Dr. Hammerton, advises her to continue her scientific research and meet her family obligations in ways that do not sacrifice her time. To do otherwise would make her, he says, "a Criminal Fool!" (284). He counsels Grace to tell her well-off sister to go to a sanitarium or live with other relatives and "As to clothes and parties—Quit!" (284). Grace is shocked by his honesty, although she is encouraged that this great scientist puts her in high company. He tells her that if "Spencer and Darwin had wasted their time as parlor ornaments—supposing they could have—would they have had a right to?" (285). Once Grace understands that her "duty" is to pursue scientific work rather than care for family or devote time to social obligations, she follows Hammerton's advice.

Readers were exhorted to follow the example set by Grace and other characters to carve out time and space for work despite the press of familial obligations and traditional notions of women's duty. Gilman promoted women's work to enable economic self-sufficiency and enhance society. Her protagonists creatively develop entrepreneurial opportunities that benefit networks, communities, and the world. Their scientific and technical solutions include developing a new drug, building social clubs and towns, solving the perennial problem of doing housework in ways that will suit both housewives and servants, and growing businesses to supply and serve healthful food and to clean houses so that women can work on what interests them. In some ways these fictions are too good to be true, but the potentials of feminism they endorse are encouraging for readers. Gilman articulated how progressive feminism's goal of providing work for women could be harnessed to entrepreneurship and collective action, arguing that individuals and society could benefit from the combination of progressive social values and capitalist methods. Hollywood adopted this formula of the feminist use of technology to solve individual and social problems, but it also restricted the success of the actor and the operation.

Katharine Hepburn's Romance with Technology

The top-rated actress on the American Film Institute's 2005 list of "50 Greatest Screen Legends," Katharine Hepburn is the subject of numerous popular biographies and fan Web sites noting her influence as a cultural icon of the New Woman.[23] According to biographers and fans, she is identified as independent and empowered, details drawn in part from Hepburn's personal life and in part from elements of her screen personae. As Roddy McDowell noted, "We take Katharine Hepburn for granted now. The sort of bravery, the wonderful lithe figure. But when she first appeared on the screen, they said, 'What's this?' She defied the law of possibility. She was a total original."[24] Her "originality" revised stereotypes of how women ought to behave socially and cinematically, reconfiguring 1930s Hollywood conventions and American cultural stereotypes of femininity, especially regarding attitudes toward work, dress, and sexuality.

Perceptions of Hepburn and Hepburn's film characterizations of women struggling to manage work and romance exemplify issues still salient for today's filmgoers. According to Rex Reed's account, "George Cukor says she swept through Hollywood in 1932 like a hurricane insulting everyone in sight—a freckled, snotty eccentric who wore men's clothes and fought senselessly with everyone in sight. She was an immediate star." Hepburn's rationalization of her "snotty" attitude deserves notice: "I had to [adopt this attitude] or they would have had me playing whores or discontented wives who always wonder whether they should go to bed with some bore."[25] From her earliest days as a film actress, Hepburn confronted authoritarian, patriarchal attitudes about females enshrined in the Hollywood studio system, but she resisted capitulating to conventions of feminine behavior and dress, whether or not this stance put her in conflict with bosses, coworkers, or audiences.[26]

Anne Edwards describes "a competitive rivalry" between Hepburn and female pioneer director Dorothy Arzner in the filming of *Christopher Strong*. Charles Higham indicates that Arzner was under pressure to meet studio expectations in directing the film and "took little or no time getting to know Kate on a personal level; they didn't really hit it off."²⁷ According to Ronald Bergan, Arzner and Hepburn's "relationship remained cool, distant and competitive. At one stage in the shooting, Arzner threatened to quit unless Kate stopped interfering with her direction."²⁸ These anecdotes provide a biographical context for recognizing how Hepburn's independence, integrity, and autonomy were fused in the minds of viewers and studio chiefs with comparable qualities belonging to characters she played. Acknowledging the seeming paradox that Hepburn was both box-office poison and star to be watched in the early 1930s, Andrew Britten argues that audiences responded favorably or unfavorably to Hepburn's roles and films based on whether they were sympathetic to the feminist values identified with her and the heroines she portrayed.²⁹

The conjunction of biographical and film narratives is a good starting point for considering how certain Hepburn films gingerly consider what happens when a woman works like a man, specifically in fields identified as traditionally masculine such as science and technology. Two films starring Hepburn, the above-mentioned *Christopher Strong* (Dir. Dorothy Arzner, 1933) and *Without Love* (Dir. Harold Bucquet, 1945), react to stereotypes about women who use technology and work in science. These narratives image heroines who are technologically and scientifically adept but ambivalent about traditional feminine desires, and they present women working in science and technology as socially radical and even monstrous. Casting Hepburn respectively as aviatrix and scientist's helpmate, the films illustrate women's work in technical fields, revealing cultural stereotypes that discourage women. In *Christopher Strong,* "A famous female flier and a member of Parliament drift into a potentially disastrous affair."³⁰ Hepburn's portrayal of Lady Cynthia Darrington emphasizes the character's interest and competence in aviation as detrimental to any future domestic bliss. In *Without Love,* the patriotic Jamie Rowan assists the war effort by supporting the research of Pat Jamieson, a scientist seeking to develop a high-altitude oxygen mask. By marrying him under an unorthodox arrangement (i.e., entering into a loveless marriage), Jamie offers him a place to locate his project (her family home) and volunteers herself as subject for the experiments. Both films emplot science and technology as empowering women to step outside the bounds of patriarchal stereotypes in entering untraditional fields, while both films also represent how Cynthia and Jamie endure unconventional domestic arrangements to foster scientific progress. The melodramatic *Christopher Strong* and the romantic comedy *Without Love* depict technically adept women who resist social conventions and sacrifice their individual desires for family and nation. Although the women's sacrifices differ in intensity, each puts her partner's needs above her own. These female protagonists contribute to science and technology in ways that indicate the anomalous status of women who enter these fields. In particular, women's dress and attitudes toward home and work reference the protagonists' submission to accepted social norms of femininity and domesticity.

Biographies represent the beginnings of Hepburn's Hollywood career in the 1930s as tainted by speculative rumors concerning her iconoclasm and identify her as resisting feminine conventions and studio pressures, particularly regarding her dress: "stories were beginning to leak out of her haughty behavior off-screen and her refusal to play the Hollywood Game, always wearing slacks and no makeup, never posing for pictures or giving interviews."[31] One anecdote told by Hepburn biographers notes how she walked through the studio lot in her underwear after management took away her dungarees as clothing unbefitting a glamorous star.[32] Another story tells of Hepburn's asociality: "she had met Mary Pickford. A few mornings later she chided [director George] Cukor, saying, 'I hope you're satisfied, I had dinner at Pickfair last night.' Cukor, taking in the full view of Kate in pants and sweater, said, 'I assume you ate in the kitchen. Certainly they'd never let you in the front door.'"[33] Cukor is also said to have described his first impression of her as "a boa constrictor on a fast."[34]

Such stories reflect a continuing fascination with apparent incompatibilities between Hepburn's private appearance and the looks of glamorous movie stars, contrasting her clothing in her off-screen and on-screen appearances. Many of her early stage and screen roles required fantasy costume, period dress, or over-the-top glamour gowns. Her portrayal of Antiope, Queen of the Amazons, in *The Warrior's Husband* performed at the Morosco Theatre in 1932, "brought her to the attention of Hollywood."[35] A publicity still of Hepburn as Antiope standing legs apart and arms clasped while dressed in a short tunic with armored breastplates and shin guards reveals her athletic build; "Nobody ever noticed me until I was in a leg show," the actress reportedly commented.[36] Hepburn's debut film performance (starring with John Barrymore and Billie Burke) in *A Bill of Divorcement* (Dir. George Cukor, 1932) required less unusual dress, as did *Break of Hearts* and *Alice Adams*, but roles in *Christopher Strong, Sylvia Scarlett, Mary, Queen of Scots, A Woman Rebels, Quality Street, Morning Glory, Little Women, Spitfire*, and *The Little Minister*, all released by RKO in the 1930s, called for unusual costumes for the roles of aviatrix, boy, Scottish queen, Victorian activist, eccentric ingenue, faith healer, and gypsy.

Hepburn's heroines were represented as abnormal, as resisting social conventions in idiosyncratically attractive ways. Early reviewers sought to "emphasise both 'beauty' and 'oddness'" in characterizing "strange beauty and inescapable magnetism"; "the high, strident, raucous, rasping voice, the straight, broad-shouldered boyish figure—perhaps they may all grate upon you, but they compel attention and they fascinate an audience"; "A slim, gaunt-featured nymph . . . with her sharp, pleasantly unpleasant voice, and a penchant for the bizarre in outfits."[37] A typical positive review of a Hepburn performance calculates how well her oddly compelling look suits the character she portrays.

Hepburn's screen characters engage in an extraordinary range of occupations that reflect American attitudes toward working women. Her most celebrated roles include playing eccentric actresses (*Stage Door, Morning Glory*) and high-spirited, attractive socialites (*Holiday, The Philadelphia Story, Bringing Up Baby*), but other films reveal interesting work choices for her film personae—librarian (*Desk Set*), aviatrix (*Christopher Strong*), faith healer (*Spitfire*), composer (*Break of Hearts*), foreign correspondent (*Woman of the Year*), attorney (*Adam's Rib*), and triple-threat athlete (*Pat and Mike*). Hepburn's characters succeed in a man's world as their behaviors and attitudes only lightly revise gender stereotypes regarding romance and domestic skills. Although Hepburn was sometimes cast as a widow or spouse rather than career woman (*Keeper of the Flame, Without Love, State of the Union, Guess Who's Coming to Dinner*), she, unlike many of her Hollywood counterparts, appeared to avoid serial marriage. Instead, she was romantically linked to Howard Hughes, Leland Hayward, John Ford, and Spencer Tracy after her unsuccessful marriage to Ludlow Ogden Smith.

A number of her screen characters were overachievers at work but with shaky domestic skills at home: confident, competent professionals attracted to romance and family who flee the confines of domesticity. Films that Hepburn made with Tracy reflect on a tension between personal relationships and professional work. Tracy insisted on top billing, and his characters emerge victorious in the battle of the sexes that he and his real-life paramour waged on-screen. Tess Harding at the end of *Woman of Year* experiences a full-scale meltdown in the kitchen when she finally returns to her husband, proclaiming her desire to concentrate on him instead of on her career as a foreign correspondent. Amanda Bonner in *Adam's Rib* is threatened with a failed marriage after facing her prosecutor husband in court, because she wins acquittal for a female client accused of the attempted murder of her husband and his mistress. A similar turnaround occurs in *Desk Set,* as I note below, for Bunny Watson accepts Dr. Richard Sumner's marriage proposal even though she realizes that his true loyalty is to the computer he invented.

Both *Christopher Strong* and *Without Love* set aside specific commentary on any shortfall in domestic skills to sketch narrative tension between aviation technology and romantic fulfillment. Hepburn's screen portrayals of the aristocratic aviatrix and heiress Lady Cynthia Darrington and the lab assistant Jamie Rowan living off her late father's and deceased husband's money reflect cultural attitudes about science and technology as well as concerns about women working in untraditional occupations or participating in extramarital liaisons. These films consider the issues of appropriate work for women and look at how women might best contribute to social progress and whether romance ought to be sacrificed to work or vice versa. More constrained than any of Gilman's protagonists, Lady Cynthia and Jamie are bound by social conventions and moral attitudes limiting women's public and private roles and are portrayed in both films as being suffocated by technology.

Christopher Strong employs melodramatic conventions that might strain the patience of the most ardent Katharine Hepburn fan.[38] Yet in its seeming anachronisms about social classes and sexual double standards, it remains as fascinating as its highly stylized costumes: where else might one see a movie star dressed elegantly as a moth, a flower, and a pilot all in the same film? Although the title creates expectations of a male lead, Arzner's film instead concentrates on depicting traditional, rebellious, modern women. Costumes decorated with touches of feathers, fur, or flowers place females in the natural world. Billie Burke plays the elegant, loving wife and mother who seems superfluous to her busy legislator husband Christopher Strong (Colin Clive) and airy socialite daughter Monica (Helen Chandler). The film's plot suggests that romance and heterosexual marriage should be enough to satisfy most women, intimating that the woman who is more passionate about her vocation and her bonds with other women instead of her male paramour is odd.

At the outset of the film, the reckless Lady Cynthia Darrington, clothed in her aviatrix outfit, and Sir Christopher Strong, the essence of aristocratic rectitude, are coincidentally brought together by a silly party game, respectively representing the odd woman and the odd man who care nothing for flirtations. Up to this point in her life, Cynthia has ignored romance, admitting to no love affairs of any kind, because she is consumed by a passion for flying, while the hard-working, respected parliamentarian Sir Christopher has eschewed extramarital liaisons to remain true to his wife—until he meets Lady Cynthia. Strong's daughter Monica sets in motion an affair between these two idiosyncratic people when she gets help from Cynthia in regularizing Monica's affair with a married man. Encouraged by Lady Cynthia, who approaches Sir Christopher on behalf of his daughter Monica, the father approves of his daughter's marriage to the divorced Harry. But in forgiving his daughter, Christopher offends his wife and aligns himself with his transgressive daughter and the exotic aviatrix who speaks for her rather than with his virtuous partner, the mother of his child.

The two couples—Cynthia and Christopher, Monica and Harry—are compared; however, the first continues an extramarital affair while the second begins to exemplify the stereotypical virtues of married life. After observing Cynthia and Christopher in a secret tryst, Monica and her new husband announce to Cynthia that they are expecting a child. Not knowing that Cynthia is also pregnant, Monica and Harry berate Cynthia for indulging in an adultery that harms Lady Strong. The young couple disagrees with Cynthia's rationalization that she and Chris are following the same modern course of action taken by Monica and Harry, who point out that Harry's first wife desired a divorce whereas Lady Strong would be destroyed if her husband deserted her.

In a study of Dorothy Arzner's films, Judith Mayne explores how the director resisted the conventions of women's movies by emphasizing relations between women instead of focusing on the romance between a man and a woman. One of the most interesting scenes in *Christopher Strong* puts the offended wife and mistress together, suggesting, despite their contrasting positions about the sanctity of marriage, that they are more alike than one might assume. They are sincere and have moral integrity even as they differ in their attitudes toward social conventions. Both Lady Strong and Lady Cynthia are willing to risk their lives for loved ones, but they symbolize women's choices in different generations, for the former is a devoted wife and mother and the latter a New Woman who strives to put career goals above romantic desire. Without knowing what caused the recent tension between Monica and Cynthia, and generously ignoring the affair between Chris and Cynthia, Lady Strong asks Monica to be kinder to Cynthia.

Lady Strong also thanks Cynthia for encouraging Monica's romance with Harry, which will produce a grandchild for the Strongs. In this scene, Lady Strong and Lady Cynthia appear as similar, yet complementary, personalities in desiring the happiness of others above their own. The women converse while standing in a doorway within the same cinematic frame; Cynthia is dressed in black with white fur trimmings, while Lady Strong wears a light-colored outfit accented with dark furs. Knowing that Cynthia is pregnant and speaking with her lover's wife, the audience understands how difficult the New Woman's position is: to fulfill her romance would mean breaking up Chris's "ideal" marriage. Cynthia cannot exult in Lady Strong's praise of her as a good friend to the family; instead it makes Cynthia feels guilty about her relationship with Chris. Chafing under Chris's request that Cynthia stop flying, and recognizing that Chris can't desert his wife, Cynthia decides to sacrifice herself to protect the Strongs' marriage. She takes an ambitious flight and breaks the altitude record, but in doing so she kills herself (and her unborn child) when she deliberately takes off her oxygen mask, passes out, and crashes the plane.

The film takes care to reproduce the ambiguities of associating women and technology. The scenes of Hepburn flying in small, open-air planes represent her in the casual, masculine outfit of the female flier made popular by Amelia Earhart and other female pioneers eager to make history. Susan Butler describes the deliberate construction of Amelia Earhart's costume as modeled on Charles Lindbergh's, noting that newsman Jake Coolidge was responsible for Earhart's "Lady Lindy" image: "He posed her mostly in her leather jacket, white-edged helmet, brown broadcloath riding 'breeks,' high-laced brown riding boots, and goggles. The theme was 'Remember Lindbergh.'"[39] Cynthia's aviator outfit is only one of her costumes, for she also wears graceful, feminine clothes—beautifully tailored dresses and ethereal ball gowns constructed out of flower petals—and appears in a moth costume that signifies her flying, frailty, and short life.[40]

Cynthia's on-camera suicide recalls these earlier scenes as she remembers her life in flashback while losing consciousness. As she recalls her life history, she hesitates slightly before killing herself even as she is setting a record for highest altitude flown. Her tombstone encapsulates her life and story in alluding to the Darrington family motto, "[C]ourage conquers death." Referencing an earlier scene in which Cynthia adds "but not love" to the motto, the tombstone avoids mentioning love in its epigraph: "Lady Cynthia Darrington, whose life and death were a source of inspiration and courage for all." Cynthia renounces Chris, but she reclaims herself in flying and embraces her death to enable him to remain with his wife.

Hepburn never played another aviator (or adulterer), but the plot, characterizations, and social criticism of *Christopher Strong* are reconfigured in her later film *Without Love,* based on a play by Philip Barry.[41] *Without Love,* a romantic comedy, alludes explicitly to *Christopher Strong* in picking up its plot thread concerning aviation altitude and exploring how a woman and a man live as married professional colleagues who work on scientific experiments to develop a high-altitude oxygen mask. According to a history of the National Institutes of Health, during World War II, "NIH and military physiologists collaborated on research into problems related to high altitude flying. They determined the altitude at which oxygen had to be administered to prevent pilots from blacking out and designed an apparatus to supply extra oxygen efficiently."[42] *Christopher Strong* incorporated references to high-altitude flying as a sign of extramarital adultery, while *Without Love* presents scientific experimentation on the high-altitude oxygen mask as a form of marital congress that temporarily subsumes sexual union.

In *Without Love,* scientist Pat Jamieson (Spencer Tracy) arrives in Washington, DC, during the Second World War to work on the secret project of creating a more efficient high-altitude oxygen mask, but he finds it difficult to secure housing and lab space. Patriotic widow Jamie Rowan revises her plans to sell her house and allows Jamieson to live there and set up his lab in the basement. Enthusiastic to become Pat's helpmate in the same way that she served her deceased husband, Jamie first offers her house and then herself, suggesting that she and Pat marry to partner on the development of the oxygen mask. Although husband and wife swear that the marriage will remain platonic, their characters do fall in love, precisely because they share certain interests—scientific research, music, and witty repartee.

Both Pat and Jamie repress certain natural desires linked in the film world with sexual passion: Pat is a secret sleepwalker who keeps a dog to help him avoid potentially embarrassing situations, while Jamie recalls the romantic passion of her first marriage and secretly yearns to experience the kind of love she had with her husband. As a romantic comedy, *Without Love* encourages audience identification with worthy principals who are awkward about finding love: the nerdy scientist who is too busy tinkering with his project to concentrate on his bride and the grieving widow who has trouble believing that she can be so lucky as to fall in love twice in her life. There is a hint of their inevitable destiny in that they share the same name; when she marries Jamie becomes Mrs. Jamie Jamieson.

In decorous fashion, the film puts them in situations near or in bed a number of times before they finally admit that they are in love with each other. Their affection appears most evident in scenes devoted to the scientific experiment, a situation requiring Jamie to suffer tortured postures. She is imaged as silenced by the oxygen mask, sneezing into it, in danger of suffocating, and being disoriented. That she must be put through these paces many times to test the equipment and procedures is elided in the film by an iterative montage. In contrast, a later demonstration for the government has Pat as the subject. This demonstration duplicates the success of Jamie's many tests in the lab while putting the inventor in the heroic posture of an aviator rather than as caged in a testing booth or suffocating in the prototype mask Jamie endures. As an experimental subject, Jamie suffers for science, akin to Georgiana in "The Birthmark," while Pat is characterized by scientific acumen and nascent romantic passion, identified by his previous attachment to the sexy Lila Vine and his sleepwalking.

The film's comic plot places the Jamiesons side-by-side in the lab while they maintain separate bedrooms. Pat sleepwalks into Jamie's room, forcing him to reveal his medical problem, but he quickly returns to his own bed. Following Pat onto the train that will bring him to Chicago to demonstrate his scientific research, Jamie ends up sharing his small sleeping compartment, where she takes the lower berth and quizzes him about poetry to determine his passions. After the scientific experiment succeeds, their romance becomes rocky as both Pat and Jamie are jealous of paramours: Pat of Paul Carrell, who formerly seduced Pat's old girlfriend Lila and now flirts with Jamie, and Jamie of Lila. Trying to get her husband's attention or a divorce, Jamie dresses up to parody Lila as an affected, heartless snob and mocks her own marital dalliance with Paul. Jamie's "Lila" costume with its feather boa evokes the ethereal glamour gowns of Cynthia Darrington, but the awkward parody suggests that Jamie has it all wrong and that Pat could never leave her for the ridiculous Lila.

Instead of *Christopher Strong*'s moralizing against extramarital dalliances that constrain the ambitions and risk the lives of independent women, *Without Love* avoids recommending adultery or promiscuity, instead privileging the relationship between the straight-arrow single scientist and the grieving widow. The film's secondary romance plot recognizes that one party in a wartime romance could get left in the lurch. Jamie's cousin Quentin (Keenan Wynn) leaves his longtime socialite fiancée Edwina Collins (Patricia Morison) for the hardbitten career woman Kitty Trimble (Lucille Ball). This triangle collapses because of the war: Quentin enlists instead of having Edwina's father use his influence to obtain a commission and chooses Kitty. Patriotism, science, and temporary sexual abnegation are promoted to win the war and the spouse.

While *Christopher Strong* imagines that there might be a better world some day, one that allows women to fulfill both ambition and love, *Without Love* proposes that true love ought to be a woman's ambition. Both films image women's desires as stronger than men's and even monstrous in being irrepressible. In *Christopher Strong*, female characters are depicted as dangerous in giving in to their impulses: Monica describes herself as bad, Cynthia is reckless, and even Lady Strong's forgiveness of Cynthia is represented as unusual, albeit generous. Three female characters in *Without Love* are man-hunters: Quentin's fiancée Edwina is domineering, his girlfriend Kitty dates many men, and even the grieving Jamie impulsively proposes marriage to Pat. Romantic passion becomes linked with intense ambition as Cynthia and Jamie share an intense desire to make scientific history. Cynthia wants to break flying records more than she wants to marry Chris and more than she values her own life and that of her unborn child. Jamie refuses to see another way of doing science without being married to a scientist, and she is willing to sacrifice all she has and does for the sake of scientific research.

The idea of woman as a different type of technical innovator or scientific helpmate is consonant with David Noble's historical survey of how the early monastic roots of science defined it as a world without women. In *Bringing up Baby* (Dir. Howard Hawks, 1938), Katharine Hepburn portrays Susan Vance, a scatterbrained heiress whose attentions to the paleontologist Dr. David Huxley (Cary Grant) drive him crazy. Huxley almost loses funding and in the film's conclusion suffers the indignity of witnessing Susan's demolition of the dinosaur skeleton he has laboriously pieced together. *Bringing up Baby* depicts a male scientist who endures a love interest, a woman who is not a scientist.[43] Less flaky than Susan and identifying with science, Hepburn's characters Cynthia Darrington and Jamie Jamieson contribute to scientific experiments in self-sacrificing, erratic, and non-specific ways. *Christopher Strong* and *Without Love* outline in dramatic and comic form the tension that makes combining relationships with work a top concern of women scientists.[44] As the previous chapter shows, science and romance are inextricably connected in modern films reflecting the persistence of traditional models of womanhood and the public understanding of science as a somewhat magical process.

Women and Computing Technology in Hollywood Films

A number of 1990s Hollywood films focus on women who employ techno-logical means to resolve romances.[45] In *Sleepless in Seattle* (Dir. Nora Ephron, 1993), Meg Ryan's character figures out (by using a desktop computer equipped with Internet access and fax capabilities) how to approach the widower whose poignant appeal for female company reached millions of radio listeners. Effi-ciently researching the history of Tom Hanks's character and jetting off to see her subject, Ryan electronically finds her man to pursue a romance that would have otherwise eluded her.[46] Nora Ephron's film wittily persuades com-puter-literate viewers that appropriating technologies such as radio, film, and computing enables romance in the Information Age. Bringing together giz-mos and old-fashioned sentiment, *Sleepless in Seattle*'s plot unites two people who appreciate technologies bridging what the continent divides; when Tom Hanks's and Meg Ryan's characters meet at the Empire State Building, they configure the romantic quest narrative as a story of how technology assists women and men in finding true love. Adapting Leo Carey's *The Shop around the Corner* (1940), Ephron's *You've Got Mail* (1998) structures another plot of technology-assisted romance for Ryan and Hanks, who play rival bookstore owners engaged in anonymous email correspondence.

Technologies of electronic communication described in *Desk Set, Disclo-sure,* and *The Net* more ominously represent conventions of romance and pro-fessional roles for women. The romance described in *Desk Set* permits women's work at the cost of stereotyping men, women, and marriage. Intent on describ-ing a culture of sexual harassment as a "virtual reality," *Disclosure* tells how a happily married man resists becoming a pawn in a executive power play engineered by his beautiful boss, an ex-girlfriend determined to rise to the top of a high-tech communication company. The predatory electronic stalking endured by the protagonist of *The Net* becomes a gendered nightmare embed-ded with references to AIDS and other sexually transmitted diseases. These films describe a chapter in twentieth-century women's history that has been elided until recently: the enabling and constraining of individual women and women's networks in relation to technological developments in computing.

Nora Ephron's parents, screenwriters Henry and Phoebe Ephron, intro-duced the subject of how computing technology encourages romantic pos-sibilities in the Hollywood comedy *Desk Set* (Dir. Walter Lang, 1957). The film's plot turns on two questions: will the new electronic brain personified as Emmy Emerac replace "the girls," the female researchers who provide answers to all sorts of questions raised at the Federal Broadcasting Network? And will the computer expert Richard Sumner (Spencer Tracy) displace the network honcho (Gig Young) who has kept the director of reference, Bunny Watson (Katharine Hepburn), on a string, romantically and professionally, for seven years? Young's character (a handsome and charming executive who comes and goes as he pleases) rises through the corporate hierarchy largely assisted by the intelligent and efficient Bunny. Because the head reference librarian meets the intellectual challenges provided by the eminently respected Richard Sumner, Ph.D., the viewer appreciates the value assigned to Bunny and her affections. We know that her sincerity, warmth, and quick intelligence must be matched in her partner, so we accept that she will be won over by the bumbling computer expert who engenders, nurtures, and admires the electronic brain.

Desk Set is affectionately dedicated with gratitude to IBM, for the audience's admiration for Bunny's virtues is meant to be matched by our amazement regarding the computer's capabilities. Hepburn acts the part of a modern working woman who is clever enough to match wits with the father of the electronic brain and with the brain itself. Bunny parries verbally with the efficiency expert and computer inventor Sumner, who realizes that Bunny's intelligence marks her as a "very rare tropical bird." A modern romance, the film resolves questions of employment and love in working magic between the two principals: Bunny learns to love both Richard Sumner and his creation, the machine made out to be her archrival, Emmy Emerac.

EMERAC, Electro Magnetic Research and Authorizing Calculator, is a fictional version of the historical ENIAC (Electronic Numerical Integrator and Calculator), the calculating computer that changed the way humans could perform tasks and the way that work associated with computing was perceived. *Desk Set* images electronic calculation by Emmy as a faster, more efficient, more accurate version of the research performed by the notable quartet of reference librarians headed by Hepburn.

These competent women await news of whether their jobs will disappear, offering a sympathetic portrait of American female labor—last to be hired, first to be fired in competitive industries. Judy Wajcman describes their predicament:

> [T]he very first computer programmers were women. Between 1940 and 1950, many women were engaged in programming, coding, or working as machine operators. Again it was due to the exigencies of war that women were recruited by the military into both civilian and military positions to work as trained mathematicians to calculate firing tables by hand for rockets and artillery

shells. When ENIAC (Electronic Numerical Integrator and Calculator), the first operational computer, was built in the United States in the early forties, these women were assigned to programme it and became known as the "ENIAC girls" (Kraft, 1979, p. 141). It was because programming was initially viewed as tedious clerical work of low status that it was assigned to women. As the complex skills and value of programming were increasingly recognized, it came to be considered creative, intellectual and demanding "men's work."[47]

Desk Set represents the battle between machine and human worker as a conflict between masculinist devotion to business economy versus the kinder, gentler world of feminine workers who share information and sympathy, but the devil is the machine and not the man who made her.

In blending two plots—romance and mystery—*Desk Set* proposes that instead of losing jobs to male coworkers, women lose jobs to computers imaged as female. Both the romantic plot concerning the rivalry between the computer expert and the network executive for Hepburn's affection and the mystery plot of what changes the computer will bring to this workplace are structured as narratives of competition, maintaining our interest by posing the question, "Will the worthy emerge victorious?" Bunny Watson wins a professional battle in proving that a reference librarian's skills can be superior to the calculating abilities of the computer, arguing that the computer should be a useful adjunct to and not a replacement for such "women's work."

But the film ends on a troubling note after Bunny agrees to marry Sumner, thereby competing with Emmy at home and at work. The viewer recognizes a potential problem: although the computer expert displays moral and intellectual superiority when compared with the glib executive who exploited Bunny, EMERAC's inventor reveals in the final scene, by repairing Emmy while romancing Bunny, that he will always "love" the computer as much as or more than Bunny. *Desk Set* characterizes Bunny as a more competent analyst than the boyfriend who counts on her to review his financial reports, as intelligent as the male Ph.D. who invented the electronic brain, and as attractive as any other woman represented, but the film offers a startling conclusion regarding technological advancement in illustrating how women should accept their place behind the machine for the greater good of society. While Bunny does not fear the computer, she appears an intuitive intelligence rather than a calculating intelligence like Emmy, who takes over rote office functions. As an ironic reward, Bunny marries the absent-minded inventor; together they will "parent" a computer, transforming Bunny from an independent career woman into a wife, mother, and adjunct to a machine.

Michael Crichton's novel *Disclosure* (1993), and the film (Dir. Barry Levinson, 1994) based on it, argue that while there is everything to be gained in promoting women according to merit, everyone will suffer if diversity counts more than technical competence in the workplace. Although differences exist between the fictional and film narratives, both texts draw on contemporary anxieties about technological merit and affirmative action to depict the dangerous reach of sexual harassment claims in high-tech companies. The film narrative calls into question the validity of gender stereotyping by describing Tom Sanders (Michael Douglas) as a successful male executive who is also a nurturing father and sensitive husband. Yet *Disclosure* is no friend to feminism, for it represents the working woman as too eager to gain power in her professions by sacrificing integrity, romance, and personal relationships.

Sanders's professional rival and former girlfriend, Meredith Johnson (Demi Moore), presents the film's most egregious example of female ambition gone awry. Johnson devours males assistants and coworkers, lies to employers and business colleagues, and rationalizes all unethical behavior as necessary if a woman is to succeed in a man's world. Following stereotype, Johnson's technical understanding is limited, so she relies on other abilities, most notably playing up her physical resemblance to the boss's deceased daughter to rise in the corporate hierarchy. An unfortunate caricature of a young woman drunk with power who is willing to commit any act to succeed, Johnson is compared by Sanders's attorney Louise Fernandez to the sterotypically arrogant male who abuses power for personal ambition.

The film highlights Johnson's malicious plot to undo Sanders's reputation as a technologically skilled and communicative production manager. Johnson's scheme depends upon her manipulating others into believing that her managerial competence outshines Sanders'; therefore, she must convince others to accept her lie that Sanders propositioned her during a late-night meeting. Sanders's colleagues, bosses, and business associates unwittingly support Johnson when she begins her campaign of deceit, but Sanders fights her accusation with every means open to him. As someone who masters technology as skillfully as Johnson manipulates people, Sanders produces an answering machine tape inadvertently recorded by his cellular phone during the meeting with Johnson, a piece of evidence that substantiates his account of events and documents his innocence. Tipped off by an anonymous email spy within the corporation that Johnson's harassment charges were a smokescreen for her devious financial scheme, Sanders accesses his company's newly developed virtual-reality archive of taped video conversations and other corporate correspondence and relies on his extensive company contacts to figure out that Johnson meddled in his division's Malaysian product line to prove her reputation as a cost-cutting genius and to diminish others' perceptions of Sanders' technical abilities.

Disclosure makes an effort to represent men and women who are not power-hungry as being more reasonable about sexual and gender issues than those who are on the make, professionally and sexually. Crichton can't resist adding an epilogue to his book punishing those who did not support Sanders by slapping harassment suits on them. The book also demonstrates how corporations reward unethical executives: Johnson gets an assignment in Paris and nets an ambassador as a husband, while the sleazy counsel who supported her schemes and sold out Sanders becomes head of the ethics committee for the California bar. *Disclosure* acknowledges that feminism has improved women's chances for professional advancement and created a domestic world where men share responsibility with women, but the novel and the film question whether we are asking too much if we expect female influence always to be an improvement. Sometimes, Crichton argues, a woman like Meredith Johnson uses being a female in a man's world as an excuse to compensate for her lack of technical understanding and social values.

Disclosure offers portraits of intelligent, competent, and kind female executives in the information technology industry who demonstrate that Johnson is an aberration, but all women in the novel and film are represented as less technologically savvy than the male characters. Sanders does not get promoted at the end of the film; instead, his guardian angel, Stephanie Kaplan, the chief financial officer who anonymously assisted his research on Johnson, is promoted on merit, that is, her financial acumen. Her loyalty to the company and her personal regard for Tom Sanders motivate her to sneak information to him via Internet email, but the reader understands that her son's supportive technical ability and access have made this mode of communication possible. Like other women in *Disclosure,* including Louise Fernandez, the otherwise competent attorney who is wowed by virtual-reality technology, and Mary Anne Hunter, the marketing executive who can barely use email, Kaplan uses computer technology without being in charge of it. Only Sanders heroically manages the machine.

Anxieties about how much an electronic machine might control human lives dominate the 1995 film *The Net,* starring Sandra Bullock as Angela Bennett. Bullock plays a plucky but ordinary young woman who overcomes every obstacle placed in her path, a role she also plays in the *Speed* films (1994, 1997) and *When You Were Sleeping* (1995). A beta tester for a software company, Angela stumbles on a lethally simple computer virus and an international plot to dismantle governmental and industrial databases. Many scenes in *The Net* are devoted to the chase as the cyberterrorists hunt down Angela in an airport, on the beach at a Mexican resort, at sea in a small boat, in the streets of Venice, in a speeding car on a California highway, amidst the labyrinthine partitions of the software firm, at a computer show in the Moscone Center, and in the streets of San Francisco during an AIDS protest.

The most suspenseful scenes in the film depict the technological search for

Angela Bennett and her concomitant research on the Praetorians whose nefarious computing program destroys an important bureaucrat, erases computer records of Angela's identity, and attacks a number of government databases. The cyberterrorists and the beta tester each access the Internet to determine what the other knows. The ideology backing up the cyberterrorists' plot—to hack into databases of the New York Stock Exchange and water and power authorities, the Los Angeles Airport, and confidential government medical records—is not well-established in the film. Rather, the viewer's attention is meant to engage quite specifically with the threat against Angela: her identity—as it can be determined by the police, the U.S. consulate in Mexico, and her employer—is changed without her knowledge. She recognizes several times in her agonizing adventure that it was easy for some hackers to figure out her personality profile (e.g., her likes and dislikes, including her predilections for Gibsons and pizzas); the extent of her personal property; her family responsibilities (she supports her mother, who has Alzheimer's disease and lives in a nursing home); and her schedule, in order to steal her assets and to replace these details of her life with more lurid, criminal "facts." A new name, arrest and property records, and family history are easily invented by the cybervillain, who accesses police records while chasing her. That this maniac made love to her during her vacation in Mexico insidiously connects technology and romance.

Angela heroically uses her technical expertise to elude being killed and to regain her identity. While she makes occasional attempts to supplement her knowledge by consulting with males, she relies on her expert understanding of computer technology honed by many hours of computer work. Angela seems like a mousy computer nerd (a "key-presser") in the first twenty minutes of film, but she becomes a heroic Internet surfer and a clever fugitive in response to the Praetorian threat.[48] Managing to eject the faux Angela and other employees of the software company by creating a false fire alarm in her workplace, Angela searches out Praetorian computer files to link the cyberconspiracy to the respected Gatekeeper computer security company. She sends the FBI evidence of Praetorian and Gatekeeper crimes, erases her spurious identity and revives her true one, and destroys the Praetorian and Gatekeeper files, all while fending off her attacker. The Net characterizes Angela as an action-adventure heroine who kills her former lover and stalker with a fire extinguisher and fixes databases to recuperate her law-abiding, property-owning identity.

The last scene of the film illustrates a tranquil vision of domesticity detailing how a woman should use computer technology to nurture her family. Angela moved her mother from the nursing home and installed her in the Venice cottage, now made inviting and comfortable. Instead of facing her computer terminal, Angela works at home while watching her mother plant flowers in the garden. The Net installs an image of woman acting as computer guru for the sake of self and mother; Angela's self-reliance and ability to care adequately for her parent support each other. The new domestic setting is startlingly attractive: a lovely, light-filled space functioning as both workplace and hospice, allowing Angela to maintain a healthy relationship her mother and see what is happening in the world around her. Yet marriage and children are missing, perhaps implying that a working computer expert can bear only so much domesticity.

Feminist Design of Technology

Feminine and feminist uses of technology are more often depicted in popular fictions, especially science fiction, rather than high culture narratives.[49] *Eve of Destruction* (Dir. Duncan Gibbins, 1991) and *Making Mr. Right* (Dir. Susan Seidelman, 1987) employ narrative conventions associating science with self-aggrandizement, ambition, and aggression, traits identified with men, while suggesting that in some near future, feminist scientists, or perhaps even feminists who are not scientifically trained, might have more beneficial influence on science and its resulting technological products. These narratives describe the capacities of two female characters, one a scientist and one not, to develop experimental technologies designed to improve human life. Both films depict robots created or deployed by women and both incorporate cultural stereotypes describing women's work in masculine domains of science and technology, stereotypes familiar to anthropologists and sociologists who study universities and corporations.[50]

Suggesting thematically that women's participation changes how technologies are created, deployed, and understood, *Eve of Destruction* and *Making Mr. Right* hint at future success for the incorporation of feminist practices. In terms of characterization and emplotment, the films explore how cyborgs blend human and artificial elements and outline how women's contributions to technologies reconfigure technological processes and products for social good. These films rely on cultural stereotypes of gender in depicting masculine and feminine engagement with technology, specifically in representing the design of the cyborg and its social relations with the humans around it. Although the tropes of destruction and creation incorporated in the films' titles indicate different genres (thriller and romance), both films establish women as less able than men to control technologies, even those designed by women. *Eve's* research scientist is punished for tweaking robotic technology, and *Mr. Right's* marketing consultant is rewarded for humanizing the robot; yet in both cases, the processes of developing and deploying technology are seen as residing outside feminine authority, for cyborgs are neutralized or empowered beyond the control of these female characters.

With roots in Western European fantasies of monsters, the cyborg has been theorized by Donna Haraway and characterized in a variety of popular films and fictions, most notably Ridley Scott's *Blade Runner* (1982), William Gibson's *Neuromancer* (1984), and Marge Piercy's *He, She, and It* (1993). Creating the cyberpunk genre, Gibson's and Scott's characters meld human and machine in dark worlds fraught with ambiguity and danger; both *Neuromancer* and *Blade Runner* describe a future full of high-tech gadgets resistant to human sympathy. Piercy's feminist science fiction novel more optimistically parallels two characters: an early modern figure of a golem created to protect a Jewish community in seventeenth-century Prague and a futuristic man-machine designed to protect a modern liberal enclave battling corporate hegemony in the twenty-first century. In the latter plot, two scientists, one male and one female, collaborate to create the robot Yod, whose capacities blend superior defense skills and sensitivity.[51] Yod becomes the paramour of a female artificial intelligence researcher (Shira Shipman) before he is sacrificed by his creators, just as his historical predecessor, the golem Joseph, is also destroyed. Piercy's novel concludes after Shira accepts that it was wrong to send Yod, a human-like machine, to his death to protect others and that she should therefore give up any hope of replacing him.

Instead of eschewing cyborg technology, Haraway takes a different position from that of Piercy's scientists in claiming that it is impossible to limit cybernetic experimentation, for it is already inextricably embodied in us and embedded in our notions of what it means to be human at the present time. Defining cyborg as "a cybernetic organism, a hybrid of machine and organism, a creature of social reality as well as a creature of fiction," "A Cyborg Manifesto" (1985, 1991) testifies to "an ironic political myth faithful to feminism, socialism, and materialism."[52] Haraway asserts, "By the late twentieth century, our time, a mythic time, we are all chimeras, theorized and fabricated hybrids of machine and organism; in short, we are all cyborgs. The cyborg is our ontology; it gives us our politics. The cyborg is a condensed image of both imagination and material reality, the two joined centers structuring any possibility of historical transformation" (435). Arguing that technology and imagination structure cultural ideas of human identity, she analyzes principles with a long history in feminist science and technology studies.[53]

Hollywood movies represent the feminine influence on science and technology as an ethical perspective and often as a feminist project intended to thwart the corrupt evils of capitalism. For example, the popular cartoon character Inspector Gadget appeared in a 1999 live-action film as a robot created by Brenda, a female scientist who supplied a heroic police officer with new body parts.[54] Brenda suggests that technological reasons for experimenting with cyborgs are insufficient, unethical, and cruel in their outcomes, an argument that the film sets within the gendered conflict between scientists: feminine ideas about scientific practice and the purposes of technology are represented as humane, in being empathetic to individuals and ethically designed for the public good, and opposed to the arrogant, selfish, profiteering pursuit of knowledge and the exploitation of a weapons technology fostered by masculine science.

In Piercy's *He, She, and It*, female scientists Malkah and Shira Shipman shape the cyborg to incorporate sensitivity and social empathy. Personality traits representing the essentially feminine, including being kind, caring, nurturing, and nonviolent, enhance the socioethical capacities of the cyborg or alien while diminishing the physical stature and cultural capital of the creature (think of the robot on *Red Dwarf* or Mr. Spock on *Star Trek*). Whether motivated by romance or morality, female scientists appear more woman than scientist in many films.

Acknowledging feminist styles of scientific and technological inquiry, these cinematic narratives resist radical reconfigurations to retreat into comfortable gendered stereotypes that put women at the margins or outside the realms of science and technology. Describing how a female robot powerfully reacts against the sexism directed toward her creator and other women, *Eve of Destruction* reconfigures the Frankenstein plot as a tale of a female scientist (played by Renée Soutendijk) balancing work and family. Dr. Simmons replicates herself in developing a military weapon in human shape, a robot named Eve VIII. Eve VIII has been designed to incorporate many human physical and mental characteristics so that she can exercise careful judgment in functioning as an undercover cybercop: she can comment on the quality of fine tailoring and can assess how much force to apply depending on circumstances. The story of a motherless female scientist who re-creates herself in machine form to overcome patriarchal oppression, *Eve of Destruction* empowers its female protagonists by technological, rather than romantic, means, but it is not a strictly feminist story. Alluding to Philippe Auguste Villiers de L'Isle-Adam's *L'Eve future* (1886), Eve VIII remains the locus of male desire designed to serve as a mechanically perfect helpmate, albeit one to fulfill military rather than domestic needs. The story of its deployment exemplifies the oppression of women in a patriarchal environment.[55]

The robot Eve physically and emotionally resembles her attractive scientist creator, for her creator's history has been embedded in her circuitry. Because Eve VIII shares Dr. Simmons's memories of pain and pleasure, the robot reacts to situations as the scientist would: becoming angry when sexually harassed and irritated when someone interferes with family time with "her" son. The robot also exhibits concern for an injured colleague and indulges in tender maternal impulses in looking for Dr. Simmons's son. The doctor represses her emotions and desires and resists any possible radical actions, but there is no check on the robot, which has no off switch, as the military operative authorized by the Pentagon to find and neutralize Eve VIII remarks.

Recruited to destroy what Dr. Simmons has created, her ally McQuade appears a no-nonsense, cynical, and bluntly spoken consultant who reveals his suspicions about elitist scientists, especially female ones. It is ambiguous whether the filmmakers deliberately link McQuade's forthrightness to ethnicity: because the African-American actor Gregory Hines plays the part, racial stereotypes are both replicated and resisted. McQuade appears a consummate professional with expertise in military operations, but his hair-trigger temper and his tendency to make profane remarks flare frequently during the time he and the doctor chase the robot. While Dr. Simmons is restrained and rational, McQuade is explosively angry about the crisis her research and her repressed personality have created. The film strains to depict how their temperaments influence and complement each other. Without looking closely at McQuade's psychology, the narrative acknowledges his distrust of science, authority figures, and women, a combination of feelings that suggests a conflict with a mother figure rather than developing an argument linking his talents to his race or personality.

Only woman's flawed psyche is dissected here, for, as Dr. Simmons quickly recognizes, Eve VIII is on a mission to rectify the scientist's past by actively confronting abuses she has endured at the hands of a drunken parent, a hostile boss, and an aggressive lover. Eve VIII strikes with deadly force against those who harmed Dr. Eve Simmons and anyone seeking to restrain the robot or those around her. Relying on the movie psychology of Alfred Hitchcock's *Marnie* (1964), the film employs flashbacks to Dr. Simmons's childhood as a basis for the robot's violent actions. At root in Eve VIII's consciousness is the traumatic memory of young Eve witnessing her drunken father causing her mother's death by accidentally pushing her into the path of car. The robot hunts down Dr. Simmons's father, who has been living under an assumed name and seeks to kill him, but he is saved because Dr. Simmons distracts the robot. The robot's next mission, to spend more time with the doctor's son Timmy, threatens the boy and his father.

Eve VIII's apocalyptic capabilities provide a suspenseful, although long-winded, climax to the film. As the twenty-four-hour clock is about to end the robot's campaign of violence by exploding her and anyone in her vicinity, McQuade and Dr. Simmons follow Eve VIII and her hostage Timmy in the New York City subway. McQuade fires a shot into the robot's left eye but only disables the robot before being injured himself. Recognizing that he must rely on the doctor to complete the task of eliminating Eve VIII, McQuade throws his gun to Dr. Simmons. Although she has avoided violence through most of the movie, she takes up the challenge of destroying the robot to protect her son. But it takes more than a gun to stop Eve VIII. The chase ends only after Dr. Simmons strikes the robot with deadly force, sticking a knife into its vulnerable area, her right eye. The film's narrative logic dictates that the robot can be eliminated only after its creator releases her repressed anger. Although it might appear that the doctor confronts a no-win scenario in choosing between the robotic version of herself, a technical creation, and her son, her biological issue, the film presents the female scientist as an excessively intellectual and technologically minded woman who must become more typically feminine to succeed. Like Piercy's fictional scientist Shira Shipman who sacrifices love and research to protect her community, Dr. Simmons destroys her technological creation to save New York and prevent an apocalypse. She is redeemed by her psychological breakthrough, although her research project must be sacrificed. The film's message reminds us that it is better to be a nurturing mother than an innovative inventor.

Acting on her creator's repressed anger, Eve VIII triggers male fears of Julia Kristeva's phallic woman and, therefore, within the film's worldview must be eliminated.[56] Destroying Eve VIII protects Eve's son and the world and allows Dr. Simmons to keep up her end of the government contract, but she has transformed herself into a vigilante using any weapon to protect the citizenry. This outcome questions whether women should engage in masculine ways with technology. The transformation of the female scientist from intellectual to action hero depends on her acting out of revenge, a stereotype associated with the female psyche, as noted in chapter 3. *Eve of Destruction* hints at a future feminist technoscience in offering the possibility of an attractive cybercop designed by a woman to defuse situations without violence, while emplotting Eve VIII's development, deployment, and destruction as the near-apocalyptic end for humanity. The robot's animation must be reversed for the world to return to a stable state; the robot is a weapon motivated by uncontrollable female rage, which ends up "a bloody mass," as typically occurs in war fantasies of violence visited upon women.[57]

Not all film androids are lethal or feared as Eve VIII. Humorously considering that a male robot might, like Frankenstein's creature at points in Shelley's novel, have a more sympathetic and humane temperament than its creator, Susan Seidelman's *Making Mr. Right* describes how a female public relations specialist is hired to teach social skills and graces to a male robot so that he might be made more endearing to the public. The private corporation Chem-Tec has developed Ulysses to perform jobs deemed hazardous for humans, such as working with explosives and going into space for long periods. When government research funds for Ulysses are threatened, the company hires

Frankie Stone (Ann Magnuson) to promote its technology to the public, which can influence the distribution of funding.

Despite her masculinized name, Frankie represents the feminine social world that must be brought into conjunction with the technological product promoted by ChemTec. She teaches the robot how to be human, learning in the process that she loves Ulysses because he is everything the uptight, obnoxious male scientist who created him is not. Although she and other single women represented in the film cannot find the right men to date, Frankie recognizes that Ulysses is more sincere, humane, and tender than his inventor Dr. Peters and the flesh-and-blood men who pursue her, such as the unctuous Dr. Ramdas and her on-again, off-again philandering politico boyfriend. While Frankie's attitudes advance the romance plot, her flaky feminine style and outrageousness conflict with the boring, stable rationality expressed by the human males, who are scientific and political authorities despite their personality flaws.

Chief Robotic Engineer Jeff Peters built Ulysses (both roles are played by John Malkovich) in his own image, even giving the robot a penis so that he would have "confidence," an elusive characteristic for women in scientific and technical fields, as social scientists document.[58] Dr. Peters barely condescends to speak with Frankie, resenting her attempts to humanize the mental, emotional, and social capacities of the android because the scientist fears that the robot he designed to live independently will be spoiled by socialization lessons. Dr. Peters scoffs at Frankie's work and criticizes her for living in "an emotional swamp" and for dragging Ulysses into that morass. That the android is a child open to new experiences is a conceit allowing Frankie to introduce him to society, including her friends. Ulysses reacts enthusiastically to all opportunities, including escaping from the lab. In one day he shops for a tuxedo with Frankie at a mall, dates the woman employee who has chased Dr. Peters, and has sex with Frankie's best friend Trish (Glenne Headly). While all three women express pleasure from their encounters with him, Trish's praise rings loudest: "He was so loving! So compassionate! So understanding of a woman's heart!" Even after she finds out he is an android, she is eager to repeat their sexual encounter.

In *Making Mr. Right*, the male scientist is the least likable character: his single-minded devotion to work and his refusal to recognize the value of human relationships and feelings make him a failure as a human being and a difficult employee and coworker. Dr. Peters resents any human interaction as wasting time that should be devoted to science, specifically, working on his technological achievement; in contrast, that technology, Ulysses, is kind, generous, and romantic. Creator and creation change places in the film: the scientist becomes more robot-like and the robot becomes more human in inverse proportion as the romance plot progresses. The male scientist's knowledge is represented in the film as narrowly conceived to achieve a place in the scientific pantheon, while Frankie's relationship with Ulysses limns how her knowledge of human relations benefits society by enhancing romance. Sending Dr. Peters into space and permitting Ulysses to stay on earth with Frankie, the movie's plot neatly resolves Frankie's romantic problems and the robot's search for a female companion. The conclusion of Seidelman's film wryly represents technological innovations as having great consequences for humanity and the individual rather than expanding scientific and technical knowledge. *Making Mr. Right* suggests that if scientific experimentation and technological innovations could be directed toward stereotypically feminine outcomes of helping others, the world might be a better place for most men and women. By sending the uptight Dr. Peters into space, the film suggests that scientific initiative to find new knowledge has its limits on earth: the scientist is a loner who eagerly undertakes a journey through the cosmos, and society prefers humanized technological products to the overly rational technoscientists who create them.

Characterizations employing stereotypical attributes of men, women, robots, and technoscientists in both films construct plots related to masculine fears about feminine power. Science and technology appear overwhelmed by feminine desires: Dr. Eve Simmons's repression and Frankie's passion supersede their respective capacities to design and evaluate innovative robots. Male experts, particularly those using scientific and technical tools and weapons, are interested in vaunting technological expertise to gain professional prestige and social approval, while female experts pursue technologies to achieve personal fulfillment and improve the world. As feminist scholars of technoscience note, girls and women often express that social interests and concerns inspire them to study and practice science and technology.[59]

Eve of Destruction and *Making Mr. Right* propose that distinguishing too carefully between human and machine is a failed endeavor, hinting that scientific interest in artificial intelligence and robotics is intertwined, perhaps in inappropriate ways, with meditating on the limits of being human. *Making Mr. Right* entertainingly represents what happens when a female publicist falls in love with an android destined to be sent into space, reconfiguring the traditional romance narrative as a story of a woman and a man-machine. While Seidelman's film suggests that robots can be better humans than their creators, *Eve of Destruction* describes what happens when a cyborg military weapon created by a woman for ostensibly peaceful purposes acts all too humanly in wreaking vengeance on the world.

Feminist values about science are represented as unconventional and somewhat threatening in these films: Dr. Simmons and Frankie recognize their iconoclasm as their projects overturn traditional (i.e., masculine) approaches to robotics and artificial intelligence. Dr. Simmons is the only woman working on the military's robotics program; her work on the peacemaker cyborg resembles Frankie's attempt to humanize the android designed to work in dangerous occupations. These films suggest that feminist values in scientific and technological enterprises will produce kinder, gentler, and therefore better, products; the feminist impulse submerged in both films suggests that public understanding and appreciation of science will increase if scientists and technologists work to improve the human condition rather than extend abstract knowledge or invent new technologies to accomplish military or corporate goals. The films discern different prospects regarding feminine influences on what are depicted as masculine domains of science and technology. *Eve's* dark pessimism about the inevitable failure of the peacemaker android contrasts with *Mr. Right's* bright optimism that cyborgs can engage in satisfying relationships with humans.

Resisting explicit feminist reconfiguration of scientific experiments and technological outcomes, these films rely on common stereotypes about male and female attitudes toward love and work. The narratives indicate that love and work are transformed by technoscience rather than transforming of it. Suggesting that cyborgs resist gender stereotypes, imaging the robot Eve as a more effective military operative than McQuade and Ulysses as a more tender lover than Dr. Peters, the films show how technology sometimes transcends gender stereotypes even if humans cannot.

But gender stereotypes also persist. *Eve of Destruction* represents a robot as a weapon tweaked by the female scientist to be a peace officer, but the robot's circuits revert to relying on stereotypically feminine motives (revenge because of abuse) in stereotypically masculine style (using guns to destroy enemies). *Making Mr. Right* outlines how feminine characteristics associated with nurturing cause a male android to become more human. Both films represent women as contributing feminine instinct and insight to a traditionally male purview to reinforce traditional roles assigned to men and women: *Eve of Destruction* criticizes the woman scientist whose repressed anger becomes her greatest personal contribution to her cyborg creation, while *Making Mr. Right* rewards the publicist for acting on her emotions and enabling the android to act on his. The films differ most in their responses to the question of what science has accomplished in creating a robot that is as human-like as possible, representing our fears of a violent, angry female cyborg and our desires for a loving male cyborg.

Referencing *Frankenstein* and *The Future Eve*, *Eve of Destruction* and *Making Mr. Right* also update the Ovidian myth of Pygmalion and Galatea in which the inanimate female statue comes alive. The artistic act of creating artificial life is represented as technological hubris in *Eve of Destruction* and *Making Mr. Right,* for male and female scientists in these narratives engage with technology from transgressive motivations: to fulfill personal desires rather than social needs. As Hillis Miller has observed, "Ovid's stories show that you always get some form of what you want, but you get it in ways that reveal what is illicit or grotesque in what you want."[60] Transgressive characters in Ovid's *Metamorphoses* end up in a state of limbo, between life and death, according to Hillis Miller: "a memorial example still present within the human community. . . . a sign that his or her fault has not been completely punished or expiated" (2). Galatea's transformation from inanimate to animate object reverses the typical transformation represented in Ovid's stories and is referenced in contrasting ways by the robots Eve and Ulysses, for their animation signifies tragic destruction in the former and romantic fulfillment in the latter.

The plots of *Eve of Destruction* and *Making Mr. Right* represent conflicts between masculine and feminine views of technoscience without resolving them. By incorporating emotional, ethical, and other social concerns in their work, Dr. Simmons and Frankie Stone offer approaches to the scientific development of technology that differ substantially from those of their male colleagues. Science and its technological applications associated with female characters appear within the films as more sympathetic and humane in their outcomes than scientific ideas and technologies in earlier literature. But the efforts of Eve and Frankie to change the larger dimensions of scientific method and practice and to develop technologies incorporating feminist principles and addressing issues of social justice are not extensively treated in the films, which remain constrained in presenting the mostly masculine, somewhat hostile environments of science and technology in the fantastic realm of science fiction. Yet, in an age when technologies such as computers and appliances with electronic chips are marketed specifically to women, and more women continue to study and practice in scientific and technological professions, viewers can hope that even the mildly feminist messages about technoscience suggested by *Eve of Destruction* and *Making Mr. Right* might inspire new cultural and film scripts representing a powerful conjunction of feminism and technology.

Conclusion
CHILDREN'S NARRATIVES

What influences children's and students' perceptions of science and technology? Paula Rayman and Belle Brett note that "social-psychological issues such as self-confidence, perceived ability, and resiliency" are linked to "female persistence in science,"[1] arguing that institutional and cultural perspectives outweigh social-psychological factors and pointing to "structural barriers . . . [that] include informal and formal exclusion: biased admission practices at graduate school, lack of opportunities for training and research, and isolation from professional and collegial networks" (390). Mary Frank Fox, Gerhard Sonnert, and Irina Nikiforova agree that the institutional environment matters; they find university "programs that regard issues, problems, and solutions of women in science and engineering" to be "rooted in 'institutional/structural-centered,' as opposed to 'individual/student-centered' perspectives are associated with the most positive outcomes in undergraduate degrees awarded to women in science and engineering."[2]

Parents, teachers, peers, involvement in STEM activities, perceptions of intrinsic value,[3] and media stereotypes affect girls' interest in STEM fields.[4] Welcoming, unbiased classroom environments and mentoring are also key.[5] Teachers are important cultural agents who can encourage students to persist in (or leave) STEM disciplines. Liz Whitelegg asserts, "Teachers need to recognize that they themselves are powerful agents of socialization, who also bring their own culturally acquired perspectives with them."[6] M. Gail Jones, Ann Howe, and Melissa J. Rua agree: "Our findings, as well as data from many other sources, are clear in their implication. Teachers cannot escape the responsibility to present science as equally appropriate for girls and boys, to expect girls to use the tools of science with facility, and to expect both boys and girls to engage thoughtfully in science activities."[7] "Female-friendly" pedagogies, which are often interactive, assist boys and girls, encourage participation in the classroom, and help determine future interest in STEM.

More girls now choose STEM courses and majors, and there is a smaller achievement gap between girls and boys in mathematics, partly due to increased curricular and extracurricular STEM opportunities for middle school and high school students. Yet, as a 2008 *Science* report indicates, "[s]tereotypes persist and are widely held by parents and teachers," and "[s]tandardized tests in the U.S. indicate girls now score just as well as boys in math."[8] Media representations of scientific careers that incorporate gendered stereotypes influence adult and student perceptions of who can become a scientist.

Asserting that popular culture media too often identify women as sex objects, psychologist Mary Pipher recommends that parents track what their daughters view.[9] She argues in *Reviving Ophelia*, "Protective space can be created by books, interests, families, churches and physical or social isolation. . . . Girls who grow up unprotected, adrift in mass culture with little protective coating and no private territory are vulnerable to many kinds of problems" (267). Melissa Milkie interviewed women's magazine editors to ask "how femininity-defining cultural institutions operate to create and sustain gender stratification."[10] She argues, "A central way women's disadvantage is maintained is through cultural beliefs and stereotypes that provide narrower, more distorted, or more harmful images about women than about men" (839).

Jocelyn Steinke agrees that "[s]tereotypical representations of scientists and engineers in the mass media can influence girls' perceptions of scientific, engineering, and technological careers" and notes an "overall paucity of images of female scientists and engineers."[11] Jennifer Gray's meta-analysis of studies about science television programs asserts that "media mentoring" supplements institutional initiatives by providing positive media role models of women in STEM: "research indicates that the symbolic modeling of positive, non-stereotypical portrayals of women in television such as female scientists, engineers, and other such characters has the potential to expand the range of options young girls deem appropriate for their gender."[12] The analysis of media can also play a critical role in educating parents, teachers, and students to recalibrate cultural norms regarding STEM careers.

Collecting and analyzing media preferences of young people reveals differences that reflect gender norms. In 2000 Dafna Lemish, Tamar Liebes, and Vered Seidmann surveyed boys and girls in 11 European countries and Israel about their media access and interests. They found gendered media preferences in their study population, with girls more interested in music, television soap operas, and reading and boys more interested in computer games, particularly violent ones, and cartoons on television; girls expressed interest in narrative computer games rather than in shooter games preferred by boys.[13] But such preferences can shift based on consumer options: there is some hope that computer games and Web sites such as Webkinz and Club Penguin aimed at young children can decrease the gender gap in computing by presenting gender-neutral content and activities online. Both boys and girls also enjoy playing Nintendogs, a series of portable Nintendo games about caring for puppies.[14] Additionally, Wii Fit, Beatles Games, and Rock Band are games that have crossover appeal for both genders and for different generations.

Seeing more female scientists and technical experts in games, on television, and in films would provide children with role models. Empirical research on media representations of science conducted by the UK Resource Centre for Women in Science, Engineering and Technology indicates that many press officers and other science communicators point to the low proportion of senior researchers who are women as a primary reason why most scientific experts presented in newspapers and on television and radio are "male, grey-haired and of a certain age."[15]

Other testimony supports that hiring more women to write and produce media affects how gender, science, and technology are represented. Connecting the number of women employed in the 1990s as producers at the U.S. cable network Nickelodeon to the increased number of female characters on children's shows, Ellen Seiter and Vicki Mayer consider the question "Does the increased representation of girls follow simply from the increased employment of women?"[16] Their historical account of the cable provider Nickelodeon's 1990s programming identity and mission acknowledges that various forces encourage a diversity of representations on the network, concluding, "The largest gains have been made in increasing the representation and variety of female characters: here the ideological commitments of individuals working at Nickelodeon have dovetailed nicely with market trends toward taking girls more seriously as a media and advertising market" (132).

Ensuring diverse representations should be complemented by a concerted effort to push against prevailing gender stereotypes. Nancy Signorelli's 1997 study of U.S. media, including television, commercials, and teenage magazines, indicates that female characters were more likely than male to be depicted in media as "talking about romance rather than at a job," although women were portrayed as "using intelligence."[17] Characterizations and plots referencing science and technology often present scientific and technically adept females as socially marginalized.

Female characters engaging with science and technology and the plots they participate in influence readers and viewers, affecting perceptions of girls' and women's opportunities and performance in STEM. Marilee Long and collaborators studied 12 episodes from four reality series (48 total episodes) about science that were aimed at children, acknowledging "that children watching television may learn attitudes, values, and behaviors depicted on screen. . . . Research shows that children are more likely to identify with characters of the same sex, and they can form attachments to recurring characters."[18] Steinke and collaborators connect television portrayals of scientists with responses to the Draw-a-Scientist Test (DAST) provided by U.S. middle school students, who drew "a male scientist who looked like the mythic stereotype of the male scientist," an image they saw on television.[19] Research from the UK Resource Centre for Women in Science, Engineering and Technology on DAST reports that while most girls drew male scientists, some girls (13% of their sample of 45 students between ages 8 and 15) drew female scientists, and all boys drew male scientists.[20]

Fictional books, television series, and films for children illustrate role models, describe STEM careers and educational pathways, reference scientific and technical topics, and teach readers and viewers about sociocultural norms affecting women's participation and performance in STEM. Children's television shows, particularly fantasy animation shows featuring superheroes or otherwise ordinary children who perform superhuman deeds, discuss science and technology in ways that often intersect with gender.

Fictional live-action series and films sometimes include children and adolescents with scientific and technical interests and abilities. For example, *Sydney White* (Dir. Joe Nussbaum, 2007) updates certain gendered features of the Snow White story while retaining others to present Sydney (Amanda Bynes) as a technically adept, assertive college freshman defeating an evil sorority sister's revenge plot. Sydney's capability with carpentry tools, her sincerity, and her lack of elitism make her more popular on the college campus than anyone else. She becomes an inspirational agent of change who spearheads a movement to ensure that all students (and not just Greeks) benefit from campus funds.

This chapter considers different genres representing gendered aspects of science and technology: animations (*Handy Manny, Powerpuff Girls; Dexter's Lab; Jimmy Neutron, Boy Genius; SpongeBob Squarepants; My Life as a Teenage Robot*), live-action fiction and reality television shows (*H2O: Just Add Water, Zoey 101, iCarly, Ned's Declassified School Survival Guide, Design Squad*), two novels for adolescents (Mary Norton's *The Borrowers* and Madeleine L'Engle's *A Wrinkle in Time*), and a film, *Ice Princess*. These narratives portray females interested and adept in using science and technology, as plots and characterizations reproduce and revise stereotypes associating certain gendered traits with scientific and technical aptitude. Such texts might encourage girls and women to pursue STEM education and careers.

Girls' Coming of Age

Two twentieth-century juvenile literature fantasy fiction series describe female adolescents who confront cultural stereotypes about women, science, and technology. Developing technical acumen, these protagonists mature by learning to take care of their families. Arrietty Clock of *The Borrowers* (1952) takes up the traditionally male occupation of borrowing to help her aging parents while they live under the floorboards of a kitchen in a large country house.[21] (Borrowers are six-inch or so beings like humans who survive by taking what they need from humans.) In the sequel, *The Borrowers Afield* (1955), Arrietty meets up with a wild young male borrower, Spiller, who assists the Clocks when they escape to a field and helps Arrietty understand that her talents are significant.[22] Like Arrietty, who uses every bit of knowledge about the material world that she can muster to survive, Meg Murry in *A Wrinkle in Time* (1962) collaborates with her brother Charles Wallace and their friend Calvin O'Keefe to find the Murrys' father after he disappears under mysterious circumstances.[23] Charles and Calvin contribute to the project of bringing Mr. Murry back to his family, but only Meg can rescue Charles Wallace after he has been inadvertently left behind on a dark planet. She undertakes a similar effort in the sequel, *A Wind in the Door* (1973), when she battles demons who threaten him.[24] For these female protagonists, acting heroically means being courageous and summoning up all one's knowledge and understanding to protect oneself and family and friends.[25]

Arrietty and Meg exercise technical and scientific skills identified as masculine and feminine in their quests. Resisting social conventions, managing adolescent anxieties, and working to protect their families, these girls access technologies while relying on their love and compassion for others. They resist doing what they are told girls should do because social conventions conflict with the emergency measures required to resolve life-threatening crises. Arrietty's mother, Homily Clock, aspires to be a high-class borrower, driving her aging husband to attempt feats of derring-do to obtain specific items from their "host's" home. Homily's desire to have the right sort of carpet and china fuels her support of Arrietty's interest in borrowing; the mother insists that since they lack a son to take up borrowing, Pod Clock must train his daughter to take up this traditionally masculine profession. Homily lets Arrietty know that a young girl must demonstrate social decorum by acting and dressing appropriately, but the mother also tells the daughter to take care of herself and her parents, and the second dictum has priority. By the time the Clocks escape from the house to take refuge in a field, Arrietty inspires the more tentative Homily, who relies on her daughter's courage. Mother and daughter develop a closer relationship while they work together to find food and shelter, and Arrietty takes pride because she is able to follow her father's example as resourceful provider.

The fourteen-year-old Arrietty occasionally takes risks that her parents disapprove of and that she sometimes regret. On her first trek to borrow, Arrietty talks to the boy in the big house and does not tell her parents about this interaction, even though it is dangerous for all the Clocks because they could be exterminated by those who fear borrowers or exploited by those wishing to capitalize on their appearance. But her clever hunches also prevent catastrophe. In *The Borrowers,* her talking with the boy encourages him to deliver food and goods to the Clocks, until his pilferage raises the suspicions of the housekeeper. In *The Borrowers Afield,* Arrietty's friendship with Spiller brings meat and protection to the Clocks, whose abilities to steal items and fashion ingenious tools from their host's property have not prepared them for coping with wildlife or rural climate. In the natural landscape, Arrietty develops into a strong, brave young woman whose doubts and anxieties fade away as she exercises her pluck, energy, and ingenuity.

Modern science fiction narratives, *A Wrinkle in Time* and *A Wind in the Door* explore imaginative elaborations of scientific principles that involve extraterrestrial travel and mind-reading. L'Engle's characterizations of Murry family members acknowledge that Meg's personality traits—anger, stubbornness, and impatience—require moderation so that she can be happier and better protect her family. Meg's affection for her brother Charles, her growing friendship with the popular Calvin, and her admiration for her parents inspire her as she fights evil forces of the universe. Mr. Murry is a physicist, and Mrs. Murry a biologist whose home laboratory allows her to do cutting-edge research while cooking dinner (39). The Murrys' scientific research creates new knowledge but leads to Mr. Murry's imprisonment and threatens Charles Wallace, problems that Meg must resolve.

Like her parents, Meg thinks like a scientist. She is a gifted mathematician who recognizes faulty assumptions and resolves life-or-death situations. The two middle children in the Murry family, the twins Sandy and Dennys, are most interested in getting along with classmates and teachers at school and raising their vegetable garden to make money, but Meg and Charles Wallace reveal extraordinary abilities in mathematics and science that make them weird to their schoolmates and suspicious to the principal, Mr. Jenkins, and to their teachers. Like most adolescents, Meg feels that her family's eccentricities inspire and weigh her down in her dealings with others. Her father's absences from home, while he is ostensibly engaged in secret government research projects, cause her embarrassment as she explains to outsiders what her mother chooses not to—that the family is intact in its unique way. Although Meg admires her mother's intelligence and beauty, she recognizes that these excellent qualities cause others envy. Meg and her mother must protect the superior Charles Wallace from his peers, who would rather beat him up every day than get to know him, and from the life-threatening disease his mother discovers he has.

Meg learns that she need not sacrifice her strengths to protect herself and her family. Although Mr. Jenkins demands that she recognize her family as dysfunctional and requiring assistance from him and others, Meg is stubborn, impatient, and angry and remains true to her family by resisting his unwanted interventions. Like Arrietty who accepts Spiller's help even though her mother has turned it down because he seems dirty and wild, Meg relies on others when necessary. In *A Wrinkle in Time,* Meg is advised by a quartet of supernatural beings, imaged as kindly aunts, who teach her that she must learn to trust herself and her ability to find her father and rescue her brother Charles. The solution Meg discovers in *A Wrinkle in Time* is love; her love for brother inspires her to fight the evil forces holding on to him. At the end of *A Wind in the Door,* Meg learns that reflecting on God's love allows her to fight the Echthroi's supernatural hold on Charles and enables her to inspire Mr. Jenkins to protect her brother from other students.

Both L'Engle and Norton represent talented young women whose characterizations blend masculine and feminine attributes and technical and scientific expertise. Arrietty and Meg perform traditional feminine tasks related to family and home while demonstrating bravery, willingness to take risks, and scientific expertise, all imaged as heroic, unconventional traits for young women. Arrietty and Meg are fictional role models for young women navigating difficult familial and social landscapes; their stories inspire many adolescents to persevere through tough times. Mary Pipher recommends to parents that media depictions denigrating women's abilities, sexuality, and intelligence should be counterbalanced by such positive messages empowering young girls to succeed by discovering themselves and establishing their moral compasses. She echoes what Catharine Maria Sedgwick's teacher in the didactic fiction *Means and Ends, or Self-Training* (1842) taught her charges: "whatever directs and subdues your passions, whatever cultivates your virtues, and whatever improves your manners, is a part of your moral *education*" (10).[26] Self-improvements increase self-esteem, which helps to buffer the individual from being overwhelmed by external forces and disagreeable persons. Sedgwick's book explains that everything one does to care for others also benefits the self, since one cannot fail to benefit from the good or goods one brings to those one loves. As old-fashioned and sentimental as this doctrine appears, the ideology of domestic love benefits Arrietty and Meg as well. Meg learns at the end of *A Wind in the Door* that loving her enemies enables her to overcome them. By drawing on better-developed skills and a revised understanding of their families, Arrietty Clock and Meg Murry battle demons of conformity to gain victory over their worst impulses and to save themselves and their families from disaster.

The film *Ice Princess* (Dir. Tim Fywell, 2005) describes a similar transformation of Casey Carlyle, a teenager about to graduate from high school who adds athletic achievement to her love of science. Casey is a science geek who becomes a top-notch competitive figure skater still interested in science. She builds on her interest in skating and her aptitude in physics to design a science project that uses video and computer programming to analyze the mathematics behind skaters' jumps, a project she hopes will gain her admission to Harvard University. Casey's mother, a college professor, encourages her daughter to pursue academics and enter the best university she can. To understand the mechanics of skating and improve her project, Casey secretly takes skating lessons with former champion and coach Tina Harwood. Casey's feminist, intellectual mother has no affection for Tina or figure skating.[27] But it is skating that excites Casey, and she becomes passionate about competing as a figure skater. Tina's own daughter Gen gives up competitive skating because she does not want to miss out on dating and socializing with friends, so Tina becomes Casey's coach. The message of the movie is that mothers should allow their daughters to make their own decisions about education and careers. Tina realizes that she should respect Gen's decision not to compete, and Casey's mother recognizes that Casey should pursue what she loves. The film concludes with Casey's mother and coach negotiating how Casey can compete as a skater while taking two university courses.

Arrietty Clock, Meg Murry, and Casey Carlyle are positive models for young girls; these young women negotiate the difficult divide of conformity and independence by acting reasonably to do what is best for them and eventually convincing their parents to respect their choices. These young women succeed without sacrificing their femininity, individuality, or relationships with their families and friends and demonstrate scientific and technical talents. They mature in appealing ways, encouraging readers to regard mathematical and scientific talents as assets to be retained and enhanced throughout one's life for intellectual and social purposes.

Gender, Science, and Technology in Television Animation

Contemporary television cartoon shows pitched at children and adults represent, resist, or reconfigure gender stereotypes about science and technology. Targeted for young children, *Handy Manny* (2006–) is a Disney animated show about a bilingual handyman who works with male and female tools who are characters in the show. Manny Garcia runs a repair shop and is hired for jobs around the town of Sheet Rock. His motto is "You break it, we fix it." He speaks English and Spanish with the town's residents and his tools, which have names and personalities: Pat, the bumbling blue hammer; Turner, a grumpy blue screwdriver; Felipe, an ambitious yellow Phillips screwdriver; Dusty, the not-so-dainty red handsaw; Stretch, the nearly perfect pink tape measure; Squeeze, a curious pair of green pliers; and Rusty, a fearful orange monkey wrench.[28] Dusty and Squeeze are female, the rest of the tools male. The tools behave according to the conventions of employees, and sometimes children, in doing their best to follow Manny's directions, but they are also friends who take care of Manny, as in "Manny's Sick Day."

The tools—tape measure, hammer, screwdriver, pliers, saw, and wrench— discuss their technical functions and their contributions to Manny's jobs, helping youngsters learn about building and repair. Manny's friends also include Kelly, a young woman who runs the hardware store; her brother Sherman, who owns and manages the shoe store; and Mr. Lopart, a middle-aged man who attempts ambitious projects for his candy store and is the least technically adept character on the show. Manny represents masculine technical acumen while Kelly portrays a technically adept female.

The most scientific character on *SpongeBob Squarepants* (1999–), an animated fantasy show about a sponge and various undersea residents of Bikini Bottom (crab, squid, starfish, puffer fish, etc.), is female: the squirrel Sandy Cheeks. Incorporating some gender stereotypes and resisting others, Sandy is an extremely competitive Texan who is a talented athlete, scientist, and mathematician. In the episode "Sandy's Rocket" (1999), Sandy takes great pains to tell SpongeBob not to mess with the rocket she has built for a space voyage, but he and Patrick take off in it while Sandy is sleeping. When SpongeBob and Patrick get back to Bikini Bottom, Sandy lets them know she is angry that they turned her "little science experiment into a disaster." In "Chimps Ahoy" (2006), Sandy's funders—Dr. Marmalade, Lord Reginald, and Professor Percy—visit Bikini Bottom to check on the progress of her research. SpongeBob and Patrick try to help Sandy by inventing a machine to impress the chimps, but the funders are instead thrilled with Sandy's invention, a banana peeler, originally designed to be a nutcracker.

Fox's long-running series *The Simpsons* (1989–) employs conventions of television situation comedies to poke fun at human foibles, many identified as negative stereotypical masculine characteristics associated with the overeating, couch-potato father Homer or his prankster, subversive son Bart. In the 1998 episode "Lisa the Simpson," daughter Lisa agonizes because her intellectual capabilities appear limited by heredity, as the official Web site description explains:

When Lisa is unable to figure out a simple brain teaser, she begins to fear that she is losing her gift of intelligence. . . . Grandpa explains to her that all Simpsons started out smart and gradually experienced a "dumbening" that left them thick as bricks. Lisa [begins] emulating Homer and Bart and their brainless ways. But this makes her unhappy, so to cheer her up, Homer gathers all the Simpson relatives he can find and tries to show her that they're not all idiots. Sadly, Lisa realizes that a lot of them are, in fact, stupid. But when she meets some of her female relatives, she is pleased to discover that many of them are doctors and businesswomen. With renewed confidence in her own intelligence, Lisa looks at the brain teaser again and figures it out immediately.[29]

In "Girls Just Want to Have Sums" (2006), Lisa disguises herself as a boy to get into the boys-only math class after the elementary school has been sex-segregated; the girls' math class teaches self-esteem and has nothing to do with numbers.[30] In "Funeral for a Fiend" (2007), Lisa installs the family's TIVO.[31] Many episodes of the show illustrate Lisa's maturity, intelligence, and general superiority and depict her talented mother Marge's forbearance with Homer's many idiocies. In "Please Homer Don't Hammer 'em" (2006), "Marge discovers her gift for carpentry but has to use Homer as a front in order to overcome people's prejudices against women builders."[32]

Four other cartoon shows incorporate and reconfigure gender stereotypes within narratives of scientific authority: *Dexter's Laboratory; Jimmy Neutron, Boy Genius; Powerpuff Girls;* and *My Life as a Teenage Robot.* In some ways, these shows follow in the footsteps of various incarnations of the *Scooby-Doo* cartoon franchise, which premiered in 1969 and included Daphne and Velma as representing respectively glamorous femininity and logical intelligence. Invoking traditional sex roles and mocking stereotypes by developing some female characters with scientific and technical aptitudes, *Dexter's Laboratory* (1996–2003); *The Adventures of Jimmy Neutron, Boy Genius* (2002–6); *Powerpuff Girls* (1998–2004); and *My Life as a Teenage Robot* (2003) associate both males and females with invention and experimentation while caricaturizing the nerdiness, absentmindedness, and egocentrism of some scientists. Blending adventure and comedy, these cartoons reconfigure stereotypes in suggesting that some girls and women in comic adventure plots are as capable as or more capable than the boys and men with whom they compete in scientific and technical fields.

Cartoon Network's *Dexter's Laboratory* characterizes twins Dexter and Dee Dee as, respectively, a "European" scientist developing new knowledge and a Valley Girl cheerleader creating havoc in her brother's lab. *Dexter's Laboratory* acknowledges ambivalence about who should have authority over science. The show's conventionalized themes include representing the male scientist as a nerd who relies on science as a social defense and an ambitious problem solver whose best efforts are misdirected. After Dexter gives Dee Dee a larger brain so that she can be his assistant, she questions Dexter and subverts his work. In the first episode of the show "Dee Deemensional," Dexter sends Dee Dee back in time to save himself, but the plan backfires when the past Dexter does not believe her. In this show, the scientist is a heroic inventor while his sister appears to him to be an enemy of science who destroys his subterranean, secret lab and whatever he produces in it.

Nickelodeon's film and television show *The Adventures of Jimmy Neutron, Boy Genius* focuses on James Isaac Neutron as a brilliant boy whose "brain blasts" help solve his friends' and family's predicaments. Compared with cool kids such as Nick Dean, Jimmy is a geek, whose archrival Cindy calls him "Nerdtron." Assisted by his friends Carl Weezer, an asthmatic lover of llamas, and Sheen, who is easily confused and obsessed with the comic figure Ultra-Lord, Jimmy portrays the scientist as a problem solver working out of a back-yard laboratory. Annoyed by girls, Jimmy creates the Girl Eating plant. He developed his dog Goddard as a super-companion and in one episode builds a robot to sell cookies. The conventions associated with the mad scientist whose overreaching ambitions create catastrophe are exemplified in the robot who sells cookies as it gives away Jimmy's gadgets to woo customers.

While Jimmy's male friends are his allies, his female counterpart, Cindy Vortex, and her girlfriends appear as childishly feminine in plotting against him. When aliens threaten Retroville, Jimmy and Cindy join forces to protect the town. In "Win, Lose, and Kaboom" (2004), the Retroville children are forced to play as a team against other planets in a game hosted by the evil genius Meldar and designed to eliminate all but the winning planet. Although Jimmy initially trusts his intelligence more than others' to save Retroville, Cindy convinces Jimmy to let other team members respond to the quiz, which results in their shared success and the town's salvation.

The Cartoon Network's series *The Powerpuff Girls* (1998–2004) depicts a team of three superhero sisters. Professor Utonium creates Blossom, Buttercup, and Bubbles out of "sugar, spice, and everything nice," and "Chemical X," aided by the professor's former assistant, the monkey Jojo, who later becomes the evil Mojo Jojo. Chemical X is a factor that changes the Girls into crime fighters with special powers. "Each girl has a distinct personality and color," but they always end up working as a team.[33] *The Powerpuff Girls* film (Dir. Craig McCracken, 2002) explains the origins and early adventures of the Girls, who discover their superpowers when they play a game of tag that wrecks Townsville. To save themselves, the Girls unknowingly "turn to the evil Mojo Jojo."[34] Spoofing Japanese superhero animation, the Powerpuff Girls are ordinary children with incredible powers, leading to many situations in which their childish traits conflict with their responsibilities as crime fighters. In "Mommy Fearest"

(1998), the Girls save Professor Utonium from Sedusa, who is disguised as "Ima Goodlady." In "Ice Sore" (1999), Blossom is embarrassed by the effects of her new ice power and refuses to use it for some time even as her sisters plead with her to save Townsville from an incoming gigantic fireball. In "Paste Makes Waste" (1999), Buttercup refuses to apologize to Elmer, a paste-eating school-mate; her behavior causes him to become a paste monster threatening every-one. Each story ends with the Girls able "to save the world before bedtime."

The girl robot protagonist ("Global Response Unit XJ9" to her scientist-creator "mom" Dr. Nora Wakeman; Jenny to her friends) of Nickelodeon's *My Life as a Teenage Robot* was also built to save the world. Each episode reveals how Jenny strives to be a normal teenage girl with feelings, a sense of humor, and the ability to communicate in social situations. For example, in "Love 'em or Lash 'em" Jenny falls in love and wants to go out with Kenny, a robot boy Dr. Wakeman recognizes as a product of her archrival. Unfortunately, Kenny's cre-ator has incorporated doglike behavior into the robot boy. After Kenny's "dog-giness" becomes evident, Jenny loses any popularity she briefly gained while having a boyfriend. Dr. Wakeman is depicted as a nerd who is more interested in science and fighting evil than in mothering; she is more concerned about preserving XJ9's superhero capacities than protecting the robot's feelings. Jenny is never afraid to neutralize attacking supervillains, but she suffers from the abuse of her high school peers Tiff and Britt and endures the attentions of Sheldon, "a budding engineer and a comic book fan."

Replicating and Resisting Gender Stereotypes in Live-Action Shows

Although one might expect cartoon characters to be more idiosyncratic than characters portrayed by actors, *Ned's Declassified School Survival Guide* presents Ned, his neighbor Jennifer Mosely (Moze), his friend Simon Cook (Cookie), and others in their middle school as a host of eccentrics. Among the "insane" teachers, the science teacher, Mr. Sweeney, wears a white lab coat and glasses and sneers at the insufficiencies of his students. In "Science Fair" (2005), Ned challenges Mr. Sweeney's theory that Ned will never win a science fair ribbon by borrowing Cookie's cyberrobotic arm and leg to present as his own project. Unfortunately, the plan goes awry. Cookie's face swells after he eats walnuts, which he does to impress his girlfriend Vanessa's grandmother, and the robotic arm and leg he demonstrates as Ned's project goes wild, making Cookie appear a monster to Vanessa's grandmother. Meanwhile, Ned, in a white lab coat and with hair made frizzy by the static electricity experiment, appears a mad scien-tist to the grandmother and viewers. Before chaos erupts, Mr. Sweeney awards

Ned a ribbon for the robotic exhibit, but after the melee Ned loses and Cookie's paper towel experiment wins because it is the only project left to be judged. The science fair episode reproduces the well-known Frankenstein tableau of mad, male scientist and frightening creature as a humorous conceit identifying the dangers of science (and science fairs).

Females as species worthy of study by scientists contribute a significant theme about gender and STEM on television. In the Australian television hit *H2O: Just Add Water* (2006–), three high school girls on the Australian Gold Coast turn into mermaids when they touch water and discover their supernatural powers. Cleo, Emma, and Rikki confide their secret to Cleo's friend Lewis, who applies his scientific knowledge to learn more about mermaids and their magic. In "The Denman Affair" Lewis interviews to become the research assistant of the accomplished, beautiful, and curious Dr. Denman, a female marine biologist. Because Dr. Denman steals the DNA sample from Cleo that Lewis has brought to the lab's powerful microscope, he refuses the scientist's tempting job offer. Lewis turns down the opportunity to travel the world and instead remains with his friends the mermaids as their protector and scientific resource because he realizes that Dr. Denman puts science above everything else, including friends and moral integrity. At the end of the first season, Dr. Denman returns in "Dr. Danger" and "A Twist in the Tail" to hunt down the mermaids. Because the girls temporarily lose their powers due to a lunar eclipse, Dr. Denman's trap at Mako Island fails to catch the mermaids. Within the narrative world, the mermaids are intuitive subjects whose scientific knowledge is not as extensive as Lewis's or Dr. Denman's. Making the female scientist (Dr. Denman) intelligent yet ambitiously selfish, and the budding male scientist (Lewis) morally superior and sympathetic to his scientific subjects, reconfigures stereotypes linking gender and science.

The divide between masculine and feminine areas of expertise extends to television representations of gender and technology. The Nickelodeon television series *iCarly* (2007–) features Freddie, the love-struck boy who lives across the hall from Carly, as the technical producer of the Web TV show of the title, while Carly and her best friend Sam create the show's content and act as on-camera hosts. The families of the central characters are mostly off-screen, except for Carly's brother Spencer and Freddy's mother. Carly's parents are in the military, and she lives with the flaky Spencer, a sculptor specializing in large pieces such as a giant coffee cup. Freddie and his overprotective mother live next door, while Sam is a school friend from a large, odd family. Sam and Carly have been friends since they were six, bonding after Sam tried to steal Carly's tuna sandwich and Carly punched her. Many episodes show Carly's resilience and maturity and focus on Spencer's shenanigans, making him the butt of many sight gags.

At least two *iCarly* episodes acknowledge that females can be more technically competent than males. In "iStakeout" (2008), Sam wins a bet with Freddie, whom she styles "a geek," because she knows "MPEG" is a computing acronym for Moving Picture Experts Group. In "iFence" (2008), Spencer fences at home with his robot and then brings Freddie along to his fencing club while Carly is stuck at home making dinner and entertaining their boring cousins the Dorfmans. Carly points out the disparity to her brother and tells him to mend his ways. In the same episode, Freddie's overprotective mother finally lets him fence and then jumps into the match to defeat his overbearing opponent. Each show includes a video clip, usually a homemade one sent by a viewer, while the iCarly.com Web site includes tips on how to shoot your own Web television show.

Dan Schneider, the producer of *iCarly*, also created the Nickelodeon show *Zoey 101* (2005–8), which focuses on a female title character, her close friends, and her school acquaintances. Zoey and her younger brother Dustin attend Pacific Coast Academy (PCA), a boarding school in Southern California. Formerly an all-boys school, PCA recently began accepting girls. In a first-season episode highlighting how girls acculturate to PCA traditions, Zoey persuades her female friends to join a basketball team and play against the boys' team, which excludes girls. Zoey is sensitive, artistically talented, and diplomatic; the show's Web site describes her as combining "brains and beauty" and being "a quick thinker."[35]

Zoey's critical decision-making and admirable creativity are often highlighted. In "The Backpack" (2005), she comes to the rescue after her roommate Nicole mistakenly sprays gooey candy on a backpack at the school store and must purchase it; Zoey decorates the backpack and turns it into a fashion accessory. She creates a boys' version of the backpack at her friend Chase's request and attracts the attention of another PCA student, Stacey, who steals Zoey's idea of decorating backpacks. When Stacey is on the verge of making a lucrative deal to sell her backpacks to the school store, Zoey designs an artistically decorated backpack with built-in massage and speakers. The development process for this enhanced backpack takes place off-screen. The viewer sees only the successful outcome of Zoey's efforts and how she spends her revenue from the bookstore arrangement: on a jukebox for the lounge that everyone can enjoy.

The subplot in "The Backpack" illustrates the idiosyncratic Quinn's ambition to create a hybrid fruit, a "banapple," which would blend her two favorite fruits, banana and apple. She combines their molecular structures into one fruit tree and creates a cyberscarecrow modeled on herself to protect the tree. Zoey's selfless invention succeeds, but Quinn's self-absorbed project does not, for the resulting fruit is poisonous. Characteristically, Zoey and Chase console Quinn, who demonstrates the lethal nature of her fruit hybrid on Stacey's bicycle seat, which withers.

In "Anger Management" (2008), Zoey observes Quinn's dietary quirkiness (she doesn't like peanuts, so she just licks the chocolate off them) and her technical abilities (she can fix Zoey's Jet X scooter). Their dialogue about repairing the scooter distinguishes having tools from being feminine. After Zoey asks for Quinn's help with the scooter, Quinn says, "I will get my tools." Zoey allows, "Maybe I should get some tools some day," but Quinn responds, "No, you are too girly to have tools." There is a certain amount of irony in this exchange, for Quinn is dressed in an outfit that includes a frilly pink shirt, headband, and sash, while Zoey is wearing a blue sweatshirt.

The show's Web site describes Quinn as

> brilliant in a mad scientist kind of way. Her room doubles as a science lab and her extra-curricular activities include inventing contraptions (a.k.a. 'Quinn-ventions') and then testing them out on unsuspecting classmates. You could say Quinn puts the 'Q' in quirky because you never know what she is going to come up with next. Sure Quinn's a little different from her classmates, but she kind of prefers it that way.

Quinn's various eccentricities include weird food preferences (for baby food), strange outfits and hairstyle, concern for her pet alpaca, propensity to invent bizarre items, and advanced understanding of science. On the fictional PCA Web site, Quinn's inventions are named and numbered, but the descriptions have been blacked out as "censored."[36] Curiously, in "Zoey's Tutor" (2006), Zoey receives help in science not from Quinn but from Logan Reese, Chase's roommate who has limited ideas of what girls can do.

In "Robot Wars" (2006), Zoey and her friends enlist Quinn to help them create a warbot to compete against the bot developed by PCA's award-winning robotics team. The robotics team of geeky boys includes three (Neil, Drew, and Wayne) who would not let Quinn join the science club because "girls and science don't mix." The boys' taunting of Quinn persuades her to overcome her reluctance to compete in a violent game, so she joins Zoey's team, which includes Lola, Chase, Michael, and Logan. Unfortunately, the narcissistic, rich Logan makes fun of Quinn; she overhears laughter and walks out on the team. Although Zoey apologizes for the teasing, Quinn refuses to return to the team to finish the bot. Zoe's team is then forced to make a deal with Miles Brody, the PCA student who knows everything. After a close battle, the geeky boys' bot defeats Zoey's team's bot; however, the teams face a rematch because the geeks violated height restrictions. Zoey's team's bot as finished by Miles is too crushed to fight again, but Quinn surprises everyone when she brings her newly designed small, purple and pink bot into the ring, endures taunting from the geeky boys ("This is why girls don't belong in the science club"), and proceeds to shoot her bot's missile into the geeky boys' bot and demolish it. After Quinn's bot wins the competition, Zoey and her friends apologize to Quinn by sending her flowers delivered by bot.

In *Zoey 101,* Quinn's character includes stereotypes associating science with wild ideas, frequent failures, and masculine confidence, but she also demonstrates positive feminine traits that transform stereotypes concerning gender and science. She is a generous person who takes Zoey in as a roommate in an early episode when Dana and Nicole are fighting, and, after a computer mix-up with rooms, Quinn later moves in with Zoey and Lola. In other episodes of the show, Quinn dates Mark, a boy in her science class ("Quinn's Date," 2005), and she helps Logan with his basketball game ("Chase's Girlfriend," 2006). Quinn and Logan date secretly in "Walk-a-Thon" (2008) and "Dinner for Two Many" (2008). In the 2008 series finale ("Chasing Zoey), they reveal their secret romance to their friends and classmates. That Quinn and the handsome, conceited, rich boy who is patient with her odd preferences are attracted to each other and that she continues her science experiments reworks stereotypes about scientifically adept girls. Similar expectations about Logan based on his wealth and narcissism are countered by his affection for Quinn and his ability to tutor science.

Reality shows such as *Top Gear* (1978–2001, 2002–) and *MythBusters* (2003–) showcase science and technology within discussion and demonstrations of technoscientific principles and products at work.[37] Aimed at adults and appealing to adolescents, these shows portray men and women doing hands-on STEM work, but men more frequently appear as scientific and technical authorities. The public television reality show *Design Squad,* which presents engineering challenges within the framework of a competition between two teams of students (high school students and college undergraduates), was created to attract high school students to engineering; it premiered on PBS stations in 2007. The show's development was based on research from the Extraordinary Women Engineers Project (EWEP), a national initiative receiving corporate and NSF support that looked at how perceptions of parents, peers, teachers, guidance counselors, and the media affected educational and career decisions of young girls. Girls responding to EWEP surveys indicated that they perceive the ideal elements of a career as "enjoyable, good working environment, making a difference, income, and flexibility," and that they considered engineering to be hard, masculine, and for people who love math and science.[38]

Recognizing the gap between what girls want and what they perceive, the EWEP report recommends developing messages "that illustrate engineering as a career that complements and supports community interests, family interests, and self-interests" (19). Co-hosted by Nate Ball and Deanne Bell, each episode of *Design Squad* follows two teams of students who work to design, build, and test prototypes (cardboard furniture, zero-gravity bike, insect sculpture) that meet the specifications of the weekly competition. Each show also introduces the audience to "engaging young engineers who demonstrate that engineering is a creative career where you get to work with great people, solve interesting problems, and design things that matter."[39] The gender balance is studiously even, while competitive elements of the show fit the winner-take-all mentality of reality television—the winner of each season wins a $10,000 scholarship from Intel—rather than the collaborative interests and good working environment mentioned by respondents in the EWEP report.

Recent fictional productions present likable female scientists who struggle against social stereotypes and expectations. Based on the 1978 children's book by Judi and Ron Barrett, the animated film *Cloudy with a Chance of Meatballs* (Dir. Phil Lord and Chris Miller, 2009) illustrates a plot in which gender, science, and technology reference and reconfigure stereotypes. The film includes a wacky scientist-inventor (he admires Nikola Tesla) and a female meteorologist (she wants to be "a real scientist") who overcome failure and fear to demonstrate technoscientific and heroic abilities. The Internet Movie Database describes these characters as "Flint Lockwood, a young inventor who dreams of creating something that will improve everyone's life . . . [and] Sam Sparks, a weathergirl covering the phenomenon who hides her intelligence behind a perky exterior." Flint and Sam share a mutual attraction to science that encourages their romance, but Sam's quest to become a scientist generally goes unmentioned in reviews.

The television show *The Big Bang Theory* (2007–) sketches a narrative arc in which science intersects with heterosexual romance and psychological maturation. This comedy sacrifices elaborate plot to showcase archetypal scientific personalities, represented by variously eccentric male, geeky Cal Tech research scientists and their commonsense, normal pretty, blonde neighbor who works as a waitress at the Cheesecake Factory. Sheldon is a child prodigy and science snob with obsessive-compulsive tendencies; his roommate Leonard is comparatively normal, although in his family he is thought of as an underachiever with a Ph.D. in astrophysics. Rounding out the group are Raj, who can correct the all-knowing Sheldon but can't speak in front of women; Howard, who shouldn't speak to women because every sentence he forms comes out as a leering proposition; and their neighbor Penny, the waitress who becomes Leonard's girlfriend. Penny's sensibility, sincerity, and sentiment make her the emotional center of most shows. Although Sheldon's intelligence allows him to be correct much of the time, his condescending attitude toward others causes him to be out of joint with his society, which takes offense at his claims such as "I'm a physicist. I have a working knowledge of the universe and all it contains."[40]

Some episodes of *The Big Bang Theory* develop Howard's romance with Bernadette, a microbiology graduate student who works at the Cheesecake Factory with Penny and who can keep up with the boys when they talk science. Bernadette's interest in Leonard's work prompts Penny to ask Sheldon for a physics tutorial in *The Gorilla Experiment* (2009); the results demonstrate that Penny can understand science but remains most fascinated by a food fact (where Fig Newtons were invented) rather than information about physics. Similarly, Leonard is unable to understand the rules of football or the dynamics of dating, and Sheldon cannot feel empathy. Each major character in *The Big Bang Theory* thus exhibits strengths and weaknesses, reflecting a blend of expected and unexpected gendered traits. The series normalizes the world of science and humanizes scientists while winking at well-known gender stereotypes.

■ ■ ■

Whether shows depicting female competence and interest in STEM can enhance the appeal of these fields, or whether students, parents, faculty, and professionals are put off by stereotypes that make scientists seem admirable competitors or lovably quirky singles looking for love, only time will tell. Television and film represent science and technology as esoteric, risky, and dangerous and therefore attractive mostly to adventurous males and odd females. After centuries of plots in print and on-screen in which science, technology, and gender are intertwined, we have come to expect, if not accept, stereotypes of femininity and masculinity in many narratives about science and technology. This book is one attempt to unpack such conventions across narrative genres and historical periods, undertaken to better understand how stereotypes are replicated, resisted, or adapted within stories referencing gender, science, and technology.

My readings are set within the context of empirical communication scholarship about viewers and their anecdotal reactions. Further empirical research into viewers' attitudes would shed more light on reactions to recent televised portrayals such as *Design Squad*'s of females and males engaging with science and technology or *The Big Bang Theory*'s romantic plots linking male and female scientists and non-scientists. Predicting what viewers and readers think is a difficult business, for individual and cultural values are diverse and change over time. The multifarious responses of fans on webzines and blogs demonstrate that consensus might not be possible.[41] The different reactions of fans when shows such as *Star Trek* or *Dr. Quinn, Medicine Woman* are cancelled or when book series such as *Harry Potter* conclude reveal that opinions differ among peers about what texts are valued and how they are interpreted. One should not assume that everyone exposed to texts representing women and men according to gendered stereotypes develops the same ideas about these texts. After all, where one parent sees a daughter "mothering" a truck and thereby behaving differently from a boy who runs a truck along the floor, another sees a girl who has become more comfortable with the truck because she is incorporating it into her play and asserting control over it.

The preceding chapters outline stereotypical configurations of gender, science, and technology in narratives and remark on the occasional deviations from such stereotypes, doing so to suggest the ways in which representations help form social norms regarding who should study and work in STEM. Viewers recognizing the incorporation of gendered stereotypes are better equipped to withstand the discrimination women face in the STEM workforce and resist such prescriptions. Consumers can avoid purchasing or watching what insults them or their children, and they can explain why they are doing so to providers and to other consumers. Further, negative stereotypes can be unraveled to produce constructive insights that improve STEM environments.

Content producers should resist the urge to replicate discriminatory stereotypes and should instead create new formulas to inspire boys *and girls* to investigate scientific principles as joyfully as the MythBusters (Adam Savage and Jamie Hyneman), as carefully as television's many forensic investigators, and as ambitiously as *Design Squad*'s contestants. Producers who develop innovative programming to spark kids' interest in science or those who commission creative programming such as PBS's *Sid the Science Guy* (2008–), which aims to teach science content to preschool kids by asking questions without incorporating stereotypes, should be commended.[42]

This book offers analyses of print and visual media as a means of enhancing the capacities of readers and viewers to identify gender stereotypes, recognize how they shape our consciousness, and work toward disassembling these formulas as natural and essential. In addition to improving interpretive capacities of individuals, media depictions of girls' and women's engagement with and authority over science and technology should be increased and given more prominence. Several organizations such as Girl Scouts, Boys & Girls Clubs of America, and FIRST® LEGO® League incorporate fun, hands-on, interactive experiences for students to become more knowledgeable about science and technology. Digital modes of communication—for example, playing computer games and watching television shows and film on the Internet—offer some opportunities for adolescents to develop their scientific and technical talents, abilities, and skills, regardless of race, class, and gender. Studying media representations of women engaging with science and technology provides opportunities for scientists to adjust their attitudes and environments and for the public to develop greater understanding of these fields.

Notes

Chapter 1

1. U.S. Senator Ron Wyden, Press Release: "Wyden Convenes Hearing on Enforcing Title IX." U.S. House Committee on Science and Technology, Press Releases: "Subcommittee Examines Ways to Break Down Barriers"; "The Science of Gender and Science."

2. Spelke and Grace, "Sex, Math, and Science"; Summers, "Remarks at NBER Conference."

3. American Sociological Association, "Statement of the American Sociological Association Council on the Causes of Gender Differences in Science and Math Career Achievement."

4. "Women and Science."

5. Songe-Möller, *Philosophy without Women*, 10.

6. Millett, *Sexual Politics*, 51.

7. Ferguson, *A Companion to Greek Tragedy*, 111–23.

8. Aeschylus, "Prometheus Bound," 139.

9. Some material in this section is adapted from Colatrella, "Science, Technology, and Literature."

10. Pollack, "Scientists Seek a New Movie Role." Also see Frayling, *Mad, Bad, and Dangerous*, for a survey of film images of scientists.

11. Fontenelle, *Conversations on the Plurality of Worlds*, advertisement blurb.

12. Mellor, *Mary Shelley*.

13. Kolodny, "Dancing through the Minefield," 185.

14. Warhol, "Physiology, Gender, and Feeling: On Cheering Up," 226.

15. See Joyrich, *Re-Viewing Reception;* Dow, *Prime-Time Feminism;* Donawerth, *Frankenstein's Daughters;* Telotte, *Replications;* Attebury, *Decoding Gender in Science Fiction;* and Yaszek, *Galactic Suburbia;* Sobchak, *Screening Space.*

16. Both literal and metaphorical uses of the word "stereotype" refer to processes

regarded as progressive for profit-making businesses because they minimize individual variations while maximizing productive output. See Colatrella, "The American Experiment in Criminal Justice and Its European Observers."

17. Birke, "In Pursuit of Difference."

18. Lubinksi and Benbow, "Sex Differences in Personal Attributes for the Development of Scientific Expertise," note greater variation in IQ between boys and girls, citing a Scottish IQ study that shows inverse bell curves for boys and girls. Hines, "Do Sex Differences in Cognition Cause the Shortage of Women in Science?," asserts that "sex differences in cognitive abilities have not been clearly linked to either organizational or activational effects of hormones" (109). Hyde, "Women in Science," reports gender differences in problem-solving ability. Also see Committee on Science, Engineering, and Public Policy, *Beyond Bias and Barriers,* 6.

19. According to COSEPUP's *Beyond Bias and Barriers,* "Studies of brain structure and function, of hormonal modulation of performance, of human cognitive development, and of human evolution provide no significant evidence for biological differences between men and women in performing science and mathematics that can account for the lower representation of women in these fields. The dramatic increase in the number of women science and engineering PhDs over the last 30 years clearly refutes long-standing myths that women innately or inherently lack the qualities needed for success; obviously, no changes in innate abilities could occur in so short a time" (25).

20. Belkin, "Diversity Isn't Rocket Science, Is It?" Other references to Hewlett's study in the paragraph are also from this article.

21. Fox, "Institutional Transformation and the Advancement of Women Faculty," 77.

22. Rosser, Fox, and Colatrella, "Developing Women's Studies."

23. Colatrella, "Feminist Narratives of Science and Technology."

24. Reports include Kitzinger et al., *Gender Stereotypes and Expertise in the Press;* Haran et al., *Screening Women in SET;* Boyce and Kitzinger, *Promoting Women in the Media;* and Whitelegg et al. *(In)visible Witnesses.* Online versions of these reports appear at http://www. ukrc4setwomen.org/. Accessed October 29, 2009.

25. Kitzinger et al., *Role Models in the Media.*

26. Steinke, "Connecting Theory and Practice," 145.

27. Kitzinger et al., *Role Models in the Media,* 21–22.

28. Dawson, *Soldier Heroes,* 48. See Pease, "Leslie Fiedler, the Rosenberg Trial, and the Formulation of an American Canon," 156: "By a Cultural Imaginary I mean, following Cornelius Castoriadis, to designate a realm wherein abide not the images of already existing social materials but the 'undetermined abstract materiality of society itself.' In relation to the Cultural Imaginary the things, objects, and individuals that society brings into existence can be said to be themselves only insofar as they are held to be self-evidently true, hence beyond debate."

29. Peril, *Pink Think.*

30. Henley, "The Power of Pink," describes the "PinkStinks" campaign of British sisters Abi and Emma Moore.

31. The book is Evans's *She Wins, You Win.* This anecdote was told during her speech at the Georgia Association for Women in Higher Education Conference, February 2004.

32. Colman, "Just a Few Favorite Indulgences"; Green, "Books: Girls Gone Wild, Idaho Style."

33. Fraser-Abder and Mehta, "Literacy for All," 210–11.

34. "Mattel Dolls Up PCs with Barbie."

35. Klugman, "A Bad Hair Day for G.I. Joe."

36. Johnson and Learned, *Don't Think Pink.*

37. Leo, "The Indignation of Barbie," "Mattel Says It Erred"; and Dowd, "Barbie Loves Math."

38. I thank Svend-Erik Larsen and Trina Moenstad for guiding my tour of Legoland operations and their interviews with me in Billund, Denmark, on October 4, 2000. I am also grateful to Karin Sorenson who arranged for me to meet these Lego employees and to Kirsten Gomard, who initiated these contacts for me.

39. Margolis and Fisher, *Unlocking the Clubhouse;* Gary Cross, *Kids' Stuff.*

40. Dean Kamen (inventor of the Segway) sponsors FIRST LEGO League (FLL), a robotics competition in the United States, which is targeted at encouraging schoolchildren to persist in studying science and technology. FLL has grown exponentially, but there are disproportionately low numbers of girls involved, although many students are interested in Legos. See FIRST LEGO League.

41. Schwartz, "Turning to Tie-Ins, Lego Thinks beyond the Brick."

42. I thank students in LCC3304: Science, Technology and Gender, Georgia Tech, fall 2001 and fall 2007, for sharing their comments about these products.

43. Similar scenarios with young children are enacted daily in schools and playgrounds. See Corinne Schiff, "Metropolitan Diary."

44. Buchanan and Peskowitz, *The Daring Book for Girls;* Iggulden and Iggulden, *The Dangerous Book for Boys.*

45. McKellar, *Math Doesn't Suck;* Inouye, *Fly Girls.*

46. Oldenziel, "Man the Maker, Woman the Consumer," 144.

47. Merchant, *The Death of Nature.*

48. Noble, *A World without Women.*

49. Rossiter, *Women Scientists in America.*

50. Keller, *A Feeling for the Organism;* Russett, *Sexual Science.*

51. Ehrenreich and English, *For Her Own Good.*

52. Baym, *American Women of Letters and the Nineteenth-Century Sciences.*

53. Wajcman, *Feminism Confronts Technology* and *Technofeminisms.*

54. Martin, "The Culture of the Telephone."

55. Scharff, "Femininity and the Electric Car."

56. Cowan, *More Work for Mother;* Cockburn and Ormrod, *Gender and Technology in the Making.*

57. Horowitz, ed., *Boys and Their Toys?*

58. These issues are salient for women in fields with long working hours and significant managerial responsibilities—positions that require education and the need to collaborate and that pressure employees to be productive, that is, positions such as those in academic science and engineering.

59. OECD, Public Understanding of Science in the OECD Member Countries.

60. Allum et al., "Science Knowledge and Attitudes across Cultures: A Meta-Analysis."

61. Turner, "School Science and Its Controversies, or Whatever Happened to Scientific Literacy?"

62. Tierney, "A New Frontier for Title IX: Science."

63. Merton, "The Matthew Effect in Science"; Rossiter, "The Matilda Effect in Science."

64. Tierney, "Tierney Lab: Male Bias or Female Choice."

65. See the Georgia Tech Center for the Study of Women, Science, and Technology (www.wst.gatech.edu) and the ADVANCE program (www.advance.gatech.edu). Virginia Tech hosts the portal to all NSF ADVANCE sites at www.advance.vt.edu. Accessed July 17, 2008.

66. Fox, "Institutional Transformation and the Advancement of Women Faculty"; Sonnert, Fox, and Adkins, "Undergraduate Women in Science and Engineering"; Fox and Mohapatra, "Social-Organizational Characteristics"; and Etzkowitz et al., *Athena Unbound.*

67. Efforts to recruit and retain more girls and women in science, mathematics, engineering, and technical disciplines have preoccupied many researchers in the United States and Europe in the decades since Title IX was enacted in 1972. See Stewart et al., eds., *Transforming Science and Engineering,* which describes initiatives developed by ADVANCE programs in U.S. universities.

68. Hanson, *Swimming against the Tide,* 1.

69. Figure C-1 in National Science Foundation, *Women, Minorities, and Persons with Disabilities.*

70. Figure D-1 in National Science Foundation, *Women, Minorities, and Persons with Disabilities.*

71. These NSF figures are cited in Belkin, "Diversity Isn't Rocket Science, Is It?"

72. Division of Science Resources Statistics, NSF, *Key Findings 2008.*

73. American Association of University Professors, *AAUP Gender Equity Indicators;* Handelsman et al., "More Women in Science."

74. The Virginia Tech ADVANCE newsletter cites ASEE's national percentage of women faculty in engineering as 11.3 percent in 2006, putting the percentage of VT female faculty in engineering at 12.5, with MIT's and Georgia Tech's percentages higher; see "ADVANCING Women at VT."

75. Sommers, "Why Can't a Woman Be More like a Man?"

76. Nelkin, *Selling Science,* 19.

77. LaFollette, "Eyes on the Stars," 262.

78. For example, see Dean, "Women in Science."

79. Weingart et al., "Of Power Maniacs and Unethical Geniuses," 281.

80. Rosenstone, "Comments on Science in the Visual Media," 336.

81. Dalle Vacche, *Diva,* 2.

82. Mulvey, "Visual Pleasure and Narrative Cinema"; Modleski, *Loving with a Vengeance,* 12; Doane, *The Desire to Desire,* 30.

83. Science and technology have historically been envisioned in literature and film as mostly male domains, although often symbolized by feminine figures. See Schiebinger, *The Mind Has No Sex,* 122; and Browner, *Profound Science and Elegant Literature,* 139.

84. *Design News* Staff, *Engineers Making a Difference;* Smallwood, "As Seen on TV," A8; and Bollag, "Award-Winning Teaching."

85. See Smallwood, "As Seen on TV." Kim Loudermilk pointed out to me how some popular television shows such as *The X-Files* (initially broadcast in 1993) and *Buffy the Vampire Slayer* (based on a 1992 film and initially broadcast in 1997) depict female characters who

mix rational understanding of science with supernatural beliefs or even powers, particularly Buffy's best friend Willow, who is both computer wizard and witch, and medical doctor Dana Sculley of *The X-Files*.

86. Cunningham et al., "Gender Representation in the NCAA News."

87. Steinke, "Cultural Representations of Gender and Science," 30.

88. Steinke et al., "Assessing Media Influences," 36–37.

89. Steinke and Long, "A Lab of Her Own?," 91.

90. Culler, *Structuralist Poetics,* 137.

91. Rabinowitz, *Before Reading,* 53. Mackey, "At Play on the Borders of the Diegetic," 619, offers a useful summary of Rabinowitz's rules: "Rules of notice help readers decide what they will pay attention to and how they will distinguish between figure and ground. Rules of signification help readers decide how to attend to what they notice: whether a narrator is reliable, for example; whether readers should assume that the physical or social norms of contemporary life apply to the actions of the story; and so forth. Rules of configuration help readers to assemble the different elements of the story to make an overall pattern. Rules of coherence, applied after the reading is concluded, are used to help the reader make the best possible sense of the text. Gaps, for example, may be reinterpreted as significant ellipses and metaphoric explanations may be invoked to establish thematic interpretations."

92. See Phelan, *Reading People, Reading Plots,* 2–3: "mimetic" aspects of characterizations referencing science and technology have corollaries in specific people who study and practice in these domains. "Synthetic" and "thematic" components of character should not be overlooked, for artificial and representative aspects of character in the narratives under discussion also convey how males and females engage with science and technology in gendered ways.

93. Valian, *Why So Slow?*

94. Brooks, *Reading for the Plot,* 10. On the influence of narrator on reader, see Zunshine, *Why We Read Fiction,* 76.

95. Warner, *From the Beast to the Blonde,* 238–39.

96. Faludi, *Backlash,* chapters 5 and 6, respectively: "Fatal and Fetal Visions: The Backlash in the Movies" and "Teen Angels and Unwed Witches: The Backlash on TV."

97. See Douglas, *Where the Girls Are,* for an analysis of 1960s and 70s American television shows; and Watson, "From *My Little Margie* to *Murphy Brown.*" Canadian guidelines are considered in Trimble, "Coming Soon to a Station Near You?," 326.

98. Douglas, "Where Have You Gone, Roseanne Barr?"

99. Bal, *Narratology,* 83.

100. Revkin, "Filmmaker Employs the Arts to Promote Sciences." Also see Perkowitz, *Hollywood Science.*

101. Haynes, *From Faust to Strangelove.*

102. Haynes, "From Alchemy to Artificial Intelligence," 244.

103. Shepherd-Barr, *Science on Stage,* 205.

104. Macdonald, *Representing Women.*

105. Flicker, "Representation of Women Scientists in Feature Films," sees six types of female scientists in films—"old maid," "male woman," "naïve expert," "evil plotter," "daughter or assistant," and "lonely heroine."

106. Gender differences are also apparent in the reactions of viewers to genres, according

to Oliver et al., "The Impact of Sex and Gender Role Self-Perception."

107. See Colatrella, *Literature and Moral Reform,* for consideration of nineteenth-century theories of reading.

108. Kenschaft, "Just a Spoonful of Sugar?," explains Disney's reconfiguration of *Mary Poppins* as a story warning upper-class parents about being too committed to work and activism. The lower-class chimney sweep and nanny inspire Mr. and Mrs. Banks to be more involved and responsible parents. Kenschaft notes that her own mother justified her choice "to interrupt graduate work for six years to become a full-time mother" after seeing Mrs. Banks's exemplary giving up of suffragette activity for her children's sake, while "another professional woman . . . thought the movie's portrayal of Mary Poppins' and Bert's beneficial relationship with Jane and Michael supported her choice to pay another person to nurture her children during the workweek while she pursued her career."

109. Paul Newman was shocked that audiences admired Hud—a selfish, suspicious, conniving young man who is eager to get his hands on his ethical father's legacy and who abuses everyone around him. Apparently the actor's charaisma and attractiveness caused audiences to see past the character's moral failings. See Lyman, "Film: No Goons in Spats, No Rat-a-Tat Dialogue."

110. Rabinowitz, *Before Reading,* 9.

111. Clough, *Feminist Thought,* 5.

112. Cole, Bracken, and Degan, *Magic School Bus Taking Flight.*

113. See Douglas, *Where the Girls Are,* chapter 6, "Genies and Witches," for an analysis of how supernatural abilities affect the characterizations of Jeannie and Samantha on *I Dream of Jeannie* and *Bewitched.*

114. Felski, *Beyond Feminist Asthetics,* cautions against privileging the aesthetic over the pop culture product.

115. Hawthorne, *Selected Tales and Sketches.*

116. Steinke and Long, "A Lab of Her Own."

Chapter 2

1. Harding, "Just Add Women and Stir?" 306–7.

2. Wylie and Nelson, "Coming to Terms with the Values of Science," 59.

3. Levine, *The Realistic Imagination,* 28.

4. For a discussion of maternity in Mary Shelley's life and work, see Mellor, *Mary Shelley.*

5. Warhol identifies sentimentalism as "effeminate" in "Preface," *Having a Good Cry,* ix–xvii.

6. The film *Frankenstein Unbound* (Dir. Roger Corman, 1990), based on Brian Aldiss's novel, also explores the analogies of big science with Frankenstein's project.

7. Hawthorne, "The Birthmark," *Selected Tales and Sketches,* 259. All quotations from the story included here are from this text.

8. Merchant, *The Death of Nature.*

9. Ibid., especially chapter 7, "Dominion over Nature."

10. Easton, *The Making of the Hawthorne Subject,* 143.

11. Weinstein, *The Literature of Labor and the Labor of Literature,* 74.

12. See Eagleton, *Literary Theory: An Introduction,* 12. The quoted text is preceded by the following: "The fact that we always interpret literary works to some extent in the light of our own concerns—indeed that in one sense of 'our own concerns' we are incapable of doing anything else—might be one reason why certain works of literature seem to retain their value across the centuries. It may be, of course, that we still share many preoccupations with the work itself; but it may also be that people have not actually been valuing the 'same' work at all, even though they may think they have. 'Our' Homer is not identical with the Homer of the Middle Ages, nor 'our' Shakespeare with that of his contemporaries; it is rather that different historical periods have constructed a 'different' Homer and Shakespeare for their own purposes, and found in these texts elements to value or devalue, though not necessarily the same ones."

13. Stolberg, "Bush's Advisers on Ethics Discuss Human Cloning," A19.

14. My thinking about the Council's reading of Hawthorne's story has been shaped by Susan Squier's talks on related subjects at various meetings of the Society for Literature, Science, and the Arts and by informal discussions with her.

15. Brainard, "Divided Bioethics Panel Recommends Moratorium on Research Cloning."

16. Annas, "Cloning and the U.S. Congress," *New England Journal of Medicine,* 1599.

17. Collingwood, *The Idea of History,* 117.

18. Child, *The Children of Mount Ida and Other Stories,* 205. All further references to the story are from this text.

19. Karcher, "Lydia Maria Child," 51. Also see Samuels, *The Culture of Sentiment.*

20. Woolrich, "The History of Refrigeration," 32.

21. Cixous, "The Laugh of the Medusa," 284.

22. Tannen, *You Just Don't Understand.*

23. My discussion here about Melville's short fictions is adapted from my argument in *Literature and Moral Reform,* 68–73.

24. For example, see Kellner's "Slaves and Shrews."

25. For more information about Melville's marriage, see the special issue "The New Melville," especially Elizabeth Renker, "Herman Melville, Wife Beating, and the Written Page," and Scott Heller, "The 'New' Melville," both of whom work to identify a "New Melville," one who "was a tyrant at home" and who is presumed to have "beat his wife." As I note in *Literature and Moral Reform* (264–65), my reading of Elizabeth Shaw Melville's letters to the Shaw family convinced me that her great admiration and respect for her husband outweighed fears she had about his doing harm to himself or others.

26. Quotations from this story and the others by Melville discussed in this chapter are taken from Melville, *The Piazza Tales and Other Prose Pieces.*

27. As Bickley, *The Method of Melville's Short Fiction,* 48, notes, "Jimmy *was* vain and artificial, but Ford could not let himself admit it."

28. The wife generally displays patient forebearance of her husband: "Now, husband," said my wife, "I am convinced that, whatever it is that causes this ticking, neither the ticking nor the table can hurt us; for we are all good Christians, I hope. I am determined to find out the cause of it, too, which time and patience will bring to light. I shall breakfast on no other table but this, so long as we live in this house. So, sit down, now that all things are ready

again, and let us quietly breakfast" (386–87).

29. See Karcher's consideration of "The Apple-Tree Table" as a satire on supernatural explanations of spiritualism mocking orthodox Christian approaches ("Philanthropy and the Occult in the Fiction of Hawthorne, Brownson, and Melville").

30. Sharkey, "Family Life ('Arrgh!') in the Comfort Zone," 33.

31. Naslund, *Ahab's Wife, or The Star-Gazer,* 380. All quotations are from this text.

32. There are literary antecedents in other works by Melville for some challenges Una faces: cannibalism is a preoccupation in *Typee* and *Omoo;* desertion is a theme in these novels, in "The Encantadas," and in the Agatha story that Melville sent to Hawthorne after hearing it from John Clifford. Melville writes about a parent's reaction to the death of a child in *Redburn* and *Israel Potter.* Naslund's novel emulates the form of *Moby-Dick* by beginning with "Extracts," which cites quotations from *Moby-Dick* and texts contemporary with it. There is also a Melvillean tone in certain episodes: Una's water breaks in her second pregnancy while she is at the shore; she lets the waters mix (502). Interlaced with Una's tale are Starbuck's and Ahab's meditations, with Starbuck commenting on her unfortunate marriage to Kit (284ff).

33. Interview with Sena Jeter Naslund reprinted at http://www.mostlyfiction.com/authorga/naslundQA.htm by permission of FSB Associates, but no longer available at time of this writing. The same details appear in Sena Jeter Naslund, "A Novelist Discovers Maria Mitchell," and in other interviews with Naslund, including Allen, "Author Says *Ahab's Wife* Is 'an epic story' of American Experience."

34. Robertson-Lorant, *Melville,* 604.

35. Kohlstedt, "Maria Mitchell and Women in Science," 130. See also Rossiter, *Women Scientists in America,* vol. 1, and Warner, "Science Education for Women in Antebellum America."

36. See Baym, "Testing Scientific Limits: Emma Willard and Maria Mitchell," in *American Women of Letters and the Nineteenth-Century Sciences.*

37. My details and phrasing are drawn from Kohlstedt's essay.

38. Una's turning away from her mother and aunt, and her friend Susan's refusal to leave her mother in slavery, provide points of contact with Stowe's *Uncle Tom's Cabin* and Frances Ellen Watkins Harper's *Iola Leroy.*

39. Instead of regarding Una as unusual for running away to sea and for marrying Ahab, readers view her as a more moderate version of reformers like Mitchell and Fuller, and her story becomes more authentic in that it stays within the historical compass allowed them.

40. See Norling, *Captain Ahab Had a Wife,* and Blum, *The View from the Masthead,* for consideration of whaling as work.

41. Barlowe, *The Scarlet Mob of Scribblers,* writes, "Women's scholarship must continue to destabilize and disrupt body(ies) of scholarship so that it presses us all to examine academic and cultural assumptions and practices that objectify, exclude, or nominalize the Other" (123).

42. See Naslund's claim that her novel is an "epic story of an American woman," revealed in Allen. Iyer's and Urquhart's reviews are excerpted at The Women's Press (www.the-womens-press.com). For other references to epic qualities, see review of the novel by Adam Dunn.

43. Kirn, "Call Me Mrs."

44. Cohan and Shires, *Telling Stories,* 79–80. See also pages 78–79: "Although romance is not fixed but, in fact, has changed in response to different historical situations, we can none-

theless offer some generalizations about this genre. Its structure paradigmatically stresses marriage and aligns that event to the story's closure in order to define a woman's social choices as personal choices (i.e. love). This transformation keeps her in the domestic sphere of the home, the site of familial relationships. Through the generic traiting of the female character in terms of integrity, emotionality, and insecurity, the domestic sphere establishes a contrast to the public space of money and property dominated by fathers and husbands. The typical traiting of the male character in terms of arrogance, dominance, emotional distance, and social position reinforces this homologous oppo-/sition of public (his)/private (hers) and economic power (his)/emotional knowledge (hers)."

45. In chapter 4 of *Literature and Moral Reform*, I consider the heterogenous style of *Moby-Dick*.

Chapter 3

1. Shields, 10.

2. Lieber's "Preface" to the U.S. edition of Gustave de Beaumont and Alexis de Toc-queville, *On the Penitentiary System in the United States and Its Application in France* (1833), xv. Also see Smith, *The Prison and the American Imagination*, 211.

3. Showalter, *The Female Malady*, surveys madness as a cultural trope identified with femininity.

4. Gould, *The Mismeasure of Man*; Cole, *Suspect Identities*.

5. Foucault, *Discipline and Punish*, 299–300: "Replacing the adversary of the sovereign, the social enemy was transformed into a deviant, who brought with him the multiple dangers of disorder, crime and madness." Sections of this chapter are adapted from Colatrella, "At optraevle kniplingen"; Colatrella, "The Significant Silence of Race: *La Cousine Bette* and 'Benito Cereno'"; and Colatrella, "Fear of Reproduction and Desire for Replication in *Dracula*."

6. Wright, *Between the Guillotine and Liberty*, describes the reform movement inaugurated by Cesar Beccaria's *Essay on Crime and Punishment* as preferring "prevention rather than punishment" (11).

7. Hugo, *Les Misérables*.

8. See Otis, "Introduction," *Literature and Science in the Nineteenth Century*, for a discussion of "affinities and differences" between literature and science (xix).

9. For a brief survey of these scientists, see "Histoire de la criminologie."

10. Gould describes the political bias of such pseudo-scientific study in *The Mismeasure of Man*.

11. Lavater, *Essays on Physiognomy*, 38 and 84.

12. Ibid., 226: "Is it not perceptible in each species whether it be warlike, defensive, enduring, weak, enjoying destruction, easy to be crushed, or crushing?"

13. Combe, *Manual of Phrenology*.

14. See Quetelet, *Research on the Propensities for Crime of Different Ages*, 38.

15. Ibid., 54: "In the inferior classes where instruction is practically nil, the habits of women approach closer to that of men."

16. Chevalier, *Laboring Classes and Dangerous Classes*, 398.

17. Geringer, "Vidocq."

18. Balzac, *A Harlot High and Low,* 443.

19. Balzac, *La Cousine Bette,* 38–39.

20. "La Bette était ... d'un entetement du mule" (85); "parfois elle ressemblait aux singes habillés en femmes" (86); she shows "une jalousie de tigre" (109).

21. Quoted in Bierne, "Adolphe Quetelet and the Origins of Positivist Criminology," 1157.

22. For a discussion of race in the novel, see Colatrella, "The Significant Silence of Race," from which this paragraph and the previous one were adapted.

23. Zola, *La Curée,* 371.

24. The translations of Zola's novel provided with page numbers in the text are from the English translation published as *The Kill.* Unpaginated translations are mine.

25. Lombroso and Ferrero, *Criminal Woman, the Prostitute, and the Normal Woman.*

26. See Lombroso and Ferrero, *The Female Offender,* 82.

27. Lombroso and Ferrero, *Criminal Woman,* 66.

28. Ibid.

29. Collins, *Dickens and Crime,* 107.

30. See Barthes, *Michelet,* for a description of Michelet's fear of blood (120).

31. See Olrik, "Le sang impur," for an analysis of Lombroso's obsession with menstruation as a symptom of female deviance.

32. As Kelly points out in *Fictional Genders,* "the undecidability of gender" represents a questioning of "the very nature of masculinity and femininity" (2).

33. Sidonie gave up her child Angelique for adoption and ended her days in a convent. See Zola's *Le Rêve* and *Le Docteur Pascal.*

34. See Roth, *Bram Stoker*; McKee, "Racialization, Capitalism, and Aesthetics in Stoker's "Dracula"; Arata, "The Occidental Tourist"; Senf, "*Dracula:* Stoker's Response to the New Woman"; Stevenson, "A Vampire in the Mirror."

35. For a summary of science in two of Stoker's fictions, see Senf, "Dracula and the Lair of White Worm," 219.

36. I thank Carol Senf for bringing these points about Van Helsing to my attention.

37. See Arata, "The Occidental Tourist"; Stevenson, "A Vampire in the Mirror"; Dijkstra, *Idols of Perversity.*

38. Stoker, *Dracula.*

39. Nuland, *Doctors,* 393–94.

40. In Dracula's castle Jonathan remarks that if Dracula had recognized the shorthand journal as being a threat, he would have surely taken it and possibly destroyed it; see *Dracula,* 40.

41. Wicke, "Vampiric Typewriting."

42. Eisenberg, Murkoff, and Hathaway. *What to Expect When You're Expecting,* 106.

43. See O'Flinn, "Production and Reproduction in the Case of *Frankenstein.*"

44. Auerbach, *Woman and the Demon,* 22.

45. Walton and Jones, *Detective Agency,* consider the politics of female detectives.

46. Haran et al., *Screening Women in SET,* 3.

47. In the series finale of *Monk* (2002–9), the daughter of Monk's deceased wife Trudy tells him that his police skills, which depend upon on his detailed, insightful observation

of crime scenes, are "a blessing" and not "a curse" because they enabled him to solve Trudy's murder after 12 years and to find the daughter she thought had died shortly after being born. Monk's obsessive-compulsive disorder is a psychiatric syndrome, and it functions in the show's diegesis in similar ways as the supernatural abilities of other detectives. Finding Trudy's daughter provides Monk with someone to love, as his assistant Natalie tells him, and, along with solving the murder, ends his trauma about Trudy's death.

48. "Biography for Catherine Willows from *CSI* (*Crime Scene Investigation*)."

49. Haran et al., *Screening Women in SET*.

Chapter 4

1. Davis-Floyd, "Birth as an American Rite of Passage," 158; Lowrey, "Understanding Reproductive Technologies as a Surveillant Assemblage."

2. Singh and Kogan, "Widening Socioeconomic Disparities in US Childhood Mortality, 1969–2000."

3. *Sicko* (Dir. Michael Moore, 2007) considers different national health care systems.

4. Numbers, "Do-It-Yourself the Sectarian Way"; and Melosh, "Every Woman Is a Nurse." A 1990 Robitussin commercial offered "Dr. Mom," still a salient image used in public health; see CBS News, "Employers Play Dr. Mom to Control H1N1."

5. Hemmings, *The Life and Times of Emile Zola*, 176.

6. My translation is from Zola, "Dépopulation," 786.

7. Zola researched theoretical positions established by Gonnard, Nitti, Bergeret, Canu, and Brochard to support his personal observation; see Baguley, *Fécondité d'Emile Zola*.

8. Knodel and van de Walle, "Fertility Decline: European Transition," 271.

9. Shorto, "No Babies?"

10. Davidson, *Revolution and the Word*, notes readers' responses to American sentimental fiction.

11. Teitelbaum and Winter, *The Fear of Population Decline*, 27–28.

12. Michelet, *La Femme*, 119.

13. Michelet, *L'Amour*, 85: "Il faut vouloir ce qu'elle veut, et la prendre au mot, la refaire, la renouveler, la *créer*."

14. Michelet rehabilitated the traditionally feared femme fatale into a "femme malade" whose menstruation wounds and incapacitates her; Moreau, *Le Sang de l'histoire*, 57, 60, and 92.

15. See Barthes, *Michelet* (120) for a description of Michelet's fear of blood.

16. Zola, *Le Roman experimental*, 133.

17. Zola, *Oeuvres complètes*, 8: 978.

18. Colatrella, *Evolution, Sacrifice, and Narrative*.

19. See Bertrand-Jennings, *L'Eros et la femme chez Zola*, 102–8.

20. Baguley, 179.

21. The Morrill Act in 1860 created land grant colleges, which also opened educational opportunities to women.

22. Wells, *Out of the Dead House*, 9–10.

23. Pringle, *Sex and Medicine*, 27.

24. The television series *Dr. Quinn, Medicine Woman* (1993–98) focused on medical cases and social challenges facing the title character, a female doctor from Boston who locates to Colorado in the late nineteenth century.

25. Howells, quoted in Parrington, *Main Currents in American Thought,* vol. 3, 248.

26. Williams, "Writing with an Ethical Purpose," 52.

27. Both Phelps and Gilman address these issues in expository works as well. See Phelps, "What Shall They Do?," "Why Shall They Do It?," "What They Are Doing," "Women and Money," "A Talk to Girls," and "A Few Words to the Girls." Gilman's ideas are explicated in *Women and Economics* (1898) and *The Man-Made World* (1911), excerpted in Schwartz's anthology *The Yellow Wallpaper and Other Writings.*

28. "The homeopaths had three central doctrines. They maintained first that diseases could be cured by drugs which produced the same symptoms when given to a healthy person. This was the homeopathic law of similars—like cures like. Second, the effects of drugs could be heightened by administering them in minute doses. The more diluted the dose, the greater the 'dynamic' effect. And third, nearly all diseases were the result of a suppressed itch, or 'psora.' The rationale for homeopathic treatment was that a patient's natural disease was somehow displaced after taking a homeopathic medicine by a weaker, but similar, artificial disease that the body could more easily overcome" (Starr, *The Social Transformation of American Medicine,* 96–97). Also see Sartisky, "Afterword," *Dr. Zay,* 274.

29. Masteller, "The Women Doctors of Howells, Phelps, and Jewett," 135.

30. Morris, "Professional Ethics and Professional Erotics in Elizabeth Stuart Phelps's *Doctor Zay,*" 92.

31. For an account of how sectarian domestic medical practices compete with the regulars' "rounds of bleedings, blisterings, and purgings," see Numbers, "Do-It-Yourself the Sectarian Way," 5.

32. See Auerbach, *Woman and the Demon;* and Gilbert and Gubar, *Madwoman in the Attic.*

33. Morantz-Sanchez, *Sympathy and Science: Women Physicians in American Medicine,* 52.

34. This view counters that of Morris, "Professional Ethics," 150. I argue that the novel is about Waldo's awakening to profession and Zay's to love, as each learns to discard preconceptions.

35. Lears, *No Place of Grace,* 221.

36. Masteller, 144.

37. Willa Cather, "Preface," *The Country of the Pointed Firs and Other Stories* (Boston: Houghton, 1925), 16, cited in *American Women Regionalists, 1850–1910,* 185.

38. Jewett, *Novels and Stories.*

39. When Joan Bascom ran away from her family as a young girl to attend college, "the whole countryside rocked with gossip" (270), but as a successful medical doctor Joan is "a source of real pride to her sister, and of indefinable satisfaction to her brother-in-law" (271).

40. For examples in English, see Stith's "The Use of the Movie 'Lorenzo's Oil' as a Teaching Tool"; Gostinger, "Adrenoleukodystrophy (ALD)"; and Burr, "Fortune Favors the Brave."

41. Jones, "Medicine and the Movies."

42. Ibid., 569.

43. Bosk and Frader apply Lewis Hyde's formulation of gift exchange to a discussion of shifting medical attitudes and practices, explaining that "AIDS has become what the French anthropologist Marcel Mauss called a 'total social phenomenon—one whose transactions are at once economic, juridical, moral, aesthetic, religious and mythological, and whose meaning cannot, therefore, be adequately described from the point of view of any single discipline'" ("AIDS and Its Impact on Medical Work," 150).

44. Goldstein, "The Implicated and the Immune: Responses to AIDS in the Arts and Popular Culture," indicates that artists and activists share credit for shaping cultural understanding: "Cultural representation, combined with political activism, forged the current consensus on AIDS" (39).

45. Works such as Shilts's *And the Band Played On* and Patton's *Inventing AIDS* chronicle the history of how medical and political authorities learned to respond to concerns voiced by gays, African Americans, intravenous drug users, and children, all of them demonized by their HIV status. These books describe political struggles in the early 1980s as symptomatic of how medical experts confronted different diseases and how Reagan-era officials reacted too slowly to the medical and political crisis because the disease appeared to affect few, and socially marginal, groups—homosexuals, Haitians, hemophiliacs, and intravenous drug users.

46. Castor, "For the Love of Lorenzo," 22.

47. Treichler, "How to Have Theory in an Epidemic," 57 and 64.

48. Sander Gilman, "Seeing the AIDS Patient," 252.

49. George Miller, who has a medical degree, indicated he envisions his films as describing mythic journeys (including *Mad Max, Lorenzo's Oil,* and *Babe, A Pig in the City*). Also see Jones, "Medicine and the Movies: Lorenzo's Oil at Century's End"; and Crawford's reference to the quest narrative at the heart of Mervyn LeRoy's film of Marie Curie in "Glowing Dishes," 74.

50. Balzac's Père Goriot and Dickens's Little Nell are only two of many characters who disappear from fiction because they are too good to exist in a troubled world. Tompkins, *Sensational Designs,* analyzes little Eva's death from consumption as a religious parable demonstrating how the innocent suffer, a lesson that can also be applied to the situation of the slaves sacrificed for the sake of their masters' greed.

51. The notice of Lorenzo's death appears at the Myelin Project site (http://www.myelin.org/). The obituary indicates he died of aspiration pneumonia; see Weil, "Lorenzo Odone," 30.

52. Saxon, "Michaela Odone, 61, the 'Lorenzo's Oil Mother.'" *New York Times.* June 13, 2000.

53. See Concar, "Lessons from Lorenzo." This interview with Augusto Odone includes his comments on studies of transplanting cells into the brain.

54. Coleman and Concar, "Pouring Cold Water on Lorenzo's Oil"; Aubourg et al., "A Two-Year Trial of Oleic and Erucic Acids"; Rizzo, "Editorial Note"; Kolata, "Experts Join in Studying Lorenzo's Oil," and "After Setbacks, Small Successes for Gene Therapy."

55. Concar, "Lorenzo's Oil Really Does Save Lives."

56. See Rubin, "Lorenzo's Oil Brings Hope for the Afflicted."

57. Kolata, "After Setbacks, Small Successes for Gene Therapy."

Chapter 5

1. I thank Laura Otis for sharing her views of scientific life and her novels and for pointing me to LabLit.com, a thoughtful, entertaining site edited by scientist and science writer Dr. Jennifer Rohn for anyone interested laboratory life and representations of it.

2. FIRST NXT blog of Katie, age 14.

3. Haran et al., *Screening Women in SET.*

4. The Internet Movie Database lists hundreds of film and television shows tagged with "babe scientist" as a keyword. Another term with different resonance is "girl geek." As "History of Girl Geeks" at GirlGeeks.org explains, "Starting with on-camera interviews and an informational website, the name originally included a question mark—GirlGeeks?—because the filmmakers wanted to explore the stereotype of the word 'geek,' meeting women who considered 'geekiness' to be an insult and others that considered it a badge of honor. Turns out that Geek was a powerful description and definitely chic, so GirlGeeks dropped the question mark and pioneered the use of rich content, mentored community, and career-enhancement commerce online to gather, train and promote women with technology skills of all kinds into better jobs."

5. From *Publishers Weekly*'s review of "Self-Experiment."

6. Cussins, "Confessions of a Bioterrorist."

7. Høeg, *Smilla's Sense of Snow.*

8. Smilla's difficult relationship with her father also sets her apart.

9. Keller, *A Feeling for the Organism.*

10. This sentence paraphrases Roberts, "The Woman Scientist in *Star Trek: Voyager*," 278.

11. Steinke, "Connecting Theory and Practice."

12. Killheffer, "Discovering Women"; Goodman, "Women of Science and the Old Boys Club."

13. Haynes, *From Faust to Strangelove;* Shepherd-Barr, *Science on Stage.*

14. Perkowitz, *Hollywood Science;* Frayling, *Mad, Bad, and Dangerous.*

15. Rossiter, *Women Scientists in America;* Noble, *A World without Women.*

16. As noted in Perkowitz, "Female Scientists on the Big Screen."

17. According to Flicker, there are six types of female scientists in films—old maid, male woman, naive expert, evil plotter, daughter or assistant, and lonely heroine ("Representation of Women Scientists in Feature Films"). See Haynes, "From Alchemy to Artificial Intelligence"; and Flicker, "Between Brains and Breasts."

18. "*Love Potion Number 9,*" RottenTomatoes.com.

19. Doane, *The Desire to Desire,* 96.

20. See "Center for the Study of Women, Science, and Technology." Since the 1970s, many U.S. universities have worked to attract and retain more women in science; intervention programs for women in STEM include the Georgia Tech Center for the Study of Women, Science, and Technology (WST). Founded in 1998, WST provides students with information about career development, arranges for mentoring, and enables networking among students and faculty.

21. Newitz and Anders, *She's Such a Geek.*

22. Flicker, "Representation of Women Scientists in Feature Films."

23. The Hollywood formula for framing this heterosexual plot as "boy-meets- girl, boy-loses-girl, boy-gets-girl" is well-known as the basis for many movies. Yet the meaning of "meets" is more complicated than one might assume. The mediation of the audience in the romance film is critical regardless of whether the characters share the same film screen. Following in a tradition stretching from Shakespeare's romances, many romantic film comedies, such as Nora Ephron's *When Harry Met Sally* (1989), *Sleepless in Seattle* (1993), and *You've Got Mail* (1998), promote the audience's learning about the protagonists more than the films illustrate characters revealing themselves to each other. Romances tend to enforce heterosexuality as normative even if they are also normalizing homosexuality. In Shakespearean comedies, a female lead masquerades as a male before revealing her true identity. In the 2006 film *She's the Man* based on Shakespeare's *Twelfth Night,* actress Amanda Bynes plays a girl taking her brother's place at a boys' prep school so that she can play soccer after her own girls' school cuts their team. In disguise as her twin, she ends up falling in love with her roommate, a male soccer player who wonders how he could feel so close to another "guy."

24. "Q and A with Nell Minow."

25. Race and ethnicity are sometimes invoked in romances as a challenge to the partners (e.g., *West Side Story, Guess Who's Coming to Dinner*). Socioeconomic class differences separate lovers in Jane Austen's and other realist novels. Temperamental differences divide male and female protagonists in comedies such as *My Girl Friday* (1940), while depicting the newspaper editor and reporter at odds and also trading witty barbs.

26. Keller, *A Feeling for the Organism,* 197.

27. Crawford, "Glowing Dishes," 71.

28. Ibid., 72.

29. Much is made of Roxanne's nudity in comic moments. See Maslin, "Steve Martin."

30. I thank Rick and Charlie Denton for pointing out the musical intertexts.

31. On the conflict between Ellie and Drumlin, see Steinke, "Women Scientists Role Models on Screen," 125.

32. Palmer responds to Ellie most ardently when she appears more feminine: nude in bed with him, dressed in a ball gown for an official reception, in pajamas just before the launch.

33. Leslie Charteris's fictions were the source of a number of films/film series about the character, and there were several television series based on Charteris's works. See "The Saint."

34. Students Elizabeth Stowe, Christy Striplin, Trevor Christensen, and Savannah Brown, in my LCC 3304 "Science, Technology, and Gender" course, noted *The Saint's* emphasis on trust and transformation in their spring 2008 team project.

35. In a featured interview on the DVD of the film, Cholodenko describes *Laurel Canyon* as a comedy-drama about a female record producer based on Joni Mitchell.

36. Potter, *Yes: Screenplay and Notes.*

37. To indicate She's voiceover narration, this dialogue appears in italics in Potter's published screenplay.

38. Shafner, "'Intuition' Rings True in World of Science."

39. Goodman, *Intuition.*

40. For a recent account of Franklin's life and work, see Maddox, *Rosalind Franklin.*

41. See Kevles, *The Baltimore Case,* 307. In 1992, "[t]he O.S.I. was taken away from the N.I.H. and reconstituted as the Office of Research Integrity (O.R.I.) within the office of the assistant secretary for health."

42. The novel's plot concerning a post-doc's accusation of lab fraud resembles elements of Kevles's *The Baltimore Case,* a nonfictional account, but Goodman's novel elaborates a romantic plot and a characterization of the accuser that are distinctly different from Kevles's account. I thank Jay Labinger for pointing to Kevles's book as a source for Goodman's novel.

Chapter 6

1. Sundin, "Gender and Technology."
2. Cowan's ideas are referenced in Pursell, "Feminism and the Rethinking of the History of Technology," 115.
3. Wajcman, *Feminism Confronts Technology* (150) and *Technofeminisms.*
4. Stanley, "Women Hold Up Two-Thirds of the Sky."
5. Menke, *Telegraphic Realism,* 163–88.
6. Light, "Programming," 296.
7. Oldenziel, *Making Technology Masculine.*
8. Vostral, *Under Wraps,* 68–69.
9. Gilbreth and Carey, *Cheaper by the Dozen,* 2.
10. From "Pioneers in Improvement and Our Modern Standard of Living."
11. The more recent *Cheaper by the Dozen* films (Dir. Shawn Levy, 2003, and Dir. Adam Shankman, 2005) are updated to revise sex roles, recasting the Gilbreth parents as a college football coach (Steve Martin) and a homemaker-turned-author (Bonnie Hunt). The first film illustrates how the father has his hands full running a household and coaching a big-league team while the mother takes off on a tour to promote her book about family life; the second shows how the father cannot resist competing with a wealthier neighbor.
12. Cowan, *More Work for Mother.*
13. Inouye, *Fly Girls;* Wosk, *Women and the Machine.*
14. Dock et al., "'But One Expects That'"; Egan, "Evolutionary Theory in the Social Philosophy of Charlotte Perkins Gilman"; Maloney, "A Feminist Looks at Education"; and Berman, "The Unrestful Cure."
15. Horace E. Scudder, the editor of *The Atlantic Monthly,* wrote to Gilman that he could not accept the story, noting, "I could not forgive myself if I made others as miserable as I have made myself." See Gilman, *The Living of Charlotte Perkins Gilman.*
16. Scharnhorst, *Charlotte Perkins Gilman: A Bibliography,* lists approximately 185 fictions published in journals or monographs from 1886 through 1916. Gilman also wrote nonfiction books and essays.
17. See Knight, *Charlotte Perkins Gilman,* regarding Gilman's use of the phrase "short sermons" in advertising for *The Forerunner.* Knight's analyses have significantly contributed to my understanding of Gilman's work and my argument about the theme of work for women as outlined in her fictions. On Gilman's ideas about evolution, see Hausman, "Sex before Gender," and Magner, "Darwinism and the Woman Question."
18. This section is adapted from Colatrella, "Work for Women."
19. See Hayden, *The Grand Domestic Revolution,* a history of domestic reform in the United States that discusses eating clubs and cooked-food delivery services, among other innovations.

20. Gilman, *What Diantha Did.*

21. References to Gilman's fictions are from Shulman's Oxford edition.

22. Kessler, *Charlotte Perkins Gilman,* 271.

23. See "50 Greatest Screen Legends." Google notes that as of December 8, 2009, there were around 1,040,000 Web sites that included information on Hepburn. Bergan, *Katharine Hepburn,* points out that in a 1995 "poll conducted among 50 critics worldwide and the general public by the *Guardian* newspaper Kate was selected as the greatest woman film star ever, alive or dead. She topped a similar poll among film-makers in *Time-Out* magazine a few months later" (186). Dougherty, "Katharine Hepburn," is one example of a fan site.

24. Quoted in Bergan, *Katharine Hepburn,* 31.

25. Katharine Hepburn, interviewed by Rex Reed, *New York Daily News,* 28 January 1979. Quoted in Britton, *Katharine Hepburn,* half-title page.

26. David Selznick reportedly remarked on her "horse face" when he viewed rushes of *A Bill of Divorcement,* and Louis B. Mayer complained about her unnatural crying in rushes for *Sea of Grass,* but Hepburn cared more about how she felt than what they, or anybody else, thought. See Bergan, *Katharine Hepburn,* 31 and 101.

27. Edwards, *A Remarkable Woman,* 96; and Higham, *Kate,* 40, quoted in Mayne, *Directed by Dorothy Arzner,* 60.

28. Bergan, *Katharine Hepburn,* 32.

29. Adorno, "The Schema of Mass Culture," argues that such fusions are the inevitable result of mass culture consumption: "The work of art becomes its own material and forms the technique of reproduction and presentation, actually a technique for the distribution of a real object. Radio broadcasts for children which intentionally play off image and reality against one another for the sake of advertising commodities and in the next moment have a Wild West hero proclaiming the virtues of some breakfast cereal, betraying the domination of image over the programme in the process, are as characteristic as the identification of film stars with their roles which is promoted by the advertising media" (64). Hepburn's mother was at one time president of the Connecticut Woman's Suffrage Association and later worked with Planned Parenthood; see Bergan, *Katharine Hepburn,* 15.

30. "Christopher Strong."

31. "Biography for Katharine Hepburn."

32. For example, see Bergan, *Katharine Hepburn,* 31.

33. Dickens, *The Films of Katharine Hepburn,* 9.

34. Bergan, *Katharine Hepburn,* 25.

35. Ibid., 23.

36. Ibid.

37. Dickens, *The Films of Katharine Hepburn,* 60, quoted in Britton, *Katharine Hepburn,* 29.

38. Based on a novel by Gilbert Frankau, the film was called by one contemporary reviewer "a drawing room tragedy" (excerpt from film review in *Time,* quoted in Dickens, *The Films of Katherine Hepburn,* 44).

39. Butler, *East to the Dawn,* 168.

40. Dalle Vache, *Diva,* discusses "the airplane fad" among Italian feminists and film stars (121ff.).

41. Martin Scorsese's 2004 film *The Aviator* represents Howard Hughes teaching

Hepburn to fly.

42. "A Short History of the National Institutes of Health."

43. I thank Dirk Vanderbeke for mentioning Grant's paleontologist to me.

44. See Levine, "Scientific Success": "Marriage has also been shown to have an adverse impact on the careers of female scientists. Data from the National Science Foundation show that female, doctoral-level scientists, and engineers are less likely to be married than are their male counterparts (66 percent versus 83 percent). Among those married, however, women are more likely to confront problems accommodating a two-career marriage—one reason being that they are twice as likely as men to have a spouse who works full-time."

45. This section is based on Colatrella, "From *Desk Set* to *The Net*."

46. In *Sleepless in Seattle,* the intertext of the 1957 film *An Affair to Remember* serves as an example of a romance gone awry because of circumstances beyond the lovers' control.

47. Wajcman, *Feminism Confronts Technology,* 158.

48. "Key-presser" is a term used for a computer programmer in Rasmussen and Håpnes, "Excluding Women from Technologies of the Future?"

49. This section is adapted from Colatrella, "Feminist Narratives of Science and Technology."

50. Fox, "Women in Science and Engineering"; Fox, "Women, Science, and Academia"; and McIlwee and Robinson, *Women in Engineering.*

51. See Deery, "The Biopolitics of Cyberspace."

52. Haraway, "A Cyborg Manifesto," 434.

53. MacKenzie and Wajcman, "Preface to the Second Edition" (xiv–xvii), note, "The social shaping of technology, which in the mid-1980s still had something of the excitement of heresy, has now become almost an orthodoxy" (xv).

54. Isaac Asimov's computer scientist in *I, Robot,* Susan Calvin, might have been a model for the filmmakers. To Roberts, "The Woman Scientist in *Star Trek, Voyager,*" Calvin appears based on Rosalind Franklin (278–79).

55. This theme and the episodic construction resemble similar features in the popular movie *Thelma and Louise* (Dir. Ridley Scott, 1991), written by Callie Khouri.

56. Kristeva, "Oscillation du 'pouvoir' au 'refus,'" 164–66.

57. Karl Theweleit, cited by Modleski, *Feminism without Women,* 62.

58. Margolis and Fisher, *Unlocking the Clubhouse;* McIlwee and Robinson, *Women in Engineering.*

59. Rosser, *Re-Engineering Female-Friendly Science;* Balsamo, "Teaching in the Belly of the Beast," 192.

60. Miller, *Versions of Pygmalion,* 1.

Chapter 7

1. Rayman and Brett, "Women Science Majors," 389.

2. Fox, Sonnert, and Nikiforova, "Successful Programs for Undergraduate Women," 333.

3. Jacobs et al., "Career Plans of Adolescents."

4. Long, Boiarsky, and Thayer, "Gender and Racial Counter-Stereotypes in Science Education Television," 255.

5. For example, see Rosser, *Re-Engineering Female Friendly Science.*

6. Whitelegg, "Girls in Science Education," 180.

7. Jones, Howe, and Rua, "Gender Differences in Students' Experiences, Interests, and Attitudes toward Science and Scientists."

8. See Hyde et al., "Diversity: Gender Similarities Characterize Math Performance" (120–24), for a consideration of how girls' achievements are rationalized as the product of hard work.

9. Pipher, *Reviving Ophelia.*

10. Milkie, "Contested Images of Femininity," 839.

11. Steinke, "Science in Cyberspace," 8.

12. Gray, "Sugar and Spice and Science." Also see Steinke, "Connecting Theory and Practice."

13. Lemish, Liebes, and Seidmann, "Gendered Media Meanings and Uses," 278.

14. Slatalla, "Cyberfamilias: Today, I Think I'll Be Hippohead"; "Nintendogs Review."

15. Boyce and Kitzinger, *Promoting Women in the Media,* 9–10.

16. Seiter and Mayer, "Diversifying Representation in Children's TV," 121.

17. Signorelli, "A Content Analysis," and Smith, "Media More Likely to Show Women Talking about Romance than at a Job."

18. Long et al., "Gender and Racial Counter-Stereotypes," 256.

19. Steinke et al., "Assessing Media Influences on Middle School-Aged Children's Perceptions of Women in Science Using the Draw-a-Scientist Test (DAST)," 51.

20. Whitelegg et al., *(In)visible Witnesses,* 15 and 20.

21. Norton, *The Borrowers.*

22. Norton, *The Borrowers Afield.*

23. L'Engle, *A Wrinkle in Time.*

24. L'Engle, *A Wind in the Door.*

25. The *Spy Kids* films directed by Robert Rodriguez focus on similar themes: *Spy Kids* (2001); *Spy Kids 2: Island of Lost Dreams* (2002); and *Spy Kids 3-D: Game Over* (2003).

26. See Sedgwick's *Means and Ends,* As the teacher quoted in the first section, "What Is education?," outlines, girls should be educated to build on their natural talents: "You are born with certain faculties. Whatever tends to develop and improve these is education. Whatever trains your mental powers, your affections, manners, and habits, is education. Your education is not limited to any period of your life, but is going on as long as you live . . ." (9). An advice manual, *Means and Ends, or Self-Training* establishes a continuing narrative thread about Mary Bond by stringing together examples of how Mary applies the didactic lessons concerning education, social relations, and domestic management. Exemplifying how one young girl enacts principles promulgated by Sedgwick, Mary, like other fictional characters, serves as a representative role model for adolescents reading the work.

27. Ebert, "Ice Princess," 311–12.

28. "Handy Manny, the New Latin Cartoon Hero."

29. "Lisa the Simpson."

30. "Girls Just Want to Have Sums."

31. "Funeral for a Fiend."

32. "Please Homer Don't Hammer 'em."

33. See Holden, "They Have a Tantrum, Then Save the World": "Each girl has a distinct

personality (and color). The redheaded Blossom (with the voice of Catherine Cavadini), the trio's levelheaded leader, and the only one whose ears perk up instead of down, is fluent in Chinese. The blond Bubbles (Tara Strong), who likes to draw, is a twittery sweet-natured aesthete, and the green-hued Buttercup (E. G. Daily), whose voice is several pitches lower than those of her sisters, is a combative warrior." '

34. "The Powerpuff Girls."

35. "Characters," *Zoey 101.* I thank Lena Denton for discussing this show and *iCarly* with me.

36. "Quinnvention Corner."

37. Other science shows directed toward children include *Beakman's World* (1993–98); *Bill Nye, the Science Guy* (1993–2002); and *Newton's Apple* (1983–98). See Long et al., and Steinke and Long, "A Lab of Her Own," for a discussion of stereotypes in television programs.

38. Extraordinary Women Engineers Project, Final Report. Also see Extraordinary Women Engineers at http://www.engineeringwomen.org/video.html.

39. Design Squad.

40. "The Big Bang Theory: The Work Song Nanocluster (#2.18)."

41. See Beach, "Research Roundup," for a consideration of students' responses.

42. For example, Linda Simensky, director of children's programming at PBS, says that she "commissioned the Jim Henson Company to create one. I really wanted daily science that you encounter every day in life. And something that models asking questions." See Blair, "Move Over MacGyver."

Bibliography

Adorno, Max. "The Schema of Mass Culture." *The Culture Industry.* Ed. J. M. Bernstein. London and New York: Routledge, 1991.

"ADVANCING Women at VT: University Statistics 2006–07." *ADVANCE Newsletter.* August 2007. http://www.advance.vt.edu/News_Events/Newsletters/07-08/Aug_2007.pdf. Accessed July 17, 2008.

Aeschylus. *Aeschylus II: The Suppliant Maidens, The Persians, Seven against Thebes, and Prometheus Bound.* Trans. David Grene. Chicago: University of Chicago Press, 1956.

Allen, Jamie. "Author Says *Ahab's Wife* Is 'An Epic Story' of American Experience." *CNN Book News.* November 8, 1999. http://www.cnn.com/books/news/9911/08/Ahab.wife/. Accessed May 14, 2009.

Allen, Polly W. *Building Domestic Liberty: Charlotte Perkins Gilman's Architectural Feminism.* Amherst: University of Massachusetts Press, 1988.

Allum, Nick, Patrick Sturgis, Dimitra Tabourazi, and Ian Brunton-Smith. "Science Knowledge and Attitudes across Cultures: A Meta-Analysis." *Public Understanding of Science* 17 (2008): 35–54.

American Association of University Professors. *AAUP Gender Equity Indicators.* 2006. www.aaup.org. Accessed May 13, 2008.

American Sociological Association. "Statement of the American Sociological Association Council on the Causes of Gender Differences in Science and Math Career Achievement: Harvard's Lawrence Summers and the Ensuing Public Debate." February 28, 2005. http://www.asanet.org/page.ww?section=Issue+Statements&name=Statement+on+Summers. Accessed July 17, 2008.

Annas, George. "Cloning and the U.S. Congress." *New England Journal of Medicine* 346.20 (May 16, 2002): 1599–1602.

Arata, Stephen D. "The Occidental Tourist: *Dracula* and the Anxiety of Reverse Colonization." *Victorian Studies* 33 (1990): 621–45.

Attebury, Brian. *Decoding Gender in Science Fiction.* New York and London: Routledge, 2002.

Atwood, Margaret. *Oryx and Crake*. New York: Doubleday, 2003.

Aubourg, Patrick et al. "A Two-Year Trial of Oleic and Erucic Acids ("Lorenzo's Oil") as Treatment for Adrenomyeloneuropathy." *The New England Journal of Medicine* (September 9, 1993): 745–52.

Auerbach, Nina. *Woman and the Demon: The Life of a Victorian Myth*. Cambridge: Harvard University Press, 1982.

Baguley, David. *Fécondité d'Emile Zola*. Toronto: University of Toronto Press, 1973.

Bal, Mieke. *Narratology: Introduction to the Theory of Narrative*. Toronto and Buffalo: University of Toronto Press, 1985.

Balsamo, Anne. "Teaching in the Belly of the Beast: Feminism in the Best of All Places." *Wild Science: Reading Feminism, Medicine, and the Media*. Ed. Janine Marchessault and Kim Sawchuk. New York and London: Routledge, 2000. 185–213.

Balzac, Honoré de. *Cousine Bette*. Trans. Marion Ayton Crawford. New York: Penguin, 1984.

———. *La Cousine Bette*. Paris: Gallimard, 1977.

———. *A Harlot High and Low*. Trans. Rayner Heppenstall. New York: Penguin, 1979.

Barlowe, Jamie. *The Scarlet Mob of Scribblers: Rereading Hester Prynne*. Carbondale: Southern Illinois University Press, 2000.

Barthes, Roland. *Michelet*. Trans. Richard Howard. New York: Hill and Wang, 1987.

Baym, Nina. *American Women of Letters and the Nineteenth-Century Sciences: Styles of Affiliation*. New Brunswick: Rutgers University Press, 2001.

Beach, Richard. "Research Roundup: Film and Television Review." *The English Journal* 66.3 (1977): 90–93.

Belkin, Lisa. "Diversity Isn't Rocket Science, Is It?" *New York Times*. May 15, 2008. E2.

Bergan, Ronald. *Katharine Hepburn: An Independent Woman*. New York: Arcade Publishing, 1996.

Berman, Jeffrey. "The Unrestful Cure: Charlotte Perkins Gilman and 'The Yellow Wallpaper.'" *The Captive Imagination: A Casebook on "The Yellow Wallpaper."* Ed. C. Golden. New York: Feminist Press, 1992. 211–41.

Bertrand-Jennings, Chantal. *L'Eros et la femme chez Zola*. Paris: Klincksieck, 1977.

Bickley, R. Bruce, Jr. *The Method of Melville's Short Fiction*. Durham: Duke University Press, 1975.

Bierne, Piers. "Adolphe Quetelet and the Origins of Positivist Criminology." *American Journal of Sociology* 92.5 (1987): 1140–69.

"The Big Bang Theory: The Work Song Nanocluster (#2.18)." 2009. Internet Movie Database. http://www.imdb.com/character/ch0064640/quotes. Accessed December 21, 2009.

"Biography for Catherine Willows from *CSI* (*Crime Scene Investigation*) (2000)." Internet Movie Database. Page last updated June 2008. http://www.imdb.com/character/ch0011010/bio. Accessed July 20, 2008.

"Biography for Katharine Hepburn." *Internet Movie Database*. http://us.imdb.com/Bio/Hepburn.+Katharine. Accessed August 4, 2008.

Birke, Linda. "In Pursuit of Difference." (1992). Republished in *The Gender and Science Reader*. Ed. Muriel Lederman and Ingrid Bartsch. London: Routledge, 2001. 309–22.

Blair, Elizabeth "Move Over MacGyver, Other Shows Make Science Fun." *NPR*. December 7, 2009. http://www.npr.org/templates/story/story.php?storyId=121146862. Accessed December 29, 2009.

Blum, Hester. *The View from the Masthead: Maritime Imagination and Antebellum America*. Chapel Hill: University of North Carolina Press, 2008.

Bollag, Burt. "Award-Winning Teaching." *The Chronicle of Higher Education* (December 1, 2006). http://chronicle.com/weekly/v53/i15/15a01001.htm. Accessed March 13, 2008.

Bosk, Charles L. and Joel E. Frader. "AIDS and Its Impact on Medical Work." *A Disease of Society: Cultural and Institutional Responses to AIDS*. Ed. Dorothy Nelkin, David P. Willis, and Scott V. Parris. New York: Cambridge University Press, 1991.

Boyce, Tammy and Jenny Kitzinger. *Promoting Women in the Media: The Role of SET Organisations and Their Science Media Communicators*. UK Resource Centre for Women in Science, Engineering and Technology. Research Report 4. March 2008.

Brainard, Jeffrey. "Divided Bioethics Panel Recommends Moratorium on Research Cloning." *The Chronicle of Higher Education* (July 12, 2002). http://chronicle.com/daily/2002/07/2002071201n.html. Accessed July 1, 2008.

Britton, Andrew. *Katharine Hepburn: Star as Feminist*. New York: Continuum, 1995.

Brooks, Peter. *Reading for the Plot: Design and Intention in Narrative*. New York: Random House, 1985.

Browner, Stephanie P. *Profound Science and Elegant Literature: Imagining Doctors in Nineteenth-Century America*. University Park: University of Pennsylvania Press, 2004.

Buchanan, Andrea J. and Miriam Peskowitz. *The Daring Book for Girls*. New York: HarperCollins, 2007.

Burr, Sandra L. "Fortune Favors the Brave: The Continuing Story of Lorenzo's Oil." http://www.law.uh.edu/healthlaw/perspectives/Research/020715Fortune.html. Accessed August 1, 2008.

Butler, Susan. *East to the Dawn: The Life of Amelia Earhart*. Reading: Addison-Wesley, 1997.

Castor, Elizabeth. "For the Love of Lorenzo." *American Health* 2 (May 1993): 20–23.

CBS News. "Employers Play Dr. Mom to Control H1N1." Trenton, NJ. November 30, 2009. http://www.cbsnews.com/stories/2009/11/30/health/main5837843.shtml. Accessed December 6, 2009.

Ceci, Stephen and Wendy Williams, eds. *Why Aren't More Women in Science?* Washington, DC: American Psychological Association, 2007.

Center for the Study of Women, Science, and Technology. Georgia Institute of Technology. http://www.wst.gatech.edu. Accessed August 9, 2008.

"Characters." *Zoey 101*. http://www.nick.com/shows/zoey_101/index.jhtml. Accessed July 29, 2008.

Chevalier, Louis. *Laboring Classes and Dangerous Classes*. Trans. Frank Jellinek. New York: Howard Fertig, 1973.

Child, Lydia Maria. *The Children of Mount Ida and Other Stories*. New York: Charles Francis, 1871.

"Christopher Strong." *Internet Movie Database*. http://www.imdb.com/title/tt0023891/. Accessed July 6, 2008.

Cixous, Hélène. "The Laugh of the Medusa." Trans. Keith Cohen and Paula Cohen. *The Signs Reader: Women, Gender, and Scholarship*. Ed. Elizabeth Abel and Emily K. Abel. Chicago: University of Chicago Press, 1983.

"Cloudy with a Chance of Meatballs." Internet Movie Database. http://www.imdb.com/title/tt0844471/synopsis. Accessed December 21, 2009.

Clough, Patricia T. *Feminist Thought: Desire, Power, and Academic Discourse.* Oxford: Blackwell, 1994.

Cockburn, Cynthia and Susan Ormrod. *Gender and Technology in the Making.* London: Sage, 1993.

Cohan, Steven and Linda M. Shires. *Telling Stories: A Theoretical Analysis of Narrative Fiction.* New York and London: Routledge, 1988.

Colatrella, Carol. "The American Experiment in Criminal Justice and Its European Observers." *National Stereotypes in Perspective: Americans in France, Frenchmen in America.* Ed. William Chew, III. Amsterdam: Rodopi, 2001. 113–41.

———. "At optraevle kniplingen." ["Unraveling the Lacemaker."] Translated into Danish by Jakob Stougaard and Thomas Teilmann Damm. Copenhagen, Denmark. *Passage* 20/21 (December 1995): 141–55.

———. "Come trasformare l'assistenza medica nell'età dell'AIDS" ["Transforming Medical Care in the Age of AIDS: Science and Parental Love in *Lorenzo's Oil*."] Translated into Italian by Cinzia Scarpino. Rome, Italy. *Ácoma: Rivista Internazionale di Studi Nordamericani* 28 (2004): 114–26.

———. "Emerson's Politics of the Novel." *Emerson at 200: Proceedings of the International Bicentennial Conference.* Rome, October 16–18, 2003. Ed. Giorgio Mariani. University of Rome, 2004. 265–277.

———. *Evolution, Sacrifice, and Narrative: Balzac, Zola, and Faulkner.* New York and London: Garland, 1990.

———. "Fear of Reproduction and Desire for Replication in *Dracula*." *The Journal of Medical Humanities* 17.3 (Spring 1996): 179–89.

———. "Feminist Narratives of Science and Technology: Artificial Life and True Love in *Eve of Destruction* and *Making Mr. Right*." *Women, Gender, and Technology.* Ed. Mary Frank Fox, Deborah Johnson, and Sue Rosser. Urbana: University of Illinois Press, 2006. 157–73.

———. "From *Desk Set* to *The Net*: Women and Computing Technology in Hollywood Films." *Canadian Review of American Studies* 31.2 (2001): 1–14.

———. *Literature and Moral Reform: Melville and the Discipline of Reading.* Gainesville: University Press of Florida, 2002.

———. "Representing Female-Friendly Science and Technology in Fiction and Film." *Women and Technology: Proceedings of the 1999 International Symposium on Technology and Society* (Piscataway: IEEE, 1999). 19–26.

———. "Science, Technology, and Literature." *The Encyclopedia of Science, Technology, and Ethics.* Ed. Carl Mitcham, Larry Arnhart, Stephanie Bird, Deborah Johnson, Raymond Spier. Farmington Hills, MI: Macmillan, 2005. 1714–23.

———. "The Significant Silence of Race: *La Cousine Bette* and 'Benito Cereno.'" *Comparative Literature* 46.3 (Summer 1994): 240–66.

———. "Work for Women: Recuperating Charlotte Perkins Gilman's Reform Fiction." *Research in Science and Technology Studies (Knowledge and Society,* vol. 12). Ed. Shirley Gorenstein. Stamford, CT: JAI Press, 2000. 53–76.

Cole, Joanna, Carolyn Bracken, and Bruce Degan. *Magic School Bus Taking Flight: A Book about Flight.* New York: Scholastic Publications, 1997.

Cole, Simon A. *Suspect Identities: A History of Fingerprinting and Criminal Identification.*

Cambridge: Harvard University Press, 2001.

Coleman, Julian and David Concar, "Pouring Cold Water on Lorenzo's Oil." *New Scientist* 6 (March 1993): 23–24.

Collingwood, R. G. *The Idea of History*. Oxford: Oxford University Press, 1956.

Collins, Philip. *Dickens and Crime*. Bloomington: Indiana University Press, 1968.

Colman, David. "Just a Few Favorite Indulgences." *New York Times Magazine*. March 23, 2008. http://www.nytimes.com/2008/03/23/fashion/23POSS.html?_r=1. Accessed December 14, 2009.

Combe, George. *Manual of Phrenology*. Boston: Marsh, Capen, Lyon, and Webb, 1839.

Committee on Science, Engineering, and Public Policy (COSEPUP). *Beyond Bias and Barriers: Fulfilling the Potential of Women in Academic Science and Engineering*. 2007. http://books.nap.edu/openbook.php?record_id=11741&page=214. Accessed August 7, 2008.

Concar, David. "Lessons from Lorenzo." *New Scientist*. January 26, 2002. http://www.newscientist.com/article/mg17323274.700-lessons-from-lorenzo.html. Accessed August 1, 2008.

———. "Lorenzo's Oil Really Does Save Lives." *New Scientist*. October 5, 2002. http://www.newscientist.com/article/mg17623630.600-lorenzos-oil-really-does-save-lives.html. Accessed August 1, 2008.

Cowan, Ruth Schwarz. *More Work for Mother: The Ironies of Household Technology from the Open Hearth to the Microwave*. New York: Basic Books, 1983.

Crawford, T. Hugh. "Glowing Dishes: Radium, Marie Curie, and Hollywood." *Biography* 23.1 (2000): 71–89.

Cross, Gary. *Kids' Stuff: Toys and the Changing World of American Childhood*. Cambridge: Harvard University Press, 1997.

Culler, Jonathan. *Structuralist Poetics*. Ithaca: Cornell University Press, 1976.

Cunningham, George B., Michael Sagas, Melanie L. Sartore, Michelle L. Amsden, and Anne Schellhase. "Gender Representation in the NCAA News: Is the Glass Half Full or Half Empty?" *Sex Roles* 50.11/12 (June 2004): 861–70.

Cussins, Charis. "Confessions of a Bioterrorist: Subject Position in Reproductive Technology." *Playing Dolly: Technocultural Formations, Fantasies, and Fictions of Assisted Reproduction*. Ed. E. Ann Kaplan and Susan Squier. New Brunswick: Rutgers University Press, 1999. 189–219.

daddytypes.com. "Pottery Barn Kids Girls and Boys." October 31, 2005. http://daddytypes.com/2005/10/31/pottery_barn_kids_girls_boys.php. Accessed December 14, 2009.

Dalle Vacche, Angela. *Diva: Defiance and Passion in Early Italian Cinema*. Austin: University of Texas Press, 2008.

Davidson, Cathy N. *Revolution and the Word: The Rise of the Novel in America*. New York: Oxford University Press, 1986.

Davis-Floyd, Robbie E. "Birth as an American Rite of Passage." *Childbirth in America*. Ed. Karen L. Michaelson. Westport: Bergin and Garvey, 1988. 153–72.

Dawson, Graham. *Soldier Heroes. British Adventure, Empire and the Imagining of Masculinities*. London: Routledge, 1994.

Dean, Cornelia. "Women in Science: The Battle Moves to the Trenches." *New York Times*. December 19, 2006. http://www.nytimes.com/2006/12/19/science/19women.html. Accessed June 29, 2008.

Deery, June. "The Biopolitics of Cyberspace: Piercy Hacks Gibson." *Future Females, The Next*

Generation: New Voices and Velocities in Feminist Science Fiction Criticism. Ed. Marleen S. Barr. Lanham, MD: Rowman and Littlefield, 2000. 87–108.

Design News Staff. *"Engineers Making a Difference: Five Engineers Find the Time to Teach Kids That Engineering Is Cool."* *Design News* (December 17, 2001): 50. Cited in "MacGyver," Wikipedia, http://en.wikipedia.org/wiki/MacGyver. Accessed March 14, 2008.

Design Squad. "About the Program." http://pbskids.org/designsquad/parentseducators/program/program_summary.html. Accessed July 27, 2008.

Dickens, Homer. *The Films of Katharine Hepburn.* New York: Citadel Press, 1971.

Dijkstra, Bram. *Idols of Perversity: Fantasies of Feminine Evil in Fin de Siècle Culture.* New York: Oxford University Press, 1986.

Division of Science Resources Statistics. National Science Foundation. *Key Findings 2008.* http://www.nsf.gov/statistics/nsf10309/content.cfm?pub_id=3996&id=4. Accessed January 3, 2010.

Doane, Mary Ann. *The Desire to Desire: The Women's Films of the 1940s.* Bloomington: Indiana University Press, 1987.

Dock, J. B., with D. R.Allen, J. Palais, and K. Tracy. "'But One Expects That'": Charlotte Perkins Gilman's 'The Yellow Wallpaper' and the Shifting Light of Scholarship." *PMLA* 111.1 (1996): 52–65.

Donawerth, Jane. *Frankenstein's Daughters: Women Writing Science Fiction.* Syracuse: Syracuse University Press, 1997.

Dougherty, Lynn Powell. "Katharine Hepburn." http://www.classicmoviefavorites.com/hepburn/. Accessed August 4, 2008.

Douglas, Susan J. *Where the Girls Are: Growing Up Female with the Media.* New York: Times Books, 1995.

———. "Where Have You Gone, Roseanne Barr?" *The Shriver Report: A Study by Maria Shriver and the Center for American Progress.* 2009. http://awomansnation.com/media.php. Accessed October 21, 2009.

Dow, Bonnie J. *Prime-Time Feminism.* Philadelphia: University of Pennsylvania Press, 1996.

Dowd, Maureen. "Barbie Loves Math." *New York Times.* February 6, 2002. http://www.nytimes.com/2002/02/06/opinion/barbie-loves-math.html. Accessed June 30, 2008.

Dunn, Adam. "Ahab's Wife." *Fiction Book Page.* http://www.bookpage.com/9910bp/fiction/ahabs_wife.html. Accessed May 14, 2009.

Eagleton, Terry. *Literary Theory: An Introduction.* Minneapolis: University of Minnesota Press, 1983.

Easton, Allison. *The Making of the Hawthorne Subject.* Columbia: University of Missouri Press, 1996.

Ebert, Roger. "Ice Princess." *Roger Ebert's Movie Yearbook 2006.* Riverside, NJ: Andrews McMeel Publishing, 2005. 311–12.

Edge: The Third Culture. http://www.edge.org/3rd_culture/debate05/debate05_index.html. Accessed June 29, 2008.

Edwards, Anne. *A Remarkable Woman: A Biography of Katharine Hepburn.* New York: Morrow, 1985; reprint, New York: Simon and Schuster, 1986.

Egan, Maureen L. "Evolutionary Theory in the Social Philosophy of Charlotte Perkins Gilman." *Hypatia* 4.1 (1989): 102–19.

Ehrenreich, Barbara and Deirdre English. *For Her Own Good.* New York: Random House,

1978; reprint 2005.

Eisenberg, Arlene, Heidi H. Murkoff, and Sandee E. Hathaway. *What to Expect When You're Expecting.* New York: Workman, 1991.

Etzkowitz, Henry, Carol Kemelgor, and Brian Uzzi. *Athena Unbound: The Advancement of Women in Science and Technology.* Cambridge: Cambridge University Press, 2000.

Evans, Gail. *She Wins, You Win.* New York: Penguin, 2003.

———. Speech. Georgia Women in Higher Education (GAWHE) Conference. Callaway Gardens, GA. February 27, 2004.

Extraordinary Women Engineers. http://www.engineeringwomen.org/video.html. Accessed July 27, 2008.

Extraordinary Women Engineers Project. Final Report. April 1995. 39 pages, p. 19. http://www.engineeringwomen.org/pdf/EWEPFinal.pdf. Accessed July 27, 2008.

Faludi, Susan. *Backlash: The Undeclared War against American Women.* New York: Crown Publishers, 1991.

Felski, Rita. *Beyond Feminist Asthetics.* Cambridge: Harvard University Press, 1989.

Ferguson, John. *A Companion to Greek Tragedy.* Austin: University of Texas Press, 1972.

Fetterley, Judith and Marjorie Pryse, eds. *American Women Regionalists, 1850–1910.* New York: W. W. Norton, 1992.

"50 Greatest Screen Legends." The American Film Institute. www.infoplease.com/ipea/A0778093.html. Accessed July 6, 2008.

First Lego League. http://www.firstlegoleague.org/. Accessed June 29, 2008.

FIRST NXT blog. Katie, age 14. "Marketing Science to Girls." The NXT Step: Lego Mindstorms. February 17, 2007. http://thenxtstep.blogspot.com/2007/02/marketing-science-to-girls.html. Accessed August 3, 2008.

Flicker, Eva. "Between Brains and Breasts—Women Scientists in Fiction Film: On the Marginalization and Sexualization of Scientific Competence." *Public Understanding of Science* 12 (2003): 307–18.

———. "Representation of Women Scientists in Feature Films: 1929 to 2003." http://www.ostina.org/index2.php?option=com_content&do_pdf=1&id=389. Accessed June 23, 2009.

Fontenelle, Bernard le Bovier de. *Conversations on the Plurality of Worlds.* Trans. H. A. Hargreaves. Berkeley: University of California Press, 1990. Advertisement at http://www.ucpress.edu/books/pages/2529.php. Accessed November 17, 2009.

Foucault, Michel. *Discipline and Punish.* Trans. Alan Sheridan. New York: Random House, 1979.

Fox, Mary Frank. "Institutional Transformation and the Advancement of Women Faculty: The Case of Academic Science and Engineering." *Higher Education: Handbook of Theory and Research,* vol. 23. Ed. J. C. Stuart. New York: Springer, 2008. 77–103, 77.

———. "Women, Science, and Academia." *Gender and Society* (2001): 654–66.

———. "Women in Science and Engineering: Theory, Practice, and Policy in Programs." *Signs* 24.1 (1998): 201–23.

——— and Sharlene Hesse-Biber. *Women at Work.* Mountain View, CA: Mayfield Publishing, 1984.

——— and Sushanta Mohapatra. "Social-Organizational Characteristics of Work and Publication Productivity among Academic Scientists in Doctoral Granting Departments." *The*

Journal of Higher Education 78 (September/October 2007): 542–71.

———, Gerhard Sonnert, and Irina Nikiforova. "Successful Programs for Undergraduate Women." *Research in Higher Education* 50 (2009): 333–53.

Frankenstein Unbound. Dir. Roger Corman, 1990.

Fraser-Abder, Pamela and Jayshree A. Mehta. "Literacy for All: Educating and Empowering Women." *Missing Links: Gender Equity in Science and Technology for Development.* Gender Working Group, United Nations Commission on Science and Technology. Ottawa: International Development Research Centre, 1995. 210–11.

Frayling, Christopher. *Mad, Bad, and Dangerous? The Scientist and Cinema.* London: Reaktion, 2005.

"Funeral for a Fiend." Season 19, Episode 8. *The Simpsons.* Original airdate 11/25/07. http://en.wikipedia.org/wiki/Funeral_for_a_Fiend. Accessed August 5, 2008.

Geringer, Joseph. "Vidocq: Convict Turned Criminal Magnifique." *Trutv Crime Library: Masterminds and Detectives.* http://www.crimelibrary.com/gangsters_outlaws/cops_others/vidocq/1.html. Accessed July 2, 2008.

Gilbert, Susan and Susan Gubar. *Madwoman in the Attic.* New Haven: Yale University Press, 1979.

Gilbreth, Frank and Ernestine Gilbreth. *Cheaper by the Dozen.* New York: HarperTorch, 2003.

Gilman, Charlotte Perkins. *The Charlotte Perkins Gilman Reader.* Ed. Ann J. Lane. New York: Pantheon Books, 1980.

———. "Coming Changes in Literature." *Forerunner* 6 (1915): 230–36; reprinted in Denise D. Knight, *Charlotte Perkins Gilman: A Study of the Short Fiction.* New York: Twayne, 1997.

———. *The Home: Its Work and Influence.* New York: Source Book Press, 1976.

———. *The Living of Charlotte Perkins Gilman: An Autobiography.* (1935). Introduction by A. J. Lane. Madison: University of Wisconsin Press, 1990.

———. *The Yellow Wallpaper.* Ed. Dale M. Bauer. Boston and New York: Bedford Books, 1998.

———. *The Yellow Wallpaper and Other Stories.* Ed. Robert Shulman. New York: Oxford Books, 1995.

———. *The Yellow Wallpaper and Other Writings.* Ed. Lynne Sharon Schwartz. New York: Bantam Books, 1989.

———. *What Diantha Did.* Durham: Duke University Press, 2005.

———. *Women and Economics.* (1898). Amherst and New York: Prometheus Books, 1994.

Gilman, Sander. "Seeing the AIDS Patient." *Disease and Representation: Images of Illness from Madness to AIDS.* Ithaca: Cornell University Press, 1988.

"Girls Just Want to Have Sums." Episode 1719. *The Simpsons.* Original airdate 4/30/06. http://www.thesimpsons.com/episode_guide/1719.htm. Accessed August 5, 2008.

Goldstein, Richard. "The Implicated and the Immune: Responses to AIDS in the Arts and Popular Culture." *A Disease of Society: Cultural and Institutional Responses to AIDS.* Ed. Dorothy Nelkin, David P. Willis, and Scott V. Parris. New York: Cambridge University Press, 1991. 17–42.

Goodman, Allegra. *Intuition.* New York: Random House, 2006.

Goodman, Walter. "Women of Science and the Old Boys Club." *New York Times.* March 29, 1995. http://www.nytimes.com/1995/03/29/arts/television-review-women-of-science-and-the-old-boys-club.html. Accessed August 3, 2008.

Gostinger, Linda. "Adrenoleukodystrophy (ALD): A Case Study Using the Film 'Lorenzo's Oil.'" http://www.accessexcellence.org/AE/AEPC/WWC/1994/adreno.php. Accessed August 1, 2008.

Gould, Stephen Jay. *The Mismeasure of Man.* New York: Norton, 1981.

Gray, Jennifer B. "Sugar and Spice and Science: Encouraging Girls through Media Mentoring." *Current Issues in Education* 8.18 (August 8, 2005). Available online at http://cie.ed.asu.edu/volume8/number18. Accessed July 22, 2008.

Green, Penelope. "Books: Girls Gone Wild, Idaho Style." *New York Times.* June 26, 2008. D3.

Handelsman, Jo, Nancy Cantor, Molly Carnes, Denice Denton, Eve Fine, Barbara Grosz, Virginia Hinshaw, Cora Marrett, Sue Rosser, Donna Shalala, and Jennifer Sheridan. "More Women in Science." *Science* 309 (2005): 1190–99.

"Handy Manny, the New Latin Cartoon Hero" *Ask Marivi?* http://www.rbird.com/movable-type/askmarivi/archives/handy-manny-the-new-latin-cartoon-hero.php. Accessed July 29, 2008.

Hanson, Sandra. *Swimming against the Tide: African American Girls and Science Education.* Philadelphia: Temple University Press, 2008.

Haran, Joan, Mwenya Chimba, Grace Reid, and Jenny Kitzinger. *Screening Women in SET: How Women in Science, Engineering and Technology Are Represented in Films and on Television.* UK Resource Centre for Women in Science, Engineering and Technology. Research Report 3. 2008.

Haraway, Donna. "A Cyborg Manifesto." (1985). *Sex/Machine.* Ed. Patrick D. Hopkins. Bloomington: Indiana University Press. 434–67.

Harding, Sandra. "Just Add Women and Stir?" *Missing Links: Gender Equity in Science and Technology for Development.* Gender Working Group, United Nations Commission on Science and Technology. Ottawa: International Development Research Centre, 1995. 306–7. http://www.idrc.ca/en/ev-29528-201-1-DO-TOPIC.html. Accessed September 12, 2010.

Hausman, Bernice L. "Sex before Gender: Charlotte Perkins Gilman and the Evolutionary Paradigm of Utopia." *Feminist Studies* 24.3 (1998): 488–510.

Hawthorne, Nathaniel. *Selected Tales and Sketches.* New York: Penguin, 1987.

Hayden, Dolores. *The Grand Domestic Revolution: A History of Feminist Designs for American Homes, Neighborhoods, and Cities.* Cambridge: MIT Press, 1985.

Haynes, Roslynn. "From Alchemy to Artificial Intelligence: Stereotypes of the Scientist in Western Literature." *Public Understanding of Science* 12 (2003): 243–53.

Haynes, Roslynn D. *From Faust to Strangelove: Representations of the Scientist in Western Literature.* Baltimore: Johns Hopkins University Press, 1994.

Heller, Scott. "The 'New' Melville." *The Chronicle of Higher Education* (April 6, 1994): A8.

Hemmings, F. W. J. *The Life and Times of Emile Zola.* New York: Scribner's, 1977.

Henley, Jon. "The Power of Pink." *The Guardian.* December 12, 2009. http://www.guardian.co.uk/theguardian/2009/dec/12/pinkstinks-the-power-of-pink. Accessed January 3, 2010.

Hines, Melissa. "Do Sex Differences in Cognition Cause the Shortage of Women in Science?" *Why Aren't More Women in Science?* Ed. Stephen Ceci and Wendy Williams. Washington, DC: American Psychological Association, 2007. 101–12.

"Histoire de la criminologie." *La Grande Encyclopédie,* vol. 6. Paris: Librairie Larousse, 1973. 3477–78.

"History of Girl Geeks." *Girl Geeks.* http://www.girlgeeks.org/about/history.shtml. Accessed August 2, 2008.

Høeg, Peter. *Smilla's Sense of Snow.* Trans. Tina Nunnally. New York: Dell, 1993.

Holden, Stephen. "They Have a Tantrum, Then Save the World." *New York Times.* July 3, 2002. http://www.nytimes.com/2002/07/03/movies/03PUFF.html. Accessed July 31, 2008.

Hopkins, Patrick D., ed. *Sex/Machine.* Bloomington: Indiana University Press, 1998.

Horowitz, Roger, ed. *Boys and Their Toys?: Masculinity, Class, and Technology.* New York and London: Routledge, 2001.

Hugo, Victor. *Les Misérables.* Trans. Lee Fahnestock and Norman MacAfee, based on the C. E. Wilbour translation. New York: New American Library, 1987.

Hyde, Janet Shibley. "Women in Science: Gender Similarities in Abilities and Sociocultural Forces." *Why Aren't More Women in Science?* Ed. Stephen Ceci and Wendy Williams. Washington, DC: American Psychological Association, 2007. 131–46.

Hyde, Janet S., Sara M. Lindberg, Marcia C. Linn, Amy B. Ellis, and Caroline C. Williams. "Diversity: Gender Similarities Characterize Math Performance." *Science* (July 25, 2008): 494–95.

Iggulden, Conn and Hal Iggulden. *The Dangerous Book for Boys.* New York: HarperCollins, 2007.

Inouye, Amy. *Fly Girls: Stories, Pictures, and Adventures from History's Most Dashing Lady Pilots.* Chicago: Girl Press, 2001.

Internet Movie Database. www.imdb.com.

Jacobs, Janis E., Laura L. Finken, Nancy Lindsley Griffin, Janet D. Wright. "Career Plans of Adolescents." *American Education Research Journal* 35.4 (1998): 681–704.

"January's Book: *Ahab's Wife* by Sena Jeter Naslund." KET [Kentucky Education Television]. http://www.ket.org/bookclub/books/2000_jul/interview.htm. Accessed July 1, 2008.

Jewett, Sarah Orne. *Novels and Stories.* New York: Library of America, 1994.

Johnson, Lisa and Andrea Learned. *Don't Think Pink: What Really Makes Women Buy—and How to Increase Your Share of This Crucial Market.* New York: American Management Association, 2004.

Jones, Anne Hudson. "Medicine and the Movies: *Lorenzo's Oil* at Century's End." *Annals of Internal Medicine* 133.7 (October 3, 2000): 567–71. http://www.annals.org/content/v01133/issue7/. Accessed June 24, 2009.

Jones, M. Gail, Ann Howe, and Melissa J. Rua. "Gender Differences in Students' Experiences, Interests, and Attitudes toward Science and Scientists." *Science Education* 84 (2000): 180–92.

Joyrich, Lynn. *Re-Viewing Reception: Television, Gender, and Postmodern Culture.* Bloomington: Indiana University Press, 1996.

Karcher, Carolyn. "Lydia Maria Child." *Dictionary of Literary Biography: American Short Story Writers before 1880.* Ed. Bobby Ellen Kimbel. Detroit: Gale Research, 1988. 43–53.

———. "Philanthropy and the Occult in the Fiction of Hawthorne, Brownson, and Melville." *The Haunted Dusk: American Supernatural Fiction, 1820–1920.* Ed. Howard Kerr, John W. Crowley, and Charles L. Crow. Athens: University of Georgia Press, 1983.

"Katharine Hepburn" by Lynn Powell Dougherty. http://www.classicmoviefavorites.com/hepburn/. Accessed August 4, 2008.

Keller, Evelyn Fox. *A Feeling for the Organism: The Life and Work of Barbara McClintock.* New

York: W. H. Freeman, 1983.

Kellner, Robert Scott. "Slaves and Shrews: Women in Melville's Short Stories." *University of Mississippi Studies in English* (1984–87): 297–310.

Kelly, Dorothy. *Fictional Genders: Role and Representation in Nineteenth-Century French Narrative*. Lincoln: University of Nebraska Press, 1989.

Kenschaft, Lori. "Just a Spoonful of Sugar?" *Girls, Boys, Books, and Toys: Gender in Children's Literatue and Culture*. Ed. Beverly Lyon Clark and Margaret R. Higgonet. Baltimore: Johns Hopkins University Press, 1999. 227–42.

Kessler, Carol F. *Charlotte Perkins Gilman: Her Progress to Utopia*. Syracuse: Syracuse University Press, 1995.

Kevles, Daniel J. *The Baltimore Case: A Trial of Politics, Science, and Character*. New York: W. W. Norton, 1998.

Killheffer, Robert K. J. "Discovering Women: Television Attempts to Alter a Cultural Bias." *Omni* 17.7 (April 1995): 27.

Kirn, Walter. "Call Me Mrs." *New York Magazine*. November 8, 1999. http://nymag.com/nymetro/arts/books/reviews/1370/. Accessed July 1, 2008.

Kitzinger, Jenny, Mwenya Chimba, Andrew Williams, Joan Haran, and Tammy Boyce. *Gender Stereotypes and Expertise in the Press: How Newspapers Represent Female and Male Scientists*. UK Resource Centre for Women in Science, Engineering and Technology. Research Report 2. March 2008.

———, Joan Haran, Mwenya Chimba, and Tammy Boyce. *Role Models in the Media: An Exploration of the Views and Experiences of Women in Science, Engineering and Technology*. UK Resource Centre for Women in Science, Engineering and Technology. Research Report 1, March 2008.

Klugman, Karen. "A Bad Hair Day for G.I. Joe." *Girls, Boys, Books, and Toys*. Baltimore: Johns Hopkins University Press, 1999. 169–82.

Knight, Denise D. *Charlotte Perkins Gilman: A Study of the Short Fiction*. New York: Twayne, 1997.

Knodel, John and Étienne van de Walle. "Fertility Decline: European Transition." *International Encyclopedia of Population*, vol. 1. New York: Macmillan, 1982. 271.

Kohlstedt, Sally. "Maria Mitchell and Women in Science." *Uneasy Careers and Intimate Lives: Women in Science, 1789–1979*. Ed. Pnina G. Abir-Am and Dorinda Outram. New Brunswick: Rutgers University Press, 1987. 129–46.

Kolata, Gina. "After Setbacks, Small Successes for Gene Therapy." *New York Times*. November 5, 2009. A19.

———. "Experts Join in Studying Lorenzo's Oil." *New York Times*. September 11, 1994. Section 1: 23.

Kolodny, Annette. "Dancing through the Minefield: Some Observations on the Theory, Practice, and Politics of Feminist Literary Criticism." (1980). *Feminisms*. Revised edition. Ed. Robyn Warhol and Diane Price Herndl. New Brunswick: Rutgers University Press, 1997. 171–90.

Kristeva, Julia. "Oscillation du 'pouvoir' au 'refus.'" ["Oscillation between Power and Denial"]. *New French Feminisms*. Ed. Elaine Marks and Isabelle de Courtivron. New York: Schocken Books, 1981. 164–66.

LaFollette, Marcel. "Eyes on the Stars: Images of Women Scientists in Popular Magazines." *Science, Technology, and Human Values* 13.3–4 (Summer–Fall 1988): 262–75.

Lavater, Johann Kaspar. *Essays on Physiognomy.* Trans. Thomas Holcroft. London: W. Tegg, 1853.

Lears, Jackson. *No Place of Grace: Antimodernism and the Transformation of American Culture.* New York: Pantheon, 1981.

Lemish, Dafna, Tamar Liebes, and Vered Seidmann. "Gendered Media Meanings and Uses." *Children and Their Changing Media Environment: A European Comparative Study.* Ed. Sonia Livingston and Moira Bovill. Mahwah, NJ: Lawrence Erlbaum, 2001. 263–82.

L'Engle, Madeleine. *A Wind in the Door.* New York: Bantam, 1973.

———. *A Wrinkle in Time.* New York: Bantam, 1962.

Leo, John. "The Indignation of Barbie." *US News and World Report.* October 4, 1992. http://www.usnews.com/usnews/opinion/articles/921012/archive_018466.htm. Accessed December 2, 2009.

Levine, George. *The Realistic Imagination.* Chicago: University of Chicago Press, 1981.

Levine, Irene S. "Scientific Success: What's Love Got to Do with It?" *Science.* May 26, 2006. http://sciencecareers.sciencemag.org/career_development/previous_issues/articles/2006_05_26/scientific_success_what_s_love_got_to_do_with_it. Accessed August 4, 2008.

Lieber, Francis. "Preface." (1833). *On the Penitentiary System in the United States and Its Application in France by Gustave de Beaumont and Alexis de Tocqueville.* Trans. Francis Lieber. Reprint, New York: Augustus M. Kelley, 1970.

Light, Jennifer. "Programming." *Gender and Technology: A Reader.* Ed. Nina E. Lerman, Ruth Oldenziel, Arwen P. Mohun. Baltimore: Johns Hopkins University Press, 2003. 294–326.

"Lisa the Simpson." Episode 917. *The Simpsons.* Original airdate 3/01/98. http://www.thesimpsons.com/episode_guide. Accessed July 28, 2008.

Lombroso, Cesare and Guglielmo Ferrero. *Criminal Woman, the Prostitute, and the Normal Woman.* Trans. Nicole Hahn Rafter and Mary Gibson. Durham: Duke University Press, 2004.

———and William Ferrero. *The Female Offender.* New York: Philosophical Library, 1958.

Long, Marilee, Greg Boiarsky, and Greg Thayer. "Gender and Racial Counter-Stereotypes in Science Education Television: A Content Analysis." *Public Understanding of Science* 10 (2001): 255–69.

Lorenzo's Oil. Dir. George Miller.

"*Love Potion Number 9.*" RottenTomatoes.com. http://www.rottentomatoes.com/m/love_potion_9/#. Accessed August 3, 2008.

Lowrey, Deborah. "Understanding Reproductive Technologies as a Surveillant Assemblage." *Sociological Perspectives* 47.4 (Winter 2004): 357–70.

Lubinksi, David S. and Camilla Persson Benbow. "Sex Differences in Personal Attributes for the Development of Scientific Expertise." *Why Aren't More Women in Science?* Ed. Stephen Ceci and Wendy Williams. Washington, DC: American Psychological Association, 2007. 79–100.

Lyman, Rick. "Film: No Goons in Spats, No Rat-a-Tat Dialogue." *New York Times.* July 14, 2002. Section 11: 20.

Macdonald, Myra. *Representing Women: Myths of Femininity in the Popular Media.* London: E. Arnold, 1995.

"MacGyver." Wikipedia, http://en.wikipedia.org/wiki/MacGyver. Accessed March 14, 2008.

MacKenzie, Donald and Judy Wajcman. "Preface to the Second Edition." *The Social Shaping of Technology.* 2nd edition. Ed. Donald MacKenzie and Judy Wajcman. Buckingham, U.K.: Open University Press, 1999.

Mackey, Margaret. "At Play on the Borders of the Diegetic: Story Boundaries and Narrative Interpretation." *Journal of Literacy Research* 35.1 (Spring 2003): 591–632.

Maddox, Brenda. *Rosalind Franklin: The Dark Lady of DNA.* New York: HarperCollins, 2002.

Magner, Lois. "Darwinism and the Woman Question." *Critical Essays on Charlotte Perkins Gilman.* Ed. J. B. Karpinski. New York: G. K. Hall, 1992.

Maloney, K. E. "A Feminist Looks at Education: The Educational Philosophy of Charlotte Perkins Gilman." *Teachers College Record* 99.3 (1998): 514–36.

Margolis, Jane and Allan Fisher. *Unlocking the Clubhouse: Women in Computing.* Cambridge: MIT Press, 2002.

Martin, Michèle. "The Culture of the Telephone." *Sex/Machine.* Ed. Patrick Hopkins. Bloomington: Indiana University Press, 1998. 50–74.

Maslin, Janet. "Steve Martin in *Roxanne.*" *New York Times.* June 19, 1987. http://movies.nytimes.com/movie/review?res=9B0DE6DF163DF93AA25755C0A961948260. Accessed August 3, 2008.

Masteller, Jean Carwile. "The Women Doctors of Howells, Phelps, and Jewett: The Conflict of Marriage and Career." *Critical Essays on Sarah Orne Jewett.* Ed. Gwen Nagel. Boston: G. K. Hall, 1984. 135–47.

"Mattel Dolls Up PCs with Barbie, Hot Wheels Touches." *C/net news.* August 3, 1999. http://news.com.com/2100–1040–229387.html. Accessed March 24, 2008.

"Mattel Says It Erred; Teen Talk Barbie Turns Silent on Math." *New York Times.* October 21, 1992. http://www.nytimes.com/1992/10/21/business/company-news-mattel-says-it-erred-teen-talk-barbie-turns-silent-on-math.html. Accessed September 12, 2010.

Mayne, Judith. *Directed by Dorothy Arzner.* Bloomington: Indiana University Press, 1994.

McIlwee, Judith S. and J. Gregg Robinson. *Women in Engineering: Gender, Power, and Workplace Culture.* Albany: State University of New York Press, 1992.

McKee, Patricia. "Racialization, Capitalism, and Aesthetics in Stoker's 'Dracula.'" *NOVEL: A Forum on Fiction* 36.1 (2002): 42–60.

McKellar, Danica. *Math Doesn't Suck.* New York: Penguin, 2007.

Mellor, Anne. *Mary Shelley: Her Life, Her Fiction, Her Monsters.* London: Routledge, 1989.

Melosh, Barbara. "Every Woman a Nurse." *"Send Us a Lady Physician": Women Doctors in America 1835–1920.* Ed. Ruth J. Abram. New York: W. W. Norton, 1985. 121–28.

Melville, Herman. *The Piazza Tales and Other Prose Pieces.* Ed. Harrison Hayford, Hershel Parker, and G. Thomas Tanselle. Evanston and Chicago: Northwestern University Press/Newberry Library, 1987.

Menke, Richard. *Telegraphic Realism.* Stanford: Stanford University Press, 2008. 163–88.

Merchant, Carolyn. *The Death of Nature.* San Francisco: Harper, 1983.

Merton, Robert K. "The Matthew Effect in Science." *Science* 159, 3810 (January 5, 1968): 56–63.

Michelet, Jules. *L'amour.* Paris: Hachette, 1859.

———. *La femme.* Paris: Flammarion, 1981.

Milkie, Melissa. "Contested Images of Femininity: An Analysis of Cultural Gatekeepers' Struggles with the 'Real Girl' Critique." *Gender and Society* 16.6 (2002): 839–59.

Miller, J. Hillis. *Versions of Pygmalion.* Cambridge: Harvard University Press, 1990.

Millett, Kate. *Sexual Politics.* (1970). Champaign-Urbana: University of Illinois Press, 2000. Text also available online at http://www.marxists.org/subject/women/authors/millett-kate/theory.htm. Accessed October 20, 2009.

Modleski, Tania. *Feminism without Women: Culture and Criticism in a Post-Feminist Age.* New York: Routledge, 1991.

———. *Loving with a Vengeance: Mass-Produced Fantasies for Women.* 2nd edition. New York: Routledge, 2007.

Morantz-Sanchez, Regina Markell. *Sympathy and Science: Women Physicians in American Medicine.* New York: Oxford University Press, 1985.

Moreau, Thérèse. *Le sang de l'histoire: Michelet, l'histoire et l'idée de la femme au XIXe siècle.* Paris: Flammarion, 1982.

Morris, Timothy. "Professional Ethics and Professional Erotics in Elizabeth Stuart Phelps's *Doctor Zay.*" *Studies in American Fiction* 21.2 (Autumn 1993): 141–52.

Mulvey, Laura. "Visual Pleasure and Narrative Cinema." *Film Theory and Criticism.* Ed. Gerald Mast and Marshall Cohen. New York: Oxford University Press, 1985. 803–16. Reprinted from *Screen* 16.3.

The Myelin Project. http://www.myelin.org/. Accessed August 1, 2008.

Naslund, Sena Jeter. *Ahab's Wife or, The Star-Gazer.* (1999). New York: HarperCollins, 2000.

———. "A Novelist Discovers Maria Mitchell." *Victoria* 14.7 (July 2000): 32–34.

National Science Foundation. *Women, Minorities, and Persons with Disabilities.* 2007 Report. http://www.nsf.gov/statistics/women/. Accessed July 16, 2008.

Nelkin, Dorothy. *Selling Science: How the Press Covers Science and Technology.* Revised edition. New York: W. H. Freeman, 1995.

"The New Melville." *American Literature* 66.1 (March 1994).

Newitz, Annalee and Charlie Anders. *She's Such a Geek: Women Write about Science, Technology, and Other Nerdy Stuff.* Emeryville, CA: Seal Press, 2006.

"Nintendogs Review." GameZone. http://nds.gamezone.com/gzreviews/r24992.htm. Accessed July 23, 2008.

Noble, David. *A World without Women.* New York: Knopf, 1992.

Norling, Lisa. *Captain Ahab Had a Wife: New England Women and the Whalefishery, 1720–1870.* Chapel Hill: University of North Carolina Press, 2000.

Norton, Mary. *The Borrowers.* Original edition 1952. New York: Harcourt Brace, 1981.

———. *The Borrowers Afield.* Original edition 1955. New York: Harcourt Brace, 1983.

Nuland, Sherwin B. *Doctors: The Biography of Medicine.* New York: Random House, 1988.

Numbers, Ronald. "Do-It-Yourself the Sectarian Way." *"Send Us a Lady Physician": Women Doctors in America 1835–1920.* Ed. Ruth J. Abram. New York: W. W. Norton, 1985: 43–54.

OECD [Organisation for Economic Co-Operation and Development]. Public Understanding of Science in the OECD Member Countries. http://www.oecd.org/document/23/0,2340,en_2649_34269_1962007_1_1_1_37417,00.html. Accessed June 12, 2008.

O'Flinn, Paul. "Production and Reproduction in the Case of *Frankenstein.*" *Popular Fictions: Essays in Literature and History.* Ed. Peter Humm, Paul Stigant, and Peter Widdowson. London: Methuen, 1986.

Oldenziel, Ruth. *Making Technology Masculine: Men, Women, and Modern Machines in America 1870–1945.* Amsterdam: Amsterdam University Press, 1999.

———. "Man the Maker, Woman the Consumer: The Consumption Junket Revisited." *Femi-

nism in Twentieth-Century Science, Technology, and Medicine. Ed. Angela N. H. Creager, Elizabeth Lunbeck, and Londa Schiebinger. Chicago: University of Chicago Press, 2001. 128–148.

Oliver, Mary Beth, Stephanie Lee Sargent, James B. Weaver, III. "The Impact of Sex and Gender Role Self-Perception on Affective Reactions to Different Types of Film." *Sex Roles* 38.1–2 (January 1998): 45–63.

Olrik, Hilde. "Le sang impur. Notes sur le concept de prostituée-née chez Lombroso." *Romantisme* 31 (1981): 167–78.

Otis, Laura, ed. *Literature and Science in the Nineteenth Century: An Anthology.* New York: Oxford University Press, 2002.

Parrington, Vernon. *Main Currents in American Thought,* vol. 3. New York: Harcourt, Brace and Company, 1930.

Patton, Cindy. *Inventing AIDS.* New York: Routledge, 1990.

Pease, Donald. "Leslie Fiedler, the Rosenberg Trial, and the Formulation of an American Canon." *boundary 2.* 17.2 (1990): 155–98.

Peiss, Kathy. *Cheap Amusements: Working Women and Leisure in Turn-of-the-Century New York.* Philadelphia: Temple University Press, 1986.

Peril, Lynn. *Pink Think: Becoming a Woman in Many Uneasy Lessons.* New York: W. W. Norton, 2002.

Perkowitz, Sidney. "Female Scientists on the Big Screen." *The Scientist.* July 21, 2006. http://www.the-scientist.com/. Accessed May 12, 2008.

———. *Hollywood Science: Movies, Science, and the End of the World.* New York: Columbia University Press, 2007.

Phelan, James. *Reading People, Reading Plots: Character, Progression, and the Interpretation of Narrative.* Chicago: University of Chicago Press, 1989.

Phelps, Elizabeth Stuart. "A Few Words to the Girls." *Woman's Journal* 3 (February 24, 1872): 62.

———. "A Talk to Girls." *Independent* 24 (January 4, 1872): 30.

———. "What Shall They Do?" *Harper's Monthly* 35 (1867): 519–23.

———. "What They Are Doing." *Independent* 23 (August 17, 1871): 1.

———. "Why Shall They Do It?" *Harper's Monthly* 36 (1868): 218–23.

———. "Women and Money." *Independent* 23 (August 24, 1871): 1.

"Pioneers in Improvement and Our Modern Standard of Living." *IW/SI News* 18 (September 1968): 37–38. Reprinted at "The Gilbreth Network." http://gilbrethnetwork.tripod.com/bio.html. Accessed July 6, 2008.

Pipher, Mary. *Reviving Ophelia: Saving the Selves of Adolescent Girls.* New York: Ballantine, 1994.

"Please Homer Don't Hammer 'em." Episode 1803. *The Simpsons.* Original airdate 9/24/06. http://www.thesimpsons.com/episode_guide/1803.htm. Accessed July 28, 2008.

Pollack, Andrew. "Scientists Seek a New Movie Role: Hero, Not Villain." *New York Times.* December 1, 1998. D1. http://www.nytimes.com/1998/12/01/science/scientists-seek-a-new-movie-role-hero-not-villain.html. Accessed December 2, 2009.

Potter, Sally. *Yes: Screenplay and Notes.* New York: Newmarket Press, 2005.

"The Powerpuff Girls." Internet Movie Database. http://www.imdb.com/title/tt0289408/plotsummary. Accessed July 31, 2008.

Pringle, Rosemary. *Sex and Medicine: Gender, Power and Authority in the Medical Profession.* Cambridge: Cambridge University Press, 1998.

Publisher Weekly's review of "Self-Experiment." *What Remains and Other Stories.* Trans. Heike Schwarzbauer and Rick Takvorian. Chicago: University of Chicago Press, 1995. Amazon. com. http://www.amazon.com/What-Remains-Other-Stories-Christa/dp/0226904954/ ref=sr_1_3?ie=UTF8&s=books&qid=1215166617&sr=1-3. Accessed July 4, 2008.

Pursell, Carroll. "Feminism and the Rethinking of the History of Technology." *Feminism in Twentieth-Century Science, Technology, and Medicine.* Ed. Angela Creager, Elizabeth Lunbeck, and Londa Schiebinger. Chicago: University of Chicago Press, 2001.

"Q and A with Nell Minow." *Romantic Movies.* Allexperts.com. http://en.allexperts.com/q/ Romantic-Movies-3173/2008/4/romance-films-pre-1950-1.htm. Accessed August 3, 2008.

Quetelet, Adolphe. *Research on the Propensities for Crime of Different Ages.* (1831). Trans. Sawyer F. Sylvester. Cincinnati: Anderson Publishing, 1984.

"Quinnvention Corner." *Pacific Coast Academy.* http://www.pacificcoastacademy.com/quinn. jhtml. Accessed July 29, 2008.

Rabinowitz, Peter. *Before Reading: Narrative Conventions and the Politics of Interpretation.* Ithaca: Cornell University Press, 1987.

Rasmussen, Bente and Tove Håpnes, "Excluding Women from Technologies of the Future? A Case Study of the Culture of Computer Science." *Sex/Machine.* Ed. Patrick D. Hopkins. Bloomington: Indiana University Press. 381–94.

Rayman, Paula and Belle Brett, "Women Science Majors: What Makes a Difference in Persistence after Graduation?" *Journal of Higher Education* 66.4 (August 1995): 388–414.

Renker, Elizabeth. "Herman Melville, Wife Beating, and the Written Page." *American Literature* 66.1 (March 1994): 123–50.

Revkin, Andrew C. "Filmmaker Employs the Arts to Promote Sciences." *New York Times.* February 1, 2005. http://www.nytimes.com/2005/02/01/science/earth/01conv.html. Accessed August 7, 2008.

Rizzo, William. "Editorial Note." *The New England Journal of Medicine* (September 9, 1993): 801–2.

Roberts, Robin. "The Woman Scientist in *Star Trek: Voyager*." *Future Females, The Next Generation: New Voices and Velocities in Feminist Science Fiction Criticism.* Ed. Marleen S. Barr. Lanham, MD: Rowman and Littlefield, 2000. 277–90.

Robertson-Lorant, Laurie. *Melville: A Biography.* Boston: University of Massachusetts Press, 1996.

Robinson, Lilian. "Killing Patriarchy: Charlotte Perkins Gilman, Murder Mystery, and Post-Feminist Propaganda." *Tulsa Studies in Women's Literature* 10.2 (1991): 273–85.

Rosenstone, Robert A. "Comments on Science in the Visual Media." *Public Understanding of Science* 12 (2003): 335–39.

Rosser, Sue V. *Re-Engineering Female Friendly Science.* New York: Teachers College Press, 1997.

———, Mary Frank Fox, and Carol Colatrella. "Developing Women's Studies in a Technological Institution." *Women's Studies Quarterly* 30.3–4 (Fall/Winter 2002): 109–25.

Rossiter, Margaret W. "The Matilda Effect in Science." *Social Studies of Science* 23 (1993): 25–341.

———. *Women Scientists in America.* 2 vols. Baltimore: Johns Hopkins University Press, 1982 and 1995.

Rotella, Elyce J. *From Home to Office*. Ann Arbor: UMI Research Press, 1981.

Roth, Phyllis. *Bram Stoker*. Boston: Twayne, 1982.

Rubin, Rita. "Lorenzo's Oil Brings Hope for the Afflicted." *USA Today*. October 12, 2002. http://www.usatoday.com/news/health/2002-10-21-lorenzo-oil-cover_x.htm. Accessed August 1, 2008.

Russett, Cynthia. *Sexual Science*. Cambridge: Harvard University Press, 1989.

Sagan, Carl. *Contact*. New York: Pocket, 1997.

"The Saint." Mysterynet.com. http://www.mysterynet.com/saint/. Accessed August 3, 2008.

Samuels, Shirley. *The Culture of Sentiment: Race, Gender, and Sentimentality in Nineteenth-Century America*. Oxford: Oxford University Press, 1992.

Sartisky, Michael. "Afterword." *Dr. Zay*. New York: Feminist Press, 1987. 259–321.

Saxon, Wolfgang. "Michaela Odone, 61, the 'Lorenzo's Oil' Mother." http://www.nytimes.com/2000/06/13/us/michaela-odone-61-the-lorenzo-oil-mother.html. Accessed August 22, 2010.

Scharff, Virginia. "Femininity and the Electric Car." *Sex/Machine*. Ed. Patrick Hopkins. Bloomington: Indiana University Press. 75–88.

Scharnhorst, Gary. *Charlotte Perkins Gilman*. Boston: Twayne, 1985.

———. *Charlotte Perkins Gilman, a Bibliography*. Lanham, MD: Scarecrow Press, 1985.

Schiebinger, Londa. *The Mind Has No Sex*. Cambridge: Harvard University Press, 1991.

Schiff, Corinne. "Metropolitan Diary." *New York Times*. March 31, 2008. http://www.nytimes.com/2008/03/31/nyregion/31diary.html. Accessed July 23, 2008.

Schwartz, Nelson D. "Turning to Tie-Ins, Lego Thinks Beyond the Brick." *New York Times*. September 6, 2009. http://www.nytimes.com/2009/09/06/business/global/06lego.html. Accessed September 29, 2009.

"The Science of Gender and Science: Pinker vs. Spelke, a Debate." *Edge: The Third Culture*. http://www.edge.org/3rd_culture/debate05/debate05_index.html. Accessed June 29, 2008.

"Science and Supermodels." January 10, 2008. http://www.scienceandsupermodels.com/2008/01/10/female-scientists-in-movies-the-top-10/. Accessed August 2, 2008.

Sedgwick, Catherine. *Means and Ends, or Self-Training*. New York: Harper Brothers, 1842.

Seiter, Ellen and Vicki Mayer. "Diversifying Representation in Children's TV: Nickelodeon's Model." *Nickelodeon Nation: The History, Politics, and Economics of America's Only TV Channel for Kids*. Ed. Heather Hendershot. New York: New York University Press, 2004.

Senf, Carol. "Dracula and the Lair of White Worm." *Gothic Studies* 2.2 (2000): 218–31.

———. "*Dracula*: Stoker's Response to the New Woman." *Victorian Studies* 26 (1982): 33–49.

Shafner, Rhonda. "'Intuition' Rings True in World of Science." *Honolulu Advertiser*. April 16, 2006. http://the.honoluluadvertiser.com/article/2006/Apr/16/il/FP604160319.html. Accessed August 3, 2008.

Sharkey, Betsy. "Family Life ('Arrgh!') in the Comfort Zone." *New York Times*. September 18, 1994. Sunday Arts and Leisure Section: 33.

Shepherd-Barr, Kirsten. *Science on Stage: From Doctor Faustus to Copenhagen*. Princeton: Princeton University Press, 2006.

Shields, Stephanie. *Speaking from the Heart: Gender and the Social Meaning of Emotion*. Cambridge: Cambridge University Press, 2002.

Shilts, Randy. *And the Band Played On.* New York: Penguin, 1988.

"A Short History of the National Institutes of Health," National Institutes of Health. http://www.history.nih.gov/exhibits/history/docs/page_06.html. Accessed July 6, 2008.

Shorto, Russell. "No Babies?" *The New York Times Magazine.* June 29, 2008. 34–41, 68–71.

Showalter, Elaine. *The Female Malady: Women, Madness, and English Culture.* New York: Pantheon, 1985.

Sicko. Dir. Michael Moore. 2007.

Signorelli, Nancy. "A Content Analysis: Reflections of Girls in the Media." April 1997. http://www.kff.org/entmedia/loader.cfm?url=/commonspot/security/getfile.cfm&PageID=14517. Accessed July 23, 2008.

Singh, G. K. and M. D. Kogan. "Widening Socioeconomic Disparities in US Childhood Mortality, 1969–2000." *American Journal of Public Health* 9 (September 2007): 1658–65.

Slatalla, Michelle. "Cyberfamilias: Today, I Think I'll Be Hippohead." *New York Times.* May 8, 2008. http://www.nytimes.com/2008/05/08cyber.html. Accessed September 10, 2010.

Smallwood, Scott. "As Seen on TV: 'CSI' and 'The X-Files' Help Build Forensic Programs." *The Chronicle of Higher Education* (July 19, 2002): A8. http://chronicle.com/weekly/v48/i45/45a00801.htm. Accessed June 25, 2009.

Smith, Caleb. *The Prison and the American Imagination.* New Haven: Yale University Press, 2009.

Smith, Dinitia. "Media More Likely to Show Women Talking about Romance than at a Job." *New York Times.* May 1, 1997. http://www.nytimes.com/1997/05/01/us/media-more-likely-to-show-women-talking-about-romance-than-at-a-job-study-says.html. Accessed July 23, 2008.

Sobchak, Vivian. *Screening Space: The American Science Fiction Film.* New York: Ungar Press, 1987; reprint, New Brunswick: Rutgers University Press, 1997.

Sommers, Christina Hoff. "Why Can't a Woman Be More like a Man?" *The American.* March/April 2008. http://www.american.com/archive/2008/march-april-magazine-contents/why-can2019t-a-woman-be-more-like-a-man. Accessed July 17, 2008.

Songe-Möller, Vigdis. *Philosophy without Women: The Birth of Sexism in Western Thought.* Trans. Peter Cripps. New York: Continuum, 2002.

Sonnert, Gerhardt, Mary Frank Fox, and Kristen Adkins. "Undergraduate Women in Science and Engineering: Effects of Faculty, Fields, and Institutions over Time." *Social Science Quarterly* 88 (December 2007): 1333–56.

Spelke, Elizabeth S. and Ariel D. Grace, "Sex, Math, and Science." *Why Aren't More Women in Science?* Ed. Stephen Ceci and Wendy Williams. Washington, DC: American Psychological Association, 2007. 57–67.

Stanley, Autumn. "Women Hold Up Two-Thirds of the Sky." *Sex/Machine.* Ed. Patrick D. Hopkins. Bloomington: Indiana University Press. 17–32.

Starr, Paul. *The Social Transformation of American Medicine.* New York: Basic Books, 1984.

Steinke, Jocelyn. "Connecting Theory and Practice: Using Televised Images of Women Scientist Role Models in Television Programming." *Journal of Broadcasting and Electronic Media* 42 (1998): 142–51.

———. "Cultural Representations of Gender and Science: Female Scientists and Engineers in Films." *Science Communication* 27.1 (2005): 27–63.

———. "Science in Cyberspace: Science and Engineering Web Sites for Girls." *Public Under-*

standing of Science 13.1 (2004): 7–74.

———. "Women Scientists Role Models on Screen: A Case Study of Contact." *Science Communication* 21.2 (December 1999): 111–36.

——— and Marilee Long. "A Lab of Her Own?: Portrayals of Female Characters in Children's Education Science Programs." *Science Communication* 18.2 (1996): 91–115.

———, Maria Knight Lapinski, Nikki Crocker, Aletta Zietsman-Thomas, Yachica Williams, Stephanie Higdon Evergreen, Sarvani Kuchibhotla. "Assessing Media Influences on Middle School-Aged Children's Perceptions of Women in Science Using the Draw-a-Scientist Test (DAST)." *Science Communication* 29.1 (September 2007): 35–64.

Stevenson, John Allen. "A Vampire in the Mirror: The Sexuality of *Dracula*." *PMLA* 103 (1988): 139–49.

Stewart, Abigail J., Janet E. Malley, and Danielle LaVaque-Manty, eds. *Transforming Science and Engineering: Advancing Academic Women*. Ann Arbor: University of Michigan Press, 2007.

Stith, Bradley J. "The Use of the Movie 'Lorenzo's Oil' as a Teaching Tool." http://carbon.cudenver.edu/~bstith/loren.htm. Accessed August 1, 2008.

Stoker, Bram. *Dracula*. (1897). Oxford: Oxford University Press, 1983.

Stolberg, Sheryl Gay. "Bush's Advisers on Ethics Discuss Human Cloning." *New York Times*. January 18, 2002. A19. http://www.nytimes.com/2002/01/18/us/bush-s-advisers-on-ethics-discuss-human-cloning.html. Accessed July 1, 2008.

Stoppard, Tom. *Arcadia*. London: Faber and Faber, 1993.

"Study Guide to Sharon Creech, *Walk Two Moons*." Sparknotes. http://www.sparknotes.com/lit/twomoons/section7.rhtml. Accessed June 29, 2008.

Summers, Lawrence. "Remarks at NBER Conference." January 14, 2005. http://www.president.harvard.edu/speeches/2005/nber.html. Accessed August 6, 2008.

Sundin, Elizabeth. "Gender and Technology—Mutually Constituting and Limiting." *Gendered Practices: Feminist Studies of Technology and Society*. Ed. Boel Berner. Department of Technology and Social Change, Linköping University, Stockholm: Almqvist & Wiksell, 1997. 249–68.

Tannen, Deborah. *You Just Don't Understand: Women and Men in Conversation*. New York: Ballantine Books, 1990.

Teitelbaum, Michael S. and Jay M. Winter. *The Fear of Population Decline*. New York: Academic Press, 1985.

Telotte, Jay. *Replications: A Robotic History of the Science Fiction Film*. Carbondale: University of Illinois Press, 1995.

Thoreau, Henry David. *Walden and Other Writings*. Ed. Brooks Atkinson. New York: Modern Library, 1992.

Tierney, John. "A New Frontier for Title IX: Science." *New York Times*. July 15, 2008. http://www.nytimes.com/2008/07/15/science/15tier.html?_. Accessed July 16, 2008.

———. "Tierney Lab: Male Bias or Female Choice." *New York Times*. July 15, 2008. http://tierneylab.blogs.nytimes.com/2008/07/14/male-bias-or-female-choice/#comments. Accessed July 16, 2008.

Tompkins, Jane. *Sensational Designs: The Cultural Work of American Fiction, 1790–1860*. New York: Oxford University Press, 1986.

Treichler, Paula. "How to Have Theory in an Epidemic: The Evolution of AIDS Treatment

Activism." *Technoculture*. Ed. Constance Penley and Andrew Ross. Minneapolis: University of Minnesota Press, 1991. 57–106.

Trimble, Linda. "Coming Soon to a Station Near You?: The CRTC Policy on Sex-Role Stereotyping." *Canadian Public Policy/Analyse de Politiques* 16.3 (1990): 326–38.

Turner, Steven. "School Science and Its Controversies, or Whatever Happened to Scientific Literacy." *Public Understanding of Science* 17 (2008): 55–72.

Tuttle, Jennifer. "Rewriting the West Cure: Charlotte Perkins Gilman, Owen Wister, and the Sexual Politics of Neurasthenia." *The Mixed Legacy of Charlotte Perkins Gilman*. Ed. C. Golden and J. Zangrando. Newark: University of Delaware Press, 2000.

U.S. House Committee on Science and Technology. "Press Release: Subcommittee Examines Ways to Break Down Barriers and Improve STEM Education Participation among Females." July 21, 2009. http://science.house.gov/press/PRArticle.aspx?NewsID=2565. Accessed November 17, 2009.

U.S. Senator Ron Wyden. "Press Releases: Wyden Convenes Hearing on Enforcing Title IX for Math, Science, Engineering Education Working to Triple Number of Women Graduating with Math, Science Degrees." October 3, 2002.

Valian, Virginia. *Why So Slow? The Advancement of Women*. Cambridge: MIT Press, 1999.

Vostral, Sharra. *Under Wraps: A History of Menstrual Hygiene Technology*. Lanham, MD: Lexington Books, 2008.

Wajcman, Judy. *Feminism Confronts Technology*. University Park: Pennsylvania State University, 1991.

——. *Technofeminisms*. Cambridge: Polity, 2001.

Walkerdine, Valerie. *Schoolgirl Fictions*. London: Verso, 1990.

Walton, Priscilla L. and Manina Jones. *Detective Agency: Women Rewriting the Hard-Boiled Tradition*. Berkeley: University of California Press, 1999.

Warhol, Robyn R. *Having a Good Cry: Effeminate Feelings and Pop-Culture Forms*. Columbus: The Ohio State University Press, 2003.

——. "Physiology, Gender, and Feeling: On Cheering Up." *Narrative* 12.2 (May 2004): 226–29.

Warner, Deborah Jean. "Science Education for Women in Antebellum America." *History of Women in the Sciences: Readings from Isis*. (1978). Ed. Sally Gregory Kohlstedt. Chicago: University of Chicago Press, 1999. 191–200.

Warner, Marina. *From the Beast to the Blonde: On Fairy Tales and Their Tellers*. New York: Noonday Press/Farrar, Straus and Giroux, 1994.

Watson, Mary Ann. "From *My Little Margie* to *Murphy Brown*: Women's Lives on the Small Screen." *Television Quarterly* 27.2 (1994): 3–24.

Weil, Martin. "Lorenzo Odone, 30; Struggle Inspired Film." *Washington Post*. May 31, 2008. B06. http://www.washingtonpost.com/wp-dyn/content/article/2008/05/30/AR2008053003014.html. Accessed August 1, 2008.

Weingart, Peter, with assistance from Claudia Muhl and Petra Pansegru. "Of Power Maniacs and Unethical Geniuses: Science and Scientists in Fiction Film." *Public Understanding of Science* 12 (2003): 279–87.

Weinstein, Cindy. *The Literature of Labor and the Labor of Literature*. Cambridge: Cambridge University Press, 1995.

Wells, Sue. *Out of the Dead House: Nineteenth-Century Women Physicians and the Writing of*

Medicine. Madison: University of Wisconsin Press, 2001.

Whitelegg, Elizabeth, Richard Holliman, Jennifer Carr, Eileen Scanlon, and Barbara Hodgson. *(In)visible Witnesses: Investigating Gendered Representations of Scientists, Technologists, Engineers and Mathematicians on U.K. Children's Television.* Research Report Series for the UK Resource Centre for Women in Science, Engineering and Technology. No. 5. March 2008.

Whitelegg, Liz. "Girls in Science Education: Of Rice and Fruit Trees." *Inventing Women: Science, Technology, and Gender.* Ed. Gill Kirkup and Laurie Smith Kellar. Cambridge: Polity Press, 1992. 178–87.

"Why Aren't More Women in Science?" *Inside Higher Ed.* January 3, 2007. http://www.insidehighered.com/news/2007/01/03/women. Accessed July 17, 2008.

Wicke, Jennifer. "Vampiric Typewriting: *Dracula* and Its Media." *ELH* 59.2 (Summer 1992): 467–93.

Williams, Susan. "Writing with an Ethical Purpose: The Case of Elizabeth Stuart Phelps." *Reciprocal Influences: Literary Production, Distribution, and Consumption in America.* Ed. Steven Fink and Susan S. Williams. Columbus: The Ohio State University Press, 1999.

Wolf, Christa. "Self-Experiment." *What Remains and Other Stories.* Trans. Heike Schwarzbauer and Rick Takvorian. Chicago: University of Chicago Press, 1995.

"Women and Science." *The NewsHour.* PBS. February 22, 2005. http://www.pbs.org/newshour/bb/science/jan-june05/harvard_02-22.html. Accessed June 29, 2008.

The Women's Press. http://www.the-womens-press.com/ahab.htm. Accessed May 14, 2009.

Woolrich, Willis R. "The History of Refrigeration; 220 Years of Mechanical and Chemical Cold: 1748–1968." *ASHRAE Journal* (July 1969): 32.

Wosk, Julie. *Women and the Machine: Representations from the Spinning Wheel to the Electronic Age.* Baltimore: Johns Hopkins University Press, 2001.

Wright, Gordon. *Between the Guillotine and Liberty: Two Centuries of the Crime Problem in France.* New York: Oxford University Press, 1983.

Yaszek, Lisa. *Galactic Suburbia.* Columbus: The Ohio State University Press, 2008.

Zola, Emile. *La Curée.* Paris: Gallimard, 1960. 371

———. "Dépopulation," *Oeuvres completes,* vol. 14. 786.

———. *Fécondité. Oeuvres completes,* vol 8.

———. *Le roman experimental.* Paris: Garnier-Flammarion, 1971. 133.

———. *Oeuvres complètes.* Ed. Henri Mitterand. Paris: Cercle de Livre Précieux, 1966.

———. *The Kill.* Trans. Arthur Goldhammer. New York: Bantam, 1954.

Zunshine, Lisa. *Why We Read Fiction: Theory of Mind and the Novel.* Columbus: The Ohio State University Press, 2006.

Index

La Cousine Bette (Balzac), 18, 26, 57–59, 198n19
Cowan, Ruth Schwarz, 12, 138, 140, 191n56, 204n2, 204n12
Crawford, T. Hugh, 116, 201n40, 203n27, 203n28
Crichton, Michael, 156, 158
Crick, Francis, 133
crime, 38; and social characteristics, 55–57; and evolution, 63–64; criminals, 25, 26, 53, 159; female offenders, 52–62, 84–85
criminal anthropology, 52–57
Crocker, Nikki, 207n19
Cross, Gary, 191n39
Crossing Jordan, 17
cryonics, 37
CSI, 17, 72, 76, 199n48; *CSI: Miami,* 17, 72; *CSI: NY,* 17, 72
Cukor, George, 145, 147
Culler, Jonathan, 19, 193n90
cultural change, 20; cultural marginality, 109; cultural sensitivity, 99; post-9/11 attitudes, 129
cultural codes, 18–22. *See also* gender
cultural ideologies, 20–22, 33
cultural imaginary, 6–7, 18
cultural scripts, 4, 168
Cunningham, George B., 193n86
La Curée [The Kill] (Zola), 18, 26, 59–62, 198n23
Curie, Marie, 116, 201n49
Curie, Pierre, 116
Cussins, Charis, 109, 202n6
cyborg, 160–68
"Cyborg Manifesto" (Haraway), 161, 206n52

D

Dalle Vacche, Angela, 16, 192n81, 205n40
Daring Book for Girls (Buchanan and Peskowitz), 10, 191n44
Dangerous Book for Boys (Iggulden and Iggulden), 10, 191n44
Darwin, Charles, 144
Davidson, Cathy N., 199n10
Davis-Floyd, Robbie E., 199n1
Dawson, Graham, 7–8, 190n28
Dean, Cornelia, 192n78
Deery, June, 206n51
Degan, Bruce, 194n112
Demme, Jonathan, 105

Denton, Charlie, 203n30
Denton, Denice, 192n73
Denton, Lena, 208n35
Denton, Rick, 203n30
"Dépopulation" (Zola), 80, 199n6
Le Depute d'Arcis (Balzac), 58
Design News, 192n84
Design Squad, 172, 184–87, 208n39
Desk Set, 148, 154–56
detectives, 17, 26
Dexter's Laboratory, 26, 172, 178–79
Dickens, Charles, 61, 201n50. See also *Hard Times; The Old Curiosity Shop*
Dickens, Homer, 205n37, 205n38
Dijkstra, Bram, 63, 198n37
Disclosure, 154, 156–58
Disclosure (Crichton), 156
Discovering Women, 110–13
discrimination, 1–2, 6, 11, 15, 29, 74, 105–6, 110, 132, 137, 187; anti-Semitism, 137; bias, 132; "chilly climate," 13, "hostile workplace," 13; patriarchal attitudes, 145; prejudices, 178, 183–84; sexism, 133, 136, 162
disease, 175. *See also* ALD; AIDS; orphan diseases
Disney, 194n108
Disney, Walt, 5
diversity, 157; diversifying science, 1, 110
Doane, Mary Ann, 16, 113, 192n82, 202n19
Dock, Julie Bates, 204n14
Le Docteur Pascal [Doctor Pascal] (Zola), 61, 82, 109, 198n33
domesticity, 5, 30, 80, 148, 159–60; domestic affairs, 72; domesticity and technology, 139–68; domestic love, 175; domestic reform, 204–5n19, 207n26; domestic technology, 12, 39, 140–45
Donawerth, Jane, 189n15
La donna delinquente (Lombroso and Ferrero), 60, 198n25, 198n26, 198n27, 198n28
Dougherty, Lynn Powell, 205n23
Douglas, Michael, 157
Douglas, Susan J., 19, 193n97, 193n98, 194n113
Douglass, Frederick, 44
Dow, Bonnie J., 189n15
Dowd, Maureen, 191n37
Dr. Breen's Practice (Howells), 86–90, 96
"Dr. Clair's Place" (Gilman), 96
Dr. Quinn, Medicine Woman, 187, 200n24

Schopenhauer, Arthur, 80
Scudder, Horace E., 204n15
Shakespeare, William, 203n23
Shalala, Donna, 192n73
Shankman, Adam, 204n11
She's Such a Geek, 115, 202n21
She's the Man, 203n23
Sheridan, Jennifer, 192n73
Shue, Elisabeth, 124
Schwartz, Nelson D., 191n41
science and faith, 130
science education, 12–14; media educating
    viewers about science, 22–25, 26; scien-
    tific experts, 171
science fiction, 5, 120, 160, 168, 174
scientific fraud, 136; scientific misconduct,
    132
scientific management, 139
scientific research, 46, 97–107, 108–37, 143–
    44, 152–53; female scientific researchers,
    11, 160
scientific truth, 136
Scooby-Doo, 178
Scorsese, Martin, 206n41
Scott, Ridley, 161, 206n55
Scrubs, 72
Sea of Grass, 205n26
Search for Extraterrestrial Intelligence
    (SETI), 120
Sedgwick, Catherine, 175, 207n26
Sedgwick, Kyra, 75
Seidelman, Susan, 160, 164
Seidmann, Vered, 170, 207n13
Seiter, Ellen, 171, 207n16
"Self-Experiment" (Wolf), 109, 202n5
Selznick, David, 205n26
Senf, Carol, 198n34, 198n35, 198n36
setting, 8, 19–21, 32, 37–38, 40–41, 47, 55, 67,
    81, 85, 91, 94, 117–22, 124, 127, 129–33,
    141, 168. *See also* mise-en-scène
sex roles, 21, 25, 42, 86, 87, 93, 97, 178,
    204n11
sexual attraction, 126–27, 130; long-term
    pair bonding, 126–27; sexual passion,
    152. *See also* romance
sex differences: in cognition, 1, 5–7; in
    crime, 54–55; sex-typed traits, 114
Sex Roles, 17
sexual deviance, 57–62
sexual discrimination. *See* discrimination
sexual harassment, 157–58

Sexual Science (Russett), 11
sexuality, 39, 46, 63–67, 70–72, 74–75, 80,
    82, 83, 115, 123, 129, 165; desexualizing
    female body, 113; normative sexuality,
    203n23
Shafner, Rhonda, 203n38
Sharkey, Betsy, 196n30
Shelley, Mary, 3–4, 28, 29, 51, 194n4
Shepherd-Barr, Kirsten, 20, 193n103, 202n13
She's Such a Geek (Newitz and Anders,
    eds.), 115, 202n21
Shields, Stephanie, 52, 197n1
Shilts, Randy, 201n45
Shires, Linda M., 50, 196–97n44
The Shop around the Corner, 154
Shorto, Russell, 199n9
Showalter, Elaine, 197n3
The Shriver Report, 19
Shulman, Robert, 205n21
Sicko, 199n3
Sid, the Science Guy, 187
Siegel, Jay, 17
Signorelli, Nancy, 171, 207n17
Simensky, Linda, 208n42
Simmons, Solon, 15
The Simpsons, 18, 22, 177, 207n29, 207n30,
    207n31, 208n32
Singh, G. K., 199n2
Skerrit, Tom, 120
Slatalla, Michelle, 207n14
slave, 45; slavery, 47. *See also* abolition
Sleepless in Seattle, 154, 203n23, 206n46
Smallwood, Scott, 192–93n85
Smilla's Sense of Snow (Høeg), 109, 202n7,
    202n8
Smith, Caleb, 197n2
Smith, Dinitia, 207n17
Smith, Ludlow Ogden, 148
Snow White, 5
Sobchak, Vivian, 189n15
social change, 16, 79–86, 97; social catego-
    ries, 188; social conventions, 109, 173;
    social engineering, 38; social marginal-
    ity, 104–5, 132, 201n45; social progress,
    35, 48, 148. *See also* cultural change
social roles, 4
Society for Literature, Science, and the Arts,
    195n14
Sommers, Christina Hoff, 14–15, 192n75
Songe-Möller, Vigdis, 189n5
Sonnert, Gerhardt, 169, 192n66, 206n2

Y

Yaszek, Lisa, 189n15
"The Yellow Wallpaper" (Gilman), 140
Yes, 26, 129–32, 203n36, 203n37
Young, Gig, 155
You've Got Mail, 203n23

Z

Zeitsman-Thomas, Aletta, 207n19
Zemeckis, Robert, 117

Zeus, 2–3
Zoey 101, 172, 182–84, 208n35, 208n36
Zola, Emile, 26, 53, 198n23, 199n6, 199n7.
    See also *La Curée* [*The Kill*]; "Dépopu-
    lation"; *Le Docteur Pascal; La Fortune
    des Rougon; Germinal;* "Letter to young
    people"; *Nana; La Rêve; Le Roman
    experimental; La Terre; La Ventre de
    Paris*
Zunshine, Lisa, 193n94